BANKS

V.

PELÉ

The Save that Shook the World

TERRY BAKER

with *Norman Giller*

NMG

NMG

**A NormanMichaelGillerEnterprises publication
in association with A1 Sporting Speakers**
© Terry Baker and Norman Giller 2008

First published in 2008 by NMG Enterprises
PO Box 3386, Ferndown, BH22 8XT

10 9 8 7 6 5 4 3 2 1

A CIP catalogue for this title is available from the British Library
ISBN 978-0-9543243-3-9

Typeset and designed by NMG Enterprises, Dorset, UK
Printed and bound in the United Kingdom by Antony Rowe Limited
Bumper's Farm, Chippenham, Wiltshire SN14 6LH

MANY OF THE PHOTOGRAPHS IN THIS BOOK HAVE BEEN KINDLY PROVIDED BY THE PREMIER AGENCY **PA PHOTOS**, WITH THANKS TO KEZIA STORR FOR HER CO-OPERATION. THERE ARE ALSO PHOTOS FROM THE PRIVATE COLLECTIONS OF GORDON BANKS AND PELÉ, AND ALSO FROM THE VAST A1 SPORTING SPEAKERS GALLERY OWNED BY TERRY AND FREDA BAKER. BEST EFFORTS HAVE BEEN MADE TO CLEAR COPYRIGHTS. THANKS TO FREDA BAKER, MICHAEL GILLER, JACKIE JONES, MIKE JONES, CHRISTOPHER JONES, DAVE BIGGS, MARK RADLEY AND LIBBY RODGER FOR THEIR PRODUCTION ASSISTANCE AND SUPPORT.

BANKS v. PELÉ CONTENTS

Sir Geoff Hurst with the Fifa World Cup, not the Jules Rimet trophy that he helped England win with his historic hat-trick at the old Wembley Stadium on July 30 1966..

BANKS v. PELÉ: The Save that Shook the World
Kick off by Sir GEOFF HURST

I was there on the pitch in Guadalajara the day that Gordon Banks made his save of a lifetime against Pelé. Looking back nearly 40 years later I still find it hard to believe that the ball didn't finish up in England's net when Pelé powered in a header that had 'goal' written all over it.

Bobby Moore, my captain for club and country, was closest to the action and he told me in the dressing-room during half-time that it was a miracle Gordon had managed to save it. The fact that so long afterwards we are still eulogising the save proves that 'a miracle' just about sums it up.

It has been almost lost in the mists of time that we went on to lose that 1970 World Cup finals match against Brazil 1-0, yet the magic of the save has lived on in the memory and is firmly cemented in the land of football legend. Hence this fascinating and quite unique book by my good friend Terry Baker, a larger-than-life entrepreneur who represents both Gordon and Pelé on the football celebrity circuit.

I cannot think of another book dedicated to just one save in a football match, but it is typical of Terry's meticulous attention to detail that he has managed to turn his memories and findings into a fascinating read. He has researched the save and the events leading up to it like a Sherlock Holmes-style detective, questioning a string of eyewitnesses and, best of all, getting the facts from the mouths of the most important people in the drama, Banks and Pelé. What a collector's item if you can get the book autographed by one or both of these giants of the beautiful game!

Terry has carried out his thorough investigation of the save with the help of sports historian Norman Giller, who was sports editor of the local West Ham paper when I was first starting out on my professional career. Norman reached the dizzy heights of chief football writer for the *Daily Express* in the same year of 1966 that was so special in my life. He has since gone on to fame as an author of more than 80 books, and admits that this is one of the more challenging books with which he has been involved.

Norman was reporting at Upton Park the night that Banksie made a save against me that, while not in the miracle class of the Pelé masterpiece, was mind-blowing to all those who saw it.

It was during a 1971-72 League Cup semi-final marathon against Stoke. In the first match at the Victoria Ground, I had scored for West Ham from the penalty spot. My style was always to smash rather than stroke penalties, and I took a long run up and hammered the ball to Gordon's right and shoulder-high into the net. This was still fresh in our minds when Gordon and I came face to face for a penalty duel in the second leg at West Ham. The match was into its last minutes and we were locked together on aggregate when Gordon upended our winger Harry Redknapp as he tried to run the ball around him. The referee had no hesitation in awarding a penalty, and my team-mates jumped about as if we had the game won. There was just the little matter left of my having to put the ball past one of the greatest goalkeepers whoever breathed.

As I placed the ball on the spot Gordon and I played mind games with each other. I looked to the corner of the net where I pretended I was going to slot the ball. But Gordon was not foxed, and decided I was going to take my usual straight down the middle approach. He read me perfectly.

I took the same long run up as at Stoke, and fired the ball with all my might. Gordon threw himself to his right and somehow managed to push the ball up against the bar and high away into the crowd for a corner.

It was a sensational save, and his team-mates carried him around the penalty area as if he was the League Cup while celebrating taking the game to a replay. We also drew that game, and in the second replay there was another incredible penalty save ... this time by none other than Bobby Moore! He took over in goal because of an injury to our 'keeper Bobby Ferguson, and saved a penalty before the ball was forced into the net in the follow-up rush. Stoke went on to win the match and the League Cup final at Wembley for the first trophy success in their history.

They could not have done it without the goalkeeping genius of Gordon Banks, and this book is a fitting tribute to one of the greatest goalkeepers ever to stand between the posts. I know that Pelé, the King, will second that opinion.

This is the never-to-be-forgotten story of their duel in the mid-day sun of Mexico.

Enjoy!

BANKS v. PELÉ: The Save that Shook the World
A Memory in a Million by TERRY BAKER

CAN one save justify a book all to itself? The answer is a resounding 'yes' when the save is made by one of the greatest goalkeepers of all against the greatest footballer ever and in the most important of all the major tournaments.

I was a fifteen-year-old schoolboy and at my most impressionable when I sat at home in Dorset watching the 1970 World Cup finals match between Brazil and England in Mexico. I looked on with disbelief as Gordon somehow managed to save a header from Pelé that would – and I say this with certainty – have beaten any other goalkeeper in the world.

It was one of those rare moments when you wonder if your eyes have deceived you. Television action replays came very slowly back in those days, and it was several minutes before we got confirmation that Gordon had pulled off a save in a million. Even as we watched the replay we wondered how on earth Banks had got from the near post to the far post to make the save. He had managed the impossible.

All these years later I am still not sure quite how he did it. It burned such a hole in my memory that long ago I decided I would at the first opportunity pay a proper tribute to what will always be a special moment in football history. Many great goals are given the glory treatment, so why not a save; well, not just a save but one that was voted the best ever in an on-line poll.

Almost as unbelievable as the save is the fact that I am now one of the few people in a position to give a totally accurate view of the goal from all sides. Nearly forty years on I find myself in the privileged role of representing not only the great Gordon Banks but also – for exclusivity of his autograph – the legendary Pelé.

So I have been able to sit at the feet of these two icons of the game and get their exclusive memories of a moment in a million.

I run a company with my wife Freda – A1 Sporting Speakers – that specialises in top-quality sporting memorabilia. For us to be interested in an item it has to be the Real McCoy and worthy of an investment. What better, I thought, than a book blessed both by Gordon Banks and Pelé on their magical moment in football history. I know as a collector myself just how precious this book will be for anybody who has it signed by one – or even better – *both* footballing legends.

There is a special limited edition being produced with the books signed exclusively

---

by both Banks and Pelé, and another less expensive copy that carries the signature of one of the giants. The autographs are a special bonus to accompany what I hope is an entertaining and enlightening read. I have done my best to stitch in interesting facts, stats and opinions that will put flesh on the story of the greatest save ever.

It is like having a report of the Battle of Waterloo, accompanied by the autographs of Wellington and Napoleon. Okay, that's a bit of a wild exaggeration, but for true football fans there have been few moments to match that battle between Gordon Banks and Pelé. Now I have managed to realise my ambition of getting it properly recorded, with exclusive input from the main participants.

I could not have produced the book without the help and guidance of my friend and near-neighbour Norman Giller, a hugely experienced and prolific sports author who was there in Mexico when Gordon made his save in a million. By enlisting the assistance of Norman and his sports statistician son, Michael, I had the best support team in putting together the story of the save and all that came before and after it.

I want to take this opportunity to thank all those who so willingly gave me their time and expertise to make sure this account of the lives and times of Banks and Pelé is completely accurate, in particular my buddy Jimmy Greaves who gave an interesting and professional insight into his playing experiences with Gordon and Pelé. I also wish to thank my wife and business partner, Freda, for her patience and encouragement in getting what has been a labour of love finished and into your hands.

Now come with me back to the start of it all and the early days of Gordon Banks, one of the two great heroes of my book ... *Banks v. Pelé, The Save that Shook the World* ...

Best wishes

Tom Baker

This Book is dedicated to my good friends
Gordon and Edson (aka Pelé), thanking them
for their friendship and co-operation,
and for showing us the way
sport should be played – with
skill, sportsmanship and
a smile.

Also to Freda (wife, business partner, lover, best friend),
Jackson, Nicole, Mum, Maria, Tara and Shelley
who all keep me going,
and James Peter Greaves, a constant inspiration.

This worn, 58-year-old photograph (above) is Gordon's first team picture from his personal scrapbook when he was keeping goal for Tinsley County Secondary Modern School. And here on the left, it's Gordon as a young professional starting out on a path that was to take him to the very peak of the football mountain.

BANKS v. Pelé: The Save that Shook the World

1. The Gordon Banks Story, the First Half

THE hands that were to become world famous as the safest in football were bruised and battered by the jobs Gordon Banks had when he left school, first as a coalbagger and then bricklayer. I have spoken to Gordon in depth to get the full facts about his early life and times, and I was amazed to find that his goalkeeping career happened more by accident than design.

Born on December 30 1937 in the steel town of Sheffield, Gordon was the youngest of four brothers. His father worked in a steel foundry until becoming a small-time bookmaker. Gordon was fifteen when he finished his formal education to work for his daily bread, first of all shovelling coal into bags before loading lorries for delivery. He then started an apprenticeship as a bricklayer. Professional football did not even enter his thoughts.

While at school he had played in goal for Sheffield Boys, but was on the wrong end of so many defeats that he became expert only at picking the ball out of the net. Money was tight, and he saw fewer than thirty League games as a kid. He would go to either Bramall Lane to watch Sheffield United play or to Hillsborough to see Wednesday, but never regularly enough to form an attachment to either club. Gordon told me:

‘It was always the goalkeepers who took my eye. I can remember seeing Bert Trautmann perform miracles between the posts for Manchester City, Bert Williams making making everything look so easy by his intelligent positioning for Wolves, big George Farm dominating the goalmouth for Blackpool, Ted Burgin always steady and reliable at the back of the Sheffield United defence and Dave McIntosh, confident and assured for Wednesday.

In my boyhood imagination I used to model myself on Trautmann, the German paratrooper who had been a prisoner-of-war and had stayed on in Engand to become one of the giants of the game as successor to the fabulous Frank Swift in Man City's goal

But I had no ambitions to emulate them when I left Tinsley County Secondary shool in the winter of 1952 to start bagging and delivering coal. I was tall and fairly hefty but without developed strength, and my work as a coalman's mate used to knacker me so much that I did not have the energy left to even think of playing football. It was a pure fluke how I got back into playing in goal. I was standing watching two teams preparing for a local league match one Saturday afternoon when a trainer recognised me from when I used to play in goal for Sheffield Boys. He told me his goalkeeper hadn't shown up and invited me to fill in for him.

My home, a terraced house in a Coronation Street setting, was just a couple of minutes away and I dashed back to get my boots. I didn't possess a pair of shorts and I played with my socks pulled up over a pair of working trousers that were covered with coal dust. The team I was playing for, working fellers with an average age of about twenty-two, held out for a 2-2 draw and I impressed them sufficiently to get invited to become their regular goalie. I was as chuffed as if I had been called up for England. Millspaugh was the name of the team, and they had unknowingly launched me on a career that was to become not just a job but a way of life.❜

Gordon's natural talent at the back of the Millspaugh defence was clear for all to see, and within a few weeks a Yorkshire League team called Romarsh Welfare invited him to join them. He did not make the best of starts, conceding twelve goals in his debut. I find it very hard to get a picture in my mind of Gordon bending down a dozen times to pick the ball out of his net.

In the next match Gordon was beaten three times, and the committee that ran the Romarsh team suggested he return to lower grade football with Millspaugh. It was like the Beatles being rejected.

During the following season with Millspaugh he was spotted by a professional scout, who recommended him to Chesterfield. The Third Division North club signed him first as an amateur and then as a part-time professional, paying him the princely sun of £2 a match. For the first time in his life, Gordon was taking his football seriously.

But it looked as if his professional career was over almost before it had started. While playing for the Chesterfield Nothern Intermediate League side he dived at the feet of a forward and got a fractured elbow as the reward for saving a certain goal. He was taken to hospital, and during an operation had a screw inserted in the elbow. Twenty or so years later he would have been nicknamed 'Bionic Banks'.

Despite the doubt of a doctor who told him he should not play football for at least a year, Gordon returned to the game after just eight weeks and was promoted to Chesterfield reserves. He doubled up as the youth team goalkeeper and Chesterfield stunned the football world by reaching the 1956 FA Youth Cup final, playing the Busby Babes of Manchester United in a cracker of a match in front of a 32,000 crowd at Old Trafford.

Back in those days the FA Youth Cup carried huge prestige, and some managers put winning it on a par with capturing the League championship. You have to remember that this was the 1950s, when footballers were earning a maximum £17 a week (later £20), and the only transfer business was for home-grown players. To win the Youth Cup convinced boardroom directors that there was something to build on for the future.

Gordon has vivid memories of the final, and recalls a young, blond-haired outside-left bombing in incredible long-range shots. His name was Bobby Charlton.

United won the match 4-3, and Gordon was so excited by the experience of playing in front of his biggest crowd to date that he decided that he wanted a long-term future in football. But before he could move his ambition forward he had a two-year hurdle to clear. He was called up for his National Service.

After doing his basic training at Catterick with the Royal Signals, Gordon was drafted to Germany where as well as finding his feet as a footballer he also found himself a wife. He met Ursula at a village dance close to Brunswick, near Hanover, where he was based. They got married after a whirlwind courtship, and Gordon sent Ursula home to Sheffield to get to know his parents during the last few weeks of his Army service. He then turned his full concentration to football and helped his regimental team mop up most of the major trophies. Gradually he was developing the confidence and positional awareness that is the stock-in-trade of any goalkeeper.

On the very day in 1958 that Gordon arrived home after his demob from the Army a Chesterfield representative was on his doorstep asking him to sign as a full-time professional at the then maximum wage of £17 a week. That was exactly the same amount that the likes of superstars like Stanley Matthews, Tom Finney, Nat Lofthouse and Bert Trautmann were earning in what were understandably known as the 'Soccer Slave' days.

It was only later that Gordon discovered the reason Chesterfield had been so anxious to sign him was because a scout employed by several clubs had been sending back excited reports about his performances with his regimental team.

Gordon was free of the hard life of bagging coal and laying bricks, and he and Ursula set up home in the small mining village of Treeton just outside Chesterfield.

He had barely established himself in the Chesterfield first-team after twenty-three League games when Leicester City moved in with a £7,000 bid. At first, Gordon was reluctant to make the move because he and Ursula were just getting settled into their new home and way of life, but he agreed to join Leicester in 1959 after the Chesterfield chairman told him the club were desperate for the money. By the standards of those days, £7,000 was a lot to pay for a virtual unknown player.

In his second season at Filbert Street, Leicester City reached the FA Cup final where they went down 2-0 to the exceptional Tottenham team that became the first side of the 20th Century to cinch the League and FA Cup double. I was a Spurs nut in those

It's the 1963 FA Cup final at Wembley and Gordon leaps to stop the ball reaching Man United striker David Herd, who scored two goals in a 3-1 victory. Among the Leicester City defenders looking on is No 4 Frank McLintock, who the following year joined Arsenal where he became a Highbury legend and leader of their 1970-71 double-winning team.

days and all these years later I can name the Tottenham team off the top of my head: Brown; Baker, Henry; Blanchflower, Norman, Mackay; Dyson or Medwin, White, Smith, Allen and Jones. My apologies for letting this get in the way of the Gordon Banks story, but I know that Gordon has a soft spot for that team too, even though he was often on the receiving end against them. They became even stronger and more stylish the following season when the one and only Jimmy Greaves joined their firing line, but I digress. Back to the Banks story.

In 1963 Leicester City were back at Wembley for an FA Cup final showdown with Matt Busby's Manchester United, which he was still rebuilding following the 1958 tragedy of the Munich air crash that wiped out the Busby Babes. For anybody of a certain age, the Babes were one of the finest teams ever to step on to a football pitch and they will always have a special place in the hearts of those lucky enough to have seen them play. New-look United, with their Scottish trio Denis Law, David Herd and

Pat Crerand in devastating form, dismantled the Leicester City defence and coasted to a 3-1 victory. Gordon recalled:

‘My memory of that 1963 FA Cup final is a sad one. I remember my Leicester team-mate Frank McLintock being close to tears as we came off with our runners-up medals. 'I hate this f****** place,' said Frank, with a sweep of his hand to indicate Wembley Stadium where he was a five-times loser..

I have never known anybody as determined to win something in football than Frank, and he knew he was going to have to leave Leicester to achieve his ambitions.

The club were frugal as far as Frank and I were concerned, and we both had long and bitter battles for improved wages. This, of course, after the maximum wage had been kicked out in 1960-61.

Frank finally moved on to Arsenal, where he was a magnificent captain of the team that won the League and FA Cup double in 1970-71. You can't stop footballers comparing their wages with players from other clubs while on international get-togethers, and I knew that most of my England team-mates were being paid at least twice as much as me each week.

I feel that I gave Leicester fantastic service in return for the poor wages they paid me, and my reward was that they more or less kicked me out after I had helped England win the World Cup in 1966. Their decision to let me go could easily have destroyed my confidence, but I made it work for me. I was twenty-eight and had won thirty-seven England caps when Leicester sold me to Stoke and handed my club jersey to teenager Peter Shilton.

In my mind I was determined to have at least another ten years at the top and to play so well that Alf Ramsey would find it impossible to drop me. After joining Stoke I was capped thirty-six more times by England.’

How best to cover Gordon's England career? To make this book even more of a collector's item, I have decided to run a summary of EVERY match that Gordon played at international level. I have enlisted the help of my co-author Norman Giller, a respected sports historian who witnessed most of Gordon's England games and he has kept a full record of every match. He collaborated on Gordon's first *Banks of England* autobiography.

We have broken the summaries down into three sections, first of all featuring the games leading up to the 1966 World Cup finals and England's Everest-peak glory at Wembley ...

Match No 1
Scotland, Wembley, 6.4.63. England lost 2-1
Banks Armfield* Byrne G. Moore Norman Flowers
Douglas ₁ Greaves Smith Melia Charlton R.

Highlights: This was Alf Ramsey's second match as England manager, and he brought Gordon Banks in for his debut after Sheffield Wednesday goalkeeper Ron Springett had carried the can for a 5-2 defeat by France in his first game in charge in Paris six weeks earlier. Both England and Scotland were down to ten men within five minutes following a collision between Bobby Smith and Scottish skipper Eric Caldow, who was carried off with a triple fracture of the leg. By the time Smith limped back on with his bruised knee bandaged 'Slim' Jim Baxter had twice beaten Gordon, first after a misplaced pass by Armfield and then from the penalty spot. Bryan Douglas scored ten minutes from the end, but the Scots deserved a victory that was masterminded by Baxter who memorably walked off with the match ball tucked up inside his jersey. This stunningly skilled showman had owned the pitch, so why not the ball? Liverpool team-mates Gerry Byrne and Jimmy Melia made their debuts. It was the first match played at the 'new' Wembley with a £500,000 roof that ran right round the stadium like a giant lip. A 98,000 crowd paid then record receipts of £76,000. **Gordon quote:** "Alf Ramsey had kicked off with two defeats and the critics were asking: 'Could this be the man to lead England to the World Cup?' From day one, I found Alf deeply knowledgeable and passionate about getting it right. He had a team pattern in his mind and was determined to find the players to fit it."

Match No 2
Brazil, Wembley, 8.5.63. Drew 1-1
Banks Armfield* Wilson Milne Norman Moore
Douglas ₁ Greaves Smith Eastham Charlton R.

Highlights: There was no Pelé, but Pepé popped up with a first-half 'banana' free-kick from 25 yards that deceived Gordon and swung into the roof of the England net. Douglas scrambled a late equalizer against the world champions. Gordon Milne was the first defensive 'ball winning' midfield player selected by Ramsey, a role that would ultimately go to Nobby Stiles. George Eastham followed his father, George senior, as

an England international, and they were the first father and son to win England caps.
Gordon quote: "Alf gave me a rollocking at half-time for falling for what he called Pepe's three-card trick. But from Alf's position on the touchline he could not have known how much bend Pepe put on the ball. I swear that if it had not gone into the net it would have done a circular tour of the stadium!"

Match No 3
Czechoslovakia, Bratislava, 20.5.63. England won 4-2
Banks   Shellito   Wilson Milne   Norman Moore*
Paine   Greaves 2   Smith 1   Eastham   Charlton R. 1

Highlights: The first victory under the Ramsey baton, and what an impressive scalp. Czechoslovakia had been runners-up in the 1962 World Cup final and included European footballer of the year Josef Masopust in their midfield. Greaves (2), Smith and Charlton scored the goals, and Ken Shellito and Terry Paine made impressive debuts. A knee injury would virtually end Shellito's career within the year. He was a beautifully balanced player who could match the speed of sprinting wingers. His early retirement would be a blow to Chelsea and England, but George Cohen was – so to speak – waiting in the wings to make the No 2 shirt his personal property. Bobby Moore captained England for the first time in place of the injured Armfield. He would go on to skipper England 90 times, equalling the record set by one of his boyhood heroes Billy Wright.
Gordon quote: "I could do nothing about either of the Czech goals and was generally pleased with my all-round display. This victory did most to lay the foundation for the club-style spirit that was always in evidence for the remainder of Alf Ramsey's reign as England manager."

Match No 4
East Germany, Leipzig, 2.6.63. England won 2-1
Banks Armfield* Wilson Milne Norman Moore
Paine Hunt 1 Smith Eastham Charlton R. 1

Highlights: Roger Hunt, playing in place of tonsilitis-victim Jimmy Greaves, scored a spectacular equaliser from thirty yards after Gordon had conceded a soft goal midway through the first-half. Bobby Charlton netted the second-half winner after a series of goalmouth misses against an outpowered East German team. An England victory in Germany would have had most managers singing their own praises, but Alf Ramsey proved he was a perfectionist expecting the highest standards when he said: "Our passing was erratic and careless and lacking in imagination. We can, and will, do much much better." But he stored in the back of his mind that England could function – and win –

without Jimmy Greaves. **Gordon quote**: "This was a best-forgotten match for me. I mistimed a dive to save a speculative shot from 30 yards and the ball rolled under my arms and into the net. I knew I was at fault and neither Alf nor my team-mates had to say anything to me. I was my own worst critic and beat myself up over that goal."

Match No 5
Wales, Ninian Park, 12.10.63. England won 4-0
Banks Armfield* Wilson   Milne Norman Moore
Paine Greaves 1 Smith 2 Eastham Charlton R. 1

Highlights: The double act of Jimmy Greaves and Bobby Smith was unstoppable. Greaves made a goal in the fifth minute for Smith who then returned the compliment before the irrepressible Greaves laid on a second goal for his beefy Tottenham team-mate. Bobby Charlton finished off the Welsh with his thirty-first goal for England, beating the record that he had held jointly with Nat Lofthouse and Tom Finney. 'Preston Plumber' Finney was a guest spectator, and said: 'Bobby will go on to score many goals for England. The record could not be held by a better player nor a nicer man. He is a credit to the game.' One true gentleman recognizing another. Bobby Charlton wore the number 11 shirt, but followed Ramsey's orders and was more withdrawn than usual ... a sign of things to come. **Gordon quote**: "There has rarely been a manager so thorough in his preparations as Alf Ramsey. In his team talk before the match he analysed the Welsh team in such detail that I think we could have played them with our eyes shut and still have won. Alf had total recall of any team he had seen play and could tell you a player's strengths and weaknesses, the foot he was likely to kick the ball with and the way in which he tackled or stood off."

Match No 6
Rest of World, Wembley, 23.10.63. England won 2-1
Banks Armfield* Wilson Milne Norman Moore
Paine 1 Greaves 1 Smith Eastham Charlton R.
Rest of the World: Yashin Santos D Schnellinger Pluskal Popluhar Masopust Kopa Law 1 Di Stefano Eusebio Gento (Subs: Soskic, Eyzaguirre, Baxter, Seeler, Puskas)

Highlights: Jinking Jimmy Greaves was the star turn on the Wembley stage in this prestige match to celebrate the Centenary of the Football Association. He might have had a first-half hat-trick but for the magnificent goalkeeping of Russia's 'Man in Black' Lev Yashin. Terry Paine gave England a first-half lead, which was cancelled out by Denis Law, and it was Greavsie who conjured the winner with just three minutes left of a memorable match. There was a wonderful moment in the first-half that captured the spirit in which the game was played. Yashin had been giving an amazing exhibition of shot stopping, and on the half hour artful dodger Greaves tried for a sixth time to beat him. He fired in a power drive that most goalkeepers would have tried to either tuck away around a post or over the bar. But the unpredictable Russian met it with a boxer's punch that sent the ball screaming back to the halfway line. Greaves and Yashin then fell into each other's arms laughing as they congratulated each other. Jimmy then at last got the better of Yashin with what he has since described as the 'greatest goal I never scored!' He threaded his way past four of the world's finest defenders before slipping the ball wide of the oncoming Yashin, but it was disallowed because the referee had – unheard by most people in the stadium – whistled for a foul against Greaves at the start of his scintillating run. What ever happened to the advantage rule, ref? **Gordon quote**: "I would have willingly paid to play in this prestigious game. I was like a kid at Christmas after the match going round getting my programme autographed by the galaxy of stars who had graced the Wembley pitch. I loved watching the legendary Yashin from the other end of the pitch, and saw just why he was rated the greatest goalkeeper of all time. Against any other goalkeeper, Greavsie would definitely have had at least a hat-trick."

Match No 7
Northern Ireland, Wembley, 20.11.63. England won 8-3
Banks Armfield* Thomson Milne Norman Moore
Paine 3 Greaves 4 Smith 1 Eastham Charlton R.

Highlights: Greaves (4) and Terry Paine (3) lit up this first match under the Wembley floodlights, and Bobby Smith scored once in what was to be his final international appearance. Smith (12) and Greaves (19) between them collected thirty-one goals in just thirteen matches together. Wolves left-back Bobby Thomson made a sound debut at the age of nineteen. It was England's sixth win in succession under Ramsey, and a mood of optimism was beginning to build with the World Cup finals bound for the birthplace of the game in 1966. Irish goalkeeper Harry Gregg, a Munich survivor, said: 'Jimmy Greaves is a genius. I have never faced a more complete finisher. He tells me he has an Irish grandmother, Katie O'Riley. We should have snapped him up!' **Gordon quote**: "Harry Gregg had my sympathy. He was an outstanding goalkeeper and pulled off some marvellous saves, but he couldn't play England on his own … particularly with Greavsie at his scintillating best. Jimmy and Bobby Smith were as good a tandem team as in any league in the world. They were the perfect partners, developing their understanding while playing together for Tottenham, Jimmy skilfully feeding off Bobby's battering-ram power."

Match No 8
Scotland, Hampden Park, 11.4.64. England lost 1-0
Banks Armfield*   Wilson Milne Norman Moore
Paine   Hunt   Byrne J.   Eastham Charlton R.

Highlights: Roger Hunt and Johnny Byrne deputised for injured Greaves and Smith on a wet and stormy afternoon at Hampden. Alan Gilzean, who was to take over from Smith as partner to Greaves at Spurs, scored the only goal of the match after Gordon had misjudged a seventy-second minute corner-kick from Davie Wilson that got held up in the near-gale force wind. A crowd of 133,245 witnessed a third Scottish victory in a row over the Auld Enemy, the first time this had happened for eighty years.
Gordon quote: "This was my first match at Hampden, and I had often heard stories that whenever there is a strong wind it gets locked in the Hampden bowl and plays all sorts of tricks with the ball. On this day, there was a gale of wet wind swirling around the ground and it was a nightmare trying to decide whether to come off my line for crosses and centres in case the ball suddenly changed course. Davie Wilson fired a corner kick high into the six-yard box. It was a goalkeeper's ball all the way and I shouted 'mine' as I left my line to collect it. But suddenly the ball was trapped by the wind and stopped as if it had brakes on it. I was left clutching thin air as Alan Gilzean stole in front of me and nodded the ball into the net with what was his specialist flick header. As the ball went into the net I swear the Hampden Roar could have been heard way down over Hadrian's Wall."

Match No 9
Uruguay, Wembley, 6.5.64. England won 2-1
Banks Cohen Wilson Milne Norman Moore*
Paine Greaves Byrne J. 2 Eastham Charlton R.

Highlights: George Cohen came in at right-back for the injured Jimmy Armfield, and partnered Ray Wilson for the first time. Ramsey's 1966 World Cup defence was taking shape. Johnny Byrne scored both England goals in an uninspiring match. A week earlier the Uruguayans had been involved in a brawl of a match with Northern Ireland in Belfast, and Alf Ramsey warned his players that on no account should they be drawn into any feuds. The result was a tame game decided by the decisive finishing of Byrne, nicknamed 'Budgie' because he was a non-stop talker both on and off the pitch. 'They were the two most satisfying goals I have ever scored,' said chirpy Byrne, who was a beautifully balanced player who used skill rather than strength to bamboozle defences.
Gordon quote: "The Uruguayans played a take-no-prisoners style of physical football

Gordon saves at the feet of Denis 'The Menace' Law, with captain Bobby Moore in close attendance.

and Alf made it very clear that on no account were we to retaliate. Little did we know then that we would be facing the Uruguayan hatchet men again in the first match of the 1966 World Cup finals."

Match No 10
Portugal, Lisbon, 17.5.64. England won 4-3
Banks Cohen Wilson Milne Norman Moore*
Thompson Greaves Byrne J. 3 Eastham Charlton R. 1

Highlights: Johnny Byrne completed a memorable hat-trick in the final moments with a beautifully disguised chip shot from the edge of the penalty area that went over the heads of three defenders and the goalkeeper and into the net. Portugal, who had led twice through the towering Torres – a 6ft 7in centre-forward – and his Benfica side-kick Eusebio, could not believe it. Liverpool dribbler Peter Thompson won his first of sixteen caps as he tried to prove to Ramsey that wingers were a necessary evil. The match was staged to mark the golden anniversary of the Portugal Football Association, and it was 17 years after England's 10-0 victory in the same picturesque setting of Portugal's National Stadium. **Gordon quote:** "Seven of us – Bobby Moore, Greavsie, Budgie Byrne, George Eastham, Bobby Charlton, Ray Wilson and yours truly– were in Alf's bad books before the match because we had gone out for a late-night drink against his orders. But he softened after we had beaten an excellent Portuguese team including Eusebio and the towering Jose Torres. Alf was not best pleased with my performance, and I was dropped for one game to teach me a lesson. It worked!"

Match No 11
USA, New York, 27.5.64. England won 10-0
Banks Cohen Thomson Bailey Norman Flowers*
Paine 2 Hunt 4 Pickering 3 Eastham (Charlton R. 1) Thompson

Highlights: Everton centre-forward Fred Pickering started his international career with a hat-trick and Roger Hunt scored four goals as England ran riot against an overwhelmed United States team. Mike Bailey, driving captain of Charlton before his move to Wolves, had a comfortable debut and would have won many more caps but for breaking a leg a few months later. Alf Ramsey had been right-back in the England team humbled 1-0 by the United States in the 1950 World Cup finals, and it was suggested to him after the match that this runaway victory had been something of a consolation. He gave the football writer putting the question one of his infamous cold-eyed stars and said: 'Nothing will ever be a consolation for that.' Clearly, an old wound that would never go away. **Gordon quote**: "It was one of the easiest games I ever played for England.

I hardly had a shot to save on a dustbowl of a pitch. Whenever I used to try to get Alf talking about that sensational defeat by the United States in the 1950 World Cup he would always change the subject. It was without doubt the lowest moment of his international career."

Match No 12
Portugal, Sao Paulo, 4.6.64. Drew 1-1
Banks Thomson Wilson Flowers Norman Moore*
Paine Greaves Byrne J. Hunt 1 Thompson

Highlights: Portugal went down to ten men when centre-forward Jose Torres was sent off for attempting to hit the referee shortly after Roger Hunt had equalised a goal by Peres. Jimmy Greaves and Johnny Byrne hit the woodwork, and Byrne had a goal disallowed but England failed to take advantage of having an extra man. Had Torres landed with his attempted punch he could have faced a life ban from football. The trouble erupted after the referee disallowed a quite obviously off-side goal by Coluna. Portuguese players hounded the referee for a full five minutes, with Torres punished for being the ring leader. England had what looked a winner from Johnny Byrne turned down five minutes from the end and a bad-tempered match ended with a 1-1 scoreline that was a fair reflection of the play that was too often polluted by the threat of violence.
Gordon quote: "This was the second game in the 'Little World Cup', with four teams taking part – Brazil, Portugal, Argentina and England. I had been left out of the first game against Brazil and watched from the touchline as Tony Waiters was beaten five times by a Pelé-inspired purple patch late in the match. Three of the goals came from the sort of free-kicks that had deceived me at Wembley a year earlier. Alf was not at all pleased, and I was recalled for this often nasty game with Portugal. I was so disappointed not to get the chance to face Pelé, who even back in 1964 was recognized as the King of football."

Match No 13
Argentina, Rio de Janeiro, 6.6.64. England lost 1-0
Banks Thomson Wilson Milne Norman Moore*
Thompson Greaves Byrne J. Eastham Charlton R.

Highlights: England held Argentina for an hour until Rojas scored in a breakaway raid seconds after the usually so reliable Greaves had missed a clear chance at the opposite end of the pitch. The Argentinians, with skipper Antonio Rattin in commanding form, then played strolling possession football to frustrate England and to clinch victory in the 'Little World Cup' tournament. Argentina won the tournament with three wins from three matches, including victory over Brazil in a vicious game that was war masquerading as sport. England returned home convinced that Argentina would be the biggest mountain between them and the 1966 World Cup. Gordon quote: "We were particularly impressed by Rattin, a butter-smooth player who bossed the midfield with style and panache. He had a moment of madness when he disputed a decision by the referee. A hint of things to come!"

Match No 14
Northern Ireland, Windsor Park, 3.10.64. England won 4-3
Banks Cohen Thomson Milne Norman Moore*
Paine Greaves 3 Pickering 1 Charlton R. Thompson

Highlights: Master poacher Jimmy Greaves scored a first-half hat-trick as England rushed to a 4-0 half-time lead, but the second-half belonged to George Best and Ireland. The young Manchester United winger tied the defenders into knots, and inspired the Irish into a fight back that had England hanging on to a one goal lead at the final whistle. Alf Ramsey gave his team a rocket after the match for becoming complacent. If it had not been for a string of superb saves by Banks, Northern Ireland's second half revival movement would have been rewarded with a remarkable victory. 'If we struggle to hold on to a 4-0 lead,' Ramsey said afterwards, 'what's going to happen if we go a goal down? We must start being more disciplined.' **Gordon quote**: "It was in this match that I first fully realized the potential of the young George Best. He had us in a panic in the second-half and I remember wishing he had been born an Englishman. Big Mo Norman, an ox of a man, was at centre-half and I looked forward to us getting a better understanding. But I missed the next three matches and by the time I was recalled poor Maurice was out of football with a broken leg received in a meaningless friendly. Football can be such a cruel game."

Match No 15
Scotland, Wembley, 10.4.65. Drew 2-2
Banks Cohen Wilson Stiles Charlton J. Moore*
Thompson Greaves 1 Bridges Byrne J. Charlton R. 1

Highlights: England did well to salvage a draw from a game in which they were reduced to only nine fit players. Ray Wilson went off at half-time with torn rib muscles, and Johnny Byrne – dropping back to replace Wilson in defence – became a limping passenger with a knee injury that virtually finished his international career. Ramsey blooded Barry Bridges, Nobby Stiles and Jack Charlton (with brother Bobby on the left wing). This was the first time that England's 1966 World Cup defence paraded together. Bobby Charlton and Jimmy Greaves gave England a commanding 2-0 lead inside the first thirty-five minutes. Denis Law scored for Scotland five minutes before half-time with a viciously swerving shot, and Ian St John equalised midway through the second-half after Cohen had cleared a Davie Wilson shot off the line. England had won the Home Championship but most neutral observers thought Alf Ramsey was being uncharacteristically overconfident when he started forecasting that England would – not might – would win the World Cup. **Gordon quote**: "This was the game in which Denis Law scored with a swerving shot that deceived me, and he was then leaping in celebration of what he thought was another goal when I catapulted back and palmed his chipped shot away for a corner. Denis, one of the game's great showmen, dropped to his knees in disbelief. 'Brilliant … you bastard!' he shouted in a mixture of appreciation and annoyance. Denis was one of those players who always had a word for you during the heat of battle. It was often a rude one, but delivered with a cheeky grin on that Danny Kaye face of his."

Match No 16
Hungary, Wembley, 5.5.65. England won 1-0
Banks Cohen Wilson Stiles   Charlton J. Moore*
Paine Greaves 1 Bridges Eastham Connelly

Highlights: Alf Ramsey's international playing career had ended the last time the Hungarians visited Wembley for their famous 6-3 victory in 1953. His long-awaited revenge was given to him by a well-constructed Jimmy Greaves goal in the sixteenth minute. Bobby Charlton failed a late fitness test and John Connelly was recalled for the first time since Ramsey's desperate first match against France. England's attacking moves were often disjointed and lacking imagination, but the most heartening sight for Ramsey was seeing the defence comfortably cope with a Hungarian forward line that was not a patch on their predecessors of 1953. Skipper Bobby Moore was exceptional at the heart of the defence. **Gordon quote:** "Alf got hold of a film of the 1953 defeat by Hungary and showed it to us during a training break. It took courage for him to screen it for us because he was one of several England players who had a stinker of a match. You could have warmed your hands on the smile on Alf's face after Greavsie's goal had given us the victory that went just a little way to wipe out his nightmare memory. Later that evening Alf got nice and relaxed after hitting his favourite tipple of gin and tonic, and he told us that the Hungarian team that beat England in the 1953 match was the greatest international side he played against in his 33 games for England. 'Ferenc Puskas,' he said, 'was a tubby man yet with explosive acceleration and great ball skills. He could have unlocked a safe with his left foot, and he gave England skipper Billy Wright the biggest chasing of his life."

Alan Ball at the start of his England career when he was just twenty and the Baby of the squad.

Match No 17
Yugoslavia, Belgrade, 9.5.65. Drew 1-1
Banks Cohen Wilson   Stiles   Charlton J. Moore*
Paine Greaves Bridges ı Ball Connelly

Highlights: Ramsey's jigsaw came closer to completion when Alan Ball made his debut, showing the energy and enthusiasm that was to make him such a vital member of the 1966 World Cup squad. Barry Bridges, Chelsea's jet-paced centre-forward, headed England's equaliser after the Yugoslavs had taken a fifteenth minute lead. England were the first foreign side to avoid defeat in Yugoslavia in a full international. "It is the proudest moment of my life," said Ballie in his Clitheroe Kid high-pitch voice after Ramsey had selected him. "I have dreamed of playing for my country ever since I first kicked a ball. There can be no greater honour. I would willingly play for nothing." **Gordon quote:** "I get choked up when I think of Ballie, who left us far too early. There has never been a prouder player to wear his country's shirt. He was the baby of the England World Cup team, but played with enormous maturity and passion."

Match No 18
West Germany, Nuremberg 12.5.65. England won 1-0
Banks Cohen Wilson Flowers Charlton J. Moore*
Paine ı Ball Jones Eastham Temple

Highlights: Derek Temple, Everton's flying winger, was called into England's injury-weakened side for what was his only cap. It was his surging run and cross that laid on the winning goal for Terry Paine in the thirty-seventh minute. Alf Ramsey experimented with a variation of a 4-3-3 formation, with Mick Jones leading the attack for the first time. This was the tenth meeting between the Germans and England and Germany were still seeking their first victory. **Gordon quote:** "It was a bit of a makeshift team because of injuries, and Alf was delighted that we managed to keep intact our record of never having been beaten by a German team in a full international."

Match No 19
Sweden, Gothenburg, 16.5.65. England won 2-1
Banks Cohen Wilson Stiles Charlton J. Moore*
Paine Ball ı Jones Eastham Connelly ı

Highlights: Alan Ball scored his first goal in international football and John Connelly snatched a seventy-fifth minute winner in a game in which the mudheap of a pitch got the better of most of the players. Nobby Stiles lost his contact lenses and a special lubricant had to be flown in from London on match day so that he could wear a spare pair. He and Ball dominated the midfield with their combination of high energy and fierce competitive spirit that would in today's non-contact game have generated a rash of red cards. The Swedish goal came following a rare mistake by Bobby Moore when he lost control of the ball in the treacherous conditions. England had finished their summer tour without defeat, and more people started to come round to the Ramsey conviction that England really could win the World Cup. **Gordon quote:** "Nobby and his big mate Alan Ball had storming games in midfield on a pitch that made every step a challenge. The pitch was flooded over every winter and used as an ice hockey rink!"

Match No 20
Northern Ireland, Wembley, 10.11.65. England won 2-1
Banks Cohen Wilson Stiles   Charlton J. Moore*
Thompson   Baker 1 Peacock 1 Charlton R. Connelly

Highlights: Joe Baker, deputising for the hospitalized, hepatitis-hit Greaves, put England in the lead in the nineteenth minute. The Irish equalised sixty seconds later when Willie Irvine turned a George Best centre through the legs of an embarrassed Gordon Banks. Persistent rain made the surface treacherous, and the Irish defenders were slithering around when Alan Peacock scored England's winner in the seventieth minute. Under gentle persuasion from Alf Ramsey – and at club level, Matt Busby – Bobby Charlton was starting to specialize in more of a withdrawn role, and he was developing into the Great Conductor. **Gordon quote:** "Oh dear, I conceded one of those goals that make goalies blush. Willie Irvine drove the ball so hard that I did not have time to get myself into position and the ball skidded thrugh my legs on a wet pudding of a pitch. Thank goodness Joe Baker and Keith Peacock scored to make my life easier, but the press still gave me a lot of stick for what was a silly goal."

Match No 21
Spain, Madrid, 8.12.65. England won 2-0
Banks Cohen Wilson Stiles Charlton J. Moore*
Ball   Hunt 1 Baker 1 (Hunter) Eastham   Charlton R.

Highlights: One of the most significant games in Alf Ramsey's managerial life. He gave full rein to his 4-3-3 formation for the first time following the experiment in Nuremberg, and the resounding victory convinced him that he had found the tactics best suited to England for the World Cup. The defence was as it would appear throughout the World Cup finals – Banks behind a back line of Cohen, Jack Charlton, Moore and Wilson. Stiles patrolled the midfield as a ball winner alongside the fetch and carrying Alan Ball, with George Eastham orchestrating things from a deep position in centre midfield (the role that would eventually become Bobby Charlton's). Here in Spain Bobby wore the number eleven shirt and was delegated an attacking role alongside out-and-out strikers Roger Hunt and Joe Baker, who spoke with such a heavy Scottish accent that many of his colleagues could not always understand him. Roger Hunt clinched victory with a classic goal on the hour after a sweeping length-of-the-pitch passing movement involving George Cohen, Bobby Charlton and Bobby Moore. The Liverpool striker was making a strong challenge for the England shirt usually worn by the absent, unwell Greaves. It was Baker who gave England an early lead on a pitch soaked by melting snow before limping off in the thirty-fifth minute with a pulled muscle. Norman 'Bites Yer Legs' Hunter became the first England player to make his debut as a substitute. **Gordon quote:** "Alan Ball famously put his hands together as Norman Hunter came running on to the pitch, and said; 'For what they are about to receive …!' I used to shudder when watching some of the tackles that Norman made, yet off the pitch he was quiet and modest and nothing like the assassin who frightened players to death."

Match No 22
Poland, Goodison Park, 5.1.66. Drew 1-1
Banks Cohen Wilson Stiles   Charlton J.   Moore*1
Ball   Hunt   Baker Eastham Harris

Highlights: Bobby Moore scored one of the two goals that decorated his 108 international appearances to cancel out Poland's lead on a glue-pot pitch at Goodison. Moore put the finishing touch to a late move started by Burnley winger Gordon Harris, deputising for the injured Bobby Charlton, and it was Jack Charlton who made the final pass that created the opening for England's skipper. This was the first match between England and Poland, and the first full international for 13 years at a Goodison ground that was to be one of the World Cup venues. Incessant rain turned the pitch into a quagmire. No doubt buoyed by his rare goal, Moore stormed into the penalty area in the closing minutes to meet a cross from the tireless Alan Ball and powered a header against the crossbar. Again, Alf Ramsey played 4-3-3, with Stiles, Ball and Eastham working together in midfield. **Gordon quote:** "A lot of people put the case that the England team should be taken out into the provinces to play foreign opposition on club grounds. Their argument was that England would play better in a club-ground atmosphere and that it would give the fans a chance to see their heroes outside London. I understood their point of view, but remain of the strong opinion that the England team *belongs* at Wembley. Despite a full house at Goodison, we found it very difficult to get properly motivated because it lacked the big-time Wembley international atmosphere. I think the new Wembley is magnificent and would have loved to have played there."

Match No 23
West Germany, Wembley, 23.2.66. England won 1-0
Banks Cohen Newton (Wilson) Moore* Charlton J. Hunter
Ball   Hunt   Stiles 1 Hurst Charlton R.

Highlights: This was to prove a dress rehearsal for the World Cup final just five months later. Nobby Stiles, wearing the number nine shirt but playing in midfield, scored the only goal of the match and of his international career. Some of the less educated football reporters wrote that Stiles had played at centre-forward and that 'Ramsey's gamble of playing him as a spearhead' paid off with a goal. They were yet to understand that shirt numbers were becoming meaningless. Little had been learned since back in the 1950s when Nandor Hidegkuti completely baffled England's defence by playing a withdrawn role in the number nine shirt. Geoff Hurst made an impressive England debut, and Keith Newton's first England game ended just before half-time when he limped off to be replaced by substitute Ray Wilson. The Germans claimed an equaliser when Heiss turned in a cross from Held, but the referee disallowed it after consulting a flag-waving linesman. The shape of things to come! The appearance together of Stiles and Hunter meant the game became a bruise on the memory of several of the Germans. **Gordon quote:** "I think Nobby was the most astonished person at Wembley when he snatched the winning goal and gave the television cameras a preview of the toothless grin that was to become so famous in the months ahead. We learnt from this game that goalkeeper Tilkowski was what we call in the trade 'a Dracula' … he didn't like crosses`!"

Match No 24
Scotland, Hampden Park, 2.4.66. England won 4-3
Banks Cohen Newton Stiles   Charlton J. Moore*
Ball   Hunt 2   Charlton R. 1 Hurst 1 Connelly

Highlights: Geoff Hurst scored his first goal for England in the nineteenth minute to start a spree that excited the 133,000 crowd but made purists wince at the procession of defensive blunders by both teams. Hunt added a second goal for England before Denis Law threw himself forward in typical dare-devil style to head Scotland's first goal just before half-time. Hunt made it 3-1 early in the second-half, and then Celtic's jinking winger Jimmy Johnstone pulled it back to 3-2 before a thunderbolt shot from Bobby Charlton restored the two-goal lead. This was Charlton in imperious form as he revelled in his role as midfield orchestrator. Johnstone, turning the England defence inside out with his dribbling runs, scored the final goal six minutes from the end with a delicate curling shot that deceived Gordon Banks. A press reporter said to Alf Ramsey immediately after the match, 'A great game to watch, Alf.' The cold blue eyes became a burning glare on the journalist. 'For you maybe,' said Alf, 'but I thought there was some appalling football played. We must be much, much tighter.' Seven-goal thrillers did not belong in the Ramsey textbook. Once a perfectionist right-back, always a perfectionist right-back. **Gordon quote:** "Jimmy Johnstone, a darting genius of a winger, spoiled he match for me wth his late goal. I thought I had all my angles covered as I advanced to meet him after he had tricked his way past two defenders. But somehow he managed to curl the ball past me and into the far corer of the net. It was a goal that I would have considered impossible."

Match No 25
Yugoslavia, Wembley, 4.5.66. England won 2-0

Banks Armfield* Wilson Peters Charlton J. Hunter
Paine Greaves ₁ Charlton R. ₁ Hurst Tambling

Highlights: Jimmy Greaves, back in the England team after his hepatitis-forced five-month lay-off, scored the first goal in the ninth minute. Bobby Charlton celebrated being elected 'Footballer of the Year' by wrapping up England's victory with another of his screaming long-range shots. Martin Peters, the player who would be described by Ramsey as 'ten years ahead of his time', twice went close to marking his debut with a goal against a highly skilled Yugoslav side. It was England's last home game before the World Cup and they responded with a powerful performance that sent a mood of optimism shooting through the country. **Gordon quote**: "Alf Ramsey used to stamp on complacency as if it was a disease. He came down hard on any player who took his England place for granted. I recall that after this match in which I did everything right, I said to to the England boss as I departed from the team hotel: 'See you, Alf.' Those famous cold eyes of his visibly widened and all he said in return was, 'Will you?' It was a lesson to me that I had to fight for my England place no matter how well I had played in previous games."

Match No 26
Finland, Helsinki, 26.6.66. England won 3-0

Banks Armfield* Wilson Peters ₁ Charlton J. ₁ Hunter
Callaghan Hunt ₁ Charlton R. Hurst Ball

Highlights: Martin Peters scored his first goal for England and the first of the match at the start of a final warm-up tour before the World Cup finals. Alan Ball failed from the penalty spot in a game remembered more for the many missed chances than those that were eventually taken by Roger Hunt and Jack Charlton (a freak goal from a last-minute shot from out on the touchline). Ian Callaghan made a lively debut alongside his Liverpool team-mate Hunt as Alf Ramsey continued his experiment of playing with just one winger. Soon, there would be none! **Gordon quote**: "Alf was trying to give as many as possible of his 22-player squad a game before the World Cup finals. Jimmy Armfield was captain, and it started a silly rumour that he was going to take over from Bobby Moore as World Cup skipper. As much as I admired Jimmy as a player and leader, I knew there was no chance that Alf would turn his back on the immaculate Moore."

Match No 27
Poland, Chorzow, 5.7.66. England won 1-0
Banks Cohen Wilson Stiles   Charlton J.   Moore*
Ball   Greaves   Charlton R. Hunt 1   Peters

Highlights: A beautifully struck shot by Roger Hunt in the thirteenth minute was enough to give England victory in this final match before the World Cup finals. This would prove to be the line-up that just twenty-five days later would win the World Cup for England, with just one exception: Hurst in place of Greaves. Alf Ramsey had unveiled his wingless wonders, and there is no doubt that he considered this his strongest line-up. Martin Peters was the man of the match, sharing scheming duties with Bobby Charlton, and having the energy to help out in both defence and attack whenever necessary. He did it all with style and grace, and it was a surprise when he failed to make Ramsey's line-up for the opening match of the World Cup six days later. **Gordon quote:** "This was the ideal final warm-up for the World Cup finals and our confidence was so high after our victory that more and more people were jumping on the bandwagon and agreeing with Alf Ramsey in believing England could become world champions."

Match No 28
Uruguay, World Cup, Wembley, 11.7.66. Drew 0-0
Banks Cohen Wilson Stiles   Charlton J.   Moore*
Ball   Greaves   Charlton R. Hunt   Connelly

Highlights: A dull and uninspiring start to the World Cup left neutrals wondering on what Alf Ramsey based his confidence that England would win the tournament. Uruguay played with nine men back in defence and defied all England's attempts to break them down. It was the first time in twelve matches that England had failed to score. John Connelly was Ramsey's one winger. The Uruguayans celebrated at the final whistle as if they had won. They had squeezed exactly what they wanted from the game with their stifling defensive tactics. It was not a pretty sight. **Gordon quote**: "As we walked down the slope towards the dressing-rooms, Jack Charlton and Bobby Moore were pulled to one side by doctors who wanted them for dope tests. Two players were

Brothers Bobby and Jack Charlton, proudly at attention. They always gave full attention to England.

selected at random after every World Cup game, and big Jack got nabbed every time. Before the tournament ended we presented him with a baby's potty and dubbed him 'England's Jimmy Riddle Champion.'"

Match No 29
Mexico, World Cup, Wembley, 16.7.66. England won 2-0
Banks Cohen Wilson Stiles Charlton J. Moore*
Paine   Greaves Charlton R. 1 Hunt 1 Peters

Highlights: Alf Ramsey had not yet completely abandoned wingers. Terry Paine was preferred to Connelly in this second game, with Martin Peters taking the place of Alan Ball in midfield. Bobby Charlton unleashed one of his magnificent twenty-five yard specials for the first goal, and Roger Hunt clinched victory after having what looked a good goal ruled offside. After the frustration of the opening match against Uruguay, this victory convinced many people that England could live up to Ramsey's expectations. Mexico were not allowed to create a single goal scoring chance by an England defence in which Bobby Moore was at his commanding best. **Gordon quote:** "Alan Ball had one of those expressive faces that glowed when he was feeling pleased and dropped to the floor when he was miserable. I thought he was going to break down and cry when Alf Ramsey told him he was not playing in this second World Cup match. We had to talk him out of walking out, and it was the best decision of his life when he decided to stay. He was to become one of the most influential of our players."

Match No 30
France, World Cup, Wembley, 20.7.66. England won 2-0
Banks Cohen Wilson Stiles Charlton J. Moore*
Callaghan Greaves Charlton R. Hunt 2 Peters

Highlights: Two smartly taken Roger Hunt goals gave England a confidence booster on their way into the World Cup quarter-finals. Ian Callaghan became the third winger tried by the England manager. Jimmy Greaves finished the match with a deep gash on his left shin, and Stiles was booked for a crunching tackle on French striker Simon. He was fortunate not to be sent off, and Ramsey ignored calls from Football Association officials that he should drop Stiles because of his competitive nature. 'If Stiles goes, so do I,' said Ramsey. And he was not feigning. He knew how vital Nobby's ball-winning performances were to the team in an era when fierce tackling midfield players were a necessary evil. **Gordon quote:** "Nobby was petrified that he was going to be banned from the tournament. His competitive play was being interpreted in some quarters as dirty, and even some British journaliss were writing that Alf should leave him out. But

I had played with Nobby long enough to know that he was never deliberately dirty. Hard yes, but then football in those days was a physically hard game. Nobby seemed about as tough as Andy Pandy when compared with some of the Argentinians we had seen on television during the World Cup. Alf told the Toothless Tiger: 'You just play your usual fair but hard game and leave me to do the worrying.'"

Match No 31
Argentina, World Cup, Wembley, 23.7.66. England won 1-0
Banks Cohen Wilson Stiles Charlton J. Moore*
Ball Hurst 1 Charlton R. Hunt Peters

Highlights: Argentina shelved their superior skills and instead concentrated on what seemed a premeditated policy of disrupting England with a spate of petty fouls. Their captain Antonio Rattin arrogantly challenged just about every decision that the referee made and was waving his arms around like a traffic policeman. Finally the referee, a little West German called Rudlof Kreitlein, could take no more of Rattin's disruptive tactics and ordered him off. It was almost comical to see the tiny figure of the referee staring up at the tall, stately looking Rattin and demanding that he leave the field. It was also very sad. It took ten minutes of argument and touchline interpretations before Rattin finally walked. Geoff Hurst, making his World Cup debut in place of the injured Greaves, headed the winning goal from a Martin Peters cross to the near post. It was a classical creation that had made-in-West Ham written all over it. For Gordon Banks, it was a record seventh successive England appearance without conceding a goal. This was the first match in which England played without a recognised winger. Ramsey's 'Wingless Wonders' were off the launching pad. Alan Ball, happy and relieved to be recalled to the team, gave a perpetual motion performance that confirmed that he was in the side to stay. **Gordon quote:** "Alf Ramsey described the Argentinians as 'animals', a heat-of-the-moment description that had diplomatic repercussions and led to official protests being made to the British ambassador in Buenos Aires. The sad fact is that Argentina were the most skilful side in the tournament, but they allowed their tempers to over-rule their talent."

No 32
Portugal, World Cup, Wembley, 26.7.66. England won 2-1
Banks Cohen Wilson Stiles Charlton J. Moore*
Ball Hurst Charlton R. 2 Hunt Peters

Highlights: This was THE classic match of the 1966 World Cup. It lacked the drama of the final, but the football played by both teams had rarely been bettered at Wembley.

The match belonged more to Bobby Charlton than anybody. He moved with the grace of a Nureyev on grass and the power of a panther. His reward was two superb goals, one drilled low into the net from a rebound after a Roger Hunt shot had been blocked, and the second, a real beauty, rifled high into the net from twenty-five yards. Seven minutes from the end England's magnificent defence conceded their first goal of the tournament when Eusebio scored from the penalty spot after Jack Charlton had handled a header from Jose Torres. Nobby Stiles performed a disciplined containing role on the great Eusebio, fresh from his stunning four-goal performance against North Korea in the quarter-final at Goodison after the Koreans had rushed three goals into the lead. Eusebio left the pitch in tears as the two teams got a standing ovation for producing a match that would live long in the memory. **Gordon quote:** "We had discussed Eusebio and his penalty taking in detail during the pre-match training, and I had made up my mind to go to my right where he always placed his penalties. My team-mates knew I was going to go to my right, but for some reason kept pointing me in that direction as Eusebio placed the ball for the spot-kick. Portuguese skipper Coluna, a wily old pro, saw the pointing fingers and whispered in Eusebio's ear. It was enough to convince me that he was telling his team-mate to change the direction of his penalty. As he kicked the ball I dived to my left. Wrong! The ball went to my right. I could have cried. It was the first goal I had conceded in 443 minutes of World Cup football, and but for those pointing fingers I might have saved it. For me, it took the edge off what I considered a magnificent team performance."

No 33
West Germany, World Cup Final, Wembley, 30.7.66. England won 4-2 (aet)
Banks Cohen Wilson Stiles   Charlton J. Moore*
Ball Hurst 3 Charlton R.   Hunt Peters 1

Highlights: Alf Ramsey decided to stick with an unchanged team. No place for fit-again Jimmy Greaves, the greatest scorer the modern English game has ever known. West Germany took the negative approach of putting Franz Beckenbauer on man-to-man marking duty against Bobby Charlton, so the two most creative players on the pitch cancelled each other out. This was manager Helmut Schoen's reaction to Charlton's spectacular show against Portugal. A rare Ray Wilson mistake on a wet surface let Helmut Haller in for a thirteenth minute goal which was equalised six minutes later when Hurst headed in a perfectly flighted free-kick from his West Ham team-mate Bobby Moore. In the 78th minute a Hurst shot was blocked and it was another West Hammer, Peters, who smacked the rebound smartly into the net to make it 2-1. England were one minute from the World Cup when Jack Charlton was adjudged to have fouled Germany's skipper Uwe Seeler. During a goalmouth scramble that followed the free-kick defender Wolfgang Weber forced the ball into the net, with skipper Bobby Moore insisting there had been a handball. Eleven minutes into extra-time, the inexhaustible Alan Ball made one of his many scampering runs past left-back Schnellinger and centred the ball. Hurst turned and fired a first-time shot against the underside of the bar, and England claimed the ball had crossed the goal-line. Swiss referee Gottfried Dienst awarded a controversial goal after consulting the Russian linesman Bakhramov. To this day, the Germans dispute the decision. Hurst ended all arguments in the final seconds when he ran on to a clearance from Bobby Moore and hammered a left foot shot past goalkeeper Hans Tilkowski to complete the first ever World Cup final hat-trick. England, just as Alf Ramsey had prophesied, were champions of the world.

Gordon quote: 'We were devastated by Germany's scrambled equalizer just seconds from the end of normal time. We had got so close only to have victory snatched away from us in the last desperate moments. It was like being pushed off Everest with just a stride to go to the summit. Alf came walking quickly and urgently towards us and while trainers Harold Shepherdson and Les Cocker massaged life back into tired limbs, Alf got to work on our minds. 'You had it won once,' he said. 'Now go out and win it again. I know how you all feel, but just look at them ...' He gestured to indicate the Germans, several of whom were lying stretched out like dead men. 'They're all knackered,' said Nobby Stiles, hardly looking a picture of freshness with his stockings rolled down to his ankles and his shirt sticking to his body with perspiration. 'We can f*** this lot!' It was Geoff Hurst's two goals in extra-time that won the Cup for us, but all of us were agreed that an equal hero was Alan Ball, who ran himself into the ground for the team. He gave the performance of his life."

We are taking a break here from Gordon's gallery of England games to start the ball rolling on the story of the life of the greatest footballer of them all, Pelé, the man who would eventually face Banks in one of the duels of the century.

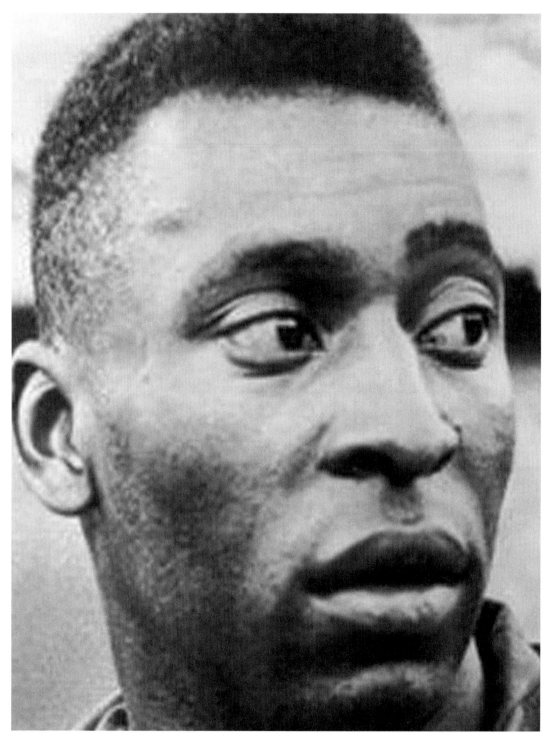

An early picture from Pelé's personal collection. He is one of the most photographed sportsmen ever.

PELÉ is one of the most written about and interviewed sportsmen of this or any other century. To maintain the unique feel we wish to have to this book, I decided the best way to give a new insight into the King of football was to present his answers to across-the-board questions on his life and times. Here are his replies to the first twenty questions, based on the years up to the 1970 World Cup finals …

How did you get your name Pelé?

'It is traditional for Brazilians to use nicknames. When I was young my family called me 'Dico' and that is still how I am known to my loved ones. The name given to me at birth was Edison Arantes Do Nascimento. The name Edison was after the inventor Thomas Edison, but I have always preferred to call myself Edson. In my early days with Santos I was called 'Gasolina', after a Brazilian singer. But Pelé is the nickname that finally stuck. The name really bugged me at first. I thought Pelé sounded horrible, and got into trouble at school one day when I punched a boy for calling me Pelé. To be honest I have never been certain about the origin but the most probable version started with a team-mate of my father's when he played for Vasco da Gama. The team-mate was a goalkeeper and was known as Bilé. I used to pretend to be him when I was about four, diving around in the goal and saying, "When I grow up I want to be like Bilé." I managed to keep pronouncing it Pilé, and that, because of the different dialects in Brazil, gradually became Pelé as it caught on at school. I hated the name right up until I started to get headlines as a young footballer, and then I thought that perhaps it was not too bad after all. Now I would not swap it for anything.'

How good a footballer was your father?

'Known as Dondinho, he was very good but very unlucky. As a centre-forward with Vasco da Gama he achieved something that I never managed, once scoring five headed goals in a single match. Those who saw him at his peak said that he was international class, but sadly he suffered a bad knee injury that forced his premature retirement when he was playing for a team called Atletico Mineiro. He and my Uncle Jorge were big influences on me in my earliest days, and they always encouraged me to play to the best of my ability.'

You were born on October 23 1940, while the World War was raging in Europe. What was it like growing up in Brazil at that time?

❝I was born in a district called Tres Coracoes, and grew up in Bauru, Sao Paulo. Like all those around us, we were a very poor family and lived in poverty. We could not even afford a proper football, and I used to play with a sock stuffed with newspaper, or sometimes with a grapefruit. It was only when I got to school that I started playing regularly with a real leather football. It was the old-fashioned type that had to be pumped up, and had very worn leather panels and a lace that could graze your face. To help my mother buy food I used to shine shoes at the Bauru Athletic Club. They were tough times, but because everybody was in the same boat I did not really appreciate just how poor we were.❞

How were you discovered and who deserves the credit for launching your career?

❝Waldemar de Brito, who had played for Brazil in the 1934 World Cup finals, was a scout for the Bauru club where I shined shoes. He saw me playing for a team we called the Shoeless Ones. We played in bare feet because we could not afford football boots. Waldemar saw enough to decide to invite me to join his Baquinho youth side, and he made sure I had a good pair of football boots for the first time in my life. When I was fifteen he took me to the famous Santos club, and I played for their juniors. Waldemar told the Santos management that I was going to become the greatest footballer ever! By the time I was sixteen I was in the Santos first-team and also got my first international call up.❞

Did you think you would get the chance to play in the 1958 World Cup finals?

❝Once I was named in the squad I was very hopeful, even though I was the youngest player at seventeen. I was called in to the team for the third match against Russia after England had held us to a goalless draw. In my next match against Wales I scored the only goal of the match, and from then on my football life was like a fairytale.❞

What do you remember of the final against host country Sweden?
❝Sweden were an exceptionally good team, playing European-style football with smooth team play and making the most of their home advantage. They took an early lead through their skilful forward Nils Liedholm, but we were always confident we could come out on top. We hit back to lead 2-1 at half-time and ten minutes into the second-half I scored what became one of my favourite goals. I caught a high, dropping ball on the thigh, hooked it over the head of my marker, and volleyed it into the net from

about the penalty spot. It was a goal scored all in one swift movement. I also managed to head our fifth goal in our 5-2 victory, and was so overcome with the emotion and excitement of it all that I cried my eyes out as the final whistle went. It was Brazil's first victory in a World Cup final and meant so much to us all. You have to realise that in Brazil football is a religion.'

Who were among your outstanding team-mates in that 1958 team?

'Vava went to Sweden as understudy to Jose Altafini, but he emerged as one of the stars of the tournament. He scored two goals against Russia and another two goals in the final. He had a very good understanding with our midfield general Didi, who always passed the ball with perfect weight and he was a free-kick specialist who was famous for his 'falling leaf' free-kick. He used to put so much spin on the ball that it would hang and curl in the air like an autumn leaf falling off a wind-swept tree.'

And how about Garrincha?

'Ah, The Legend! He and I made our World Cup debuts together against Russia, and he was responsible for laying on Vava's two goals. He was such a free spirit that coaches did not quite know how to handle him. Manoel, his real name, was a cripple at birth and an operation left one leg shorter than the other and both legs were bowed. But when a ball was at his feet he could be the most bewitching and bewildering winger in the world. He made more headlines with his life off the pitch than on it, but I will always remember him with affection for his skill as a footballer. We played together 59 times for Brazil, and were never on the losing side.'

What difference did helping Brazil win the World Cup make to your life?

'It suddenly went mad! I gradually became financially comfortable and was able to give my parents the things they deserved from life. We did not earn anything like the fortunes today's footballers are picking up, but I was much better off than earlier generations of players. From being unknown, I was getting offers to endorse and sponsor things. It was all quite a shock to the system and needed getting used to.'

Tell us about your greatest goal that came a year after the 1958 World Cup.

'You will be referring to a goal I scored against Brazilian club Juventus at their Rua Javari Stadium in August 1959. I flick headed the ball past one defender, then a second and then a third, all the time heading the ball. The goalkeeper came towards me and I

Garrincha and Pelé, who were never in a beaten Brazilian team in 59 internationals together.

then headed it over him and into the net. It completed my hat-trick, and even the home fans were kind enough to applaud it. Just a couple of years ago I attended a ceremony at the stadium where they unveiled a statute of me heading the ball as a reminder of that goal. There were no television cameras at league matches in those days, and for a film made in 2004 they reconstructed the goal using digital techniques. It was a goal of which I was very proud.'

A year later another goal was marked with a special plaque.

'This was against Fluminense at the Maracana Stadium in Rio. I dribbled the ball through the defence – some reporters counted eight players that I went past – before beating the goalkeeper. It was voted the 'most beautiful' goal ever scored at the Maracana, which is of course our national stadium. You have to remember that I concentrated on scoring the goals, and I left the descriptions to others. All I know is that to me goals are the only thing that matter in football, and I was lucky to score a lot of them.'

You did not enjoy the 1962 World Cup in Chile?

'I enjoyed the fact that Brazil successfully defended the World Cup, beating Czechoslovakia in the final after eliminating England in the quarter-final. But a pulled muscle meant I missed the closing stages of the tournament, although I had the consolation of winning a medal as a member of the squad. I was so pleased with the two-goal debut of my deputy Amarildo against Spain that I jumped fully clothed into the team bath after the match to congratulate him!'

By then you were the target for every major club in Europe.

'Yes, I could have taken my pick of the best clubs in Italy or Spain, but when it became public that I was wanted abroad there was a huge public outcry. The Government stepped in and declared me an official national treasure of Brazil, so therefore not for export. It was a huge honour for me, but I often wonder what I might have achieved against the challenge of disciplined European defences.'

Santos were the dominant force in Brazil while you were playing?

'We won more than 30 trophies when I was with the club, but don't run away with the idea that Santos were a one-man team. I had team-mates of the quality of Zito, Pepe and Coutinho, and we had a great understanding. We specialised in having outstanding individualists but also good team tactics with everybody pulling their weight.'

The 1966 World Cup in England was your unhappiest?

'It was a horrible experience. I had so looked forward to playing in the country that gave organised football to the world. But the tournament was far too physical, with violent defenders kicking the individual players out of the game. When we played Portugal in our third match I was brutally tackled half a dozen times before I had to limp off the pitch. It was my lowest moment in football, and I vowed then never to play World Cup football again.'

What did you think of the winning England team?

'They were hard but fair, and in Bobby Moore, Bobby Charlton and Geoff Hurst had world-class players. In goal, of course, was the formidable Gordon Banks, who did not concede a single goal until the semi-finals. There is no question that England had the best defence in the finals, but their attack lacked consistency. I often wonder what

Eusebio offers comfort as Pelé pays the price of being a marked man in the 1966 World Cup finals.

might have happened in the quarter-final if Argentina had kept their tempers. It was fitting that England won the final against West Germany, another very physical side. But I was very surprised they played without the great Jimmy Greaves. All in all, I thought they were very disappointing finals with too much emphasis on the physical rather than the skilful side of football. In 1966 it was hardly the Beautiful Game.'

Who did you consider the outstanding individual in the 1966 finals?

'It had to be Eusebio. He scored nine goals, and his performance against North Korea in the quarter-finals was one of the great one-man displays. He scored four goals and almost single handed dragged Portugal into the semi-final after they had gone down 3-0 in the first fifteen minutes. The only satisfying moment for me was scoring with a direct free-kick against Bulgaria in our opening match. It meant I had become the first player in history to score in three successive World Cup final tournaments. But it was no consolation for the way I was kicked out of the match against Portugal.'

You reached an astonishing milestone in 1969 when you scored your 1,000th goal.

'This was against Vasca da Gama at my beloved Maracana Stadium. I scored from the penalty spot and the game was held up for ten minutes while everybody celebrated. I had been on 999 goals for several games, and I felt a load had been lifted off my shoulders when I at last got that 1,000th goal. It was probably the worst penalty I ever took! I had a special golden shirt presented to me on the pitch, and Santos declared the day – November 19 – 'Pelé Day.' Great moments like these you never ever forget.'

What restored your appetite for the World Cup?

'My 1,000th goal made me realise I still had much to give, even though there was some politics when my old international team-mate Mario Zagalo took over from Joao Saldanha as Brazil's coach. I sensed we could win the Jules Rimet trophy for a record third time, and I wanted to be part of that history. I had got the bad feelings of the 1966 tournament out of my system, and felt we had the players to win the trophy again.'

How did you react when you heard that champions England were in your group?

'We were quietly confident we could beat them. In 1969 we had managed to win 2-1 in a friendly match in Rio after England had led 1-0 at half-time. Gordon Banks had saved a penalty against our captain Carlos Alberto, and I found myself greatly respecting his composure and his ability ....'

Match No 34
Northern Ireland, Windsor Park, 22.10.66. England won 2-0
Banks Cohen Wilson Stiles   Charlton J. Moore*
Ball   Hurst Charlton R.   Hunt ₁ Peters ₁

Highlights: The Irish, with George Best and Derek Dougan in menacing mood, battled desperately to overcome Engand in their first match as world champions, but they were sunk by a goal in each half by first Roger Hunt and then Martin Peters. The match deteriorated into a bad tempered encounter, and in the closing minutes Linfield winger Billy Ferguson was ordered off after a savage tackle on Alan Ball. **Gordon quote:** "Bobby Moore's attention during the build up to the match was claimed by the Inland Revenue, who announced they would be taxing the £1,000 bonus collected by each of the 22 players in our World Cup winning squad. On behalf of the team, skipper Bobby took the Taxman to the steps of the law courts before they relented and agreed to make it tax free. I know that I'm biased but I would suggest that this was a disgraceful way to treat heroes. Can you imagine what the bonuses would be today for an England team winning the World Cup! We almost had to beg for our rewards."

Match No 35
Czechoslovakia, Wembley, 2.11.66. Drew 0-0
Banks   Cohen Wilson Stiles   Charlton J. Moore*
Ball   Hurst Charlton R.   Hunt Peters

Highlights: This was the sixteenth match since the summer of 1965 in which England had not conceded a goal. The Czechs came only to defend, and their nine-man blanket defence smothered the England attack. Unbeaten in a run of eighteen matches, England had lost only once in their last twenty-nine games, but this was a below-par performance that disappointed the 75,000 crowd. For the record, this was only the second goalless draw in fifty-eight post-war full internationals at Wembley. The only other one was the World Cup curtain-raiser against Uruguay. **Gordon quote:** "We were choked not to win this first match back at Wembley since the World Cup ... almost literally choked by a Czech team that were interested only in going home without conceding a goal. I was a spectator for much of the match because our opponents played only two forwards upfield throughout the game. My sympathy was with the crowd. They deserved something better for their money."

Match No 36
Wales, Wembley, 16.11.66. England won 5-1
Banks Cohen Wilson Stiles Charlton J. 1 Moore*
Ball Hurst 2 Charlton R. 1 Hunt Peters 1 o.g.

Highlights: The Charlton brothers were both on the score-sheet and Geoff Hurst netted twice against a Welsh team that telegraphed their tactics by continually trying to play long balls to their twin strikers Wyn Davies and Ron Davies. Apart from a consolation headed goal by Wyn Davies, the England defence comfortably controlled the Welsh attack by shutting out their supply line from the wings. With both the Home Championship and qualification for the European championships at stake, the game had a hard competitive edge and the final scoreline flattered the world champions who were helped by an own goal from one of the hardest workers on the pitch, Terry Hennessey. Bobby Moore, playing in his fiftieth international, was exceptional in an England defence that was at its dominant best. **Gordon quote:** "Little did we know it then, but this was the last time the World Cup winning team would play together. All these years later I can say with confidence that this was the greatest England defence of all time. In our last 25 matches we conceded only 15 goals, and we kept a blank sheet in 16 of the games. The defence rests!"

Match No 37
Scotland, Wembley, 15.4.67. England lost 3-2
Banks Cohen Wilson Stiles Charlton J. 1 Moore*
Ball Greaves Charlton R. Hurst 1 Peters

Highlights: Scotland claimed they were world champions after handing England their first defeat in twenty matches, but it was something of a hollow victory against a team reduced to eight fit players. Jack Charlton hobbled at centre-foward for much of the match with a broken toe, Ray Wilson was a limping passenger after getting a kick on the ankle, and Jimmy Greaves was reduced to half pace by a knock in his comeback match. Denis Law was at his tormenting best and gave Scotland the lead after twenty-eight minutes, and it remained at 1-0 until a four-goal rush in the last twelve minutes. Celtic winger Bobby Lennox made it 2-0 before Jack Charlton bravely pulled one back. Gordon Banks was beaten at the near post by Jim McCalliog and then Hurst headed home a Bobby Charlton cross. Nobby Stiles, Denis Law's Manchester United team-mate, said later: 'I knew the Scots were taking it very seriously when Denis came on to the pitch wearing shinpads. I had never seen him wear them before.' Four of the Scottish team helped Celtic become the first British club to win the European Cup the following month. The newly knighted Sir Alf Ramsey said: 'Scotland deserved their victory, but I hope they will accept it as a fact rather than an excuse when I say we were heavily handicapped by injuries.' **Gordon quote:** "There was an amusing postscript to the match. Our team coach, with a police escort to speed us through the heavy traffic, slowed down at a crossroads about a mile from Wembley where an army of Scottish supporters were celebrating their win at a pub on the corner. They saw the coach, thought it was theirs and started to do victory jigs and to chant 'Scot-land … Scot-land …' Suddenly it dawned on them that they were cheering the *English* team. I have never seen such a quick change of mood. Suddenly beer bottles and glasses rained on our coach as our driver put his foot down and got us away unharmed. Goodness knows what they would have done had Scotland lost the game! As it was, for years afterwards they claimed their victory meant they were the true world champions."

Match No 38
Wales, Ninian Park, 21.10.67. England won 3-0
Banks Cohen Newton Mullery Charlton J. Moore*
Ball 1 Hunt Charlton R. 1 Hurst Peters 1

Highlights: The match turned on a magnificent save by Gordon Banks. Wales were having the better of the early play in a rainstorm when his Stoke team-mate Roy Vernon fired a shot from point-blank range. Somehow Banks managed to fist the ball off target, and from then on England took command. Martin Peters and Bobby Charlton scored a goal each and Alan Ball netted from the penalty spot. Mike England stood like a man mountain in the middle of the Welsh defence, and gave added ammunition to his Tottenham supporters who claimed with some justification that he was the best centre-half in Britain. **Gordon quote:** "That save against Roy Vernon was one of the greatest of my career. I leapt forward just as he connected and managed to fist the ball off target. 'And I thought you were my pal,' Roy joked as he sportingly acknowledged my save with a pat on the shoulder. It was the sort of good sportsmanship that was commonplace in those days despite the fierceness of the competition."

Match No 39
Northern Ireland, Wembley, 22.11.67. England won 2-0
Banks Cohen Wilson Mullery Sadler Moore*
Thompson Hunt Charlton R.1 Hurst 1 Peters

Highlights: Versatile David Sadler made his debut at centre-half against a Northern Ireland team missing their two key forwards George Best and Derek Dougan. Goals from Geoff Hurst and Bobby Charlton clinched victory in an undistinguished match that fell flat the moment it was announced just before the kick-off that both Best and Dougan

Sir Bobby Charlton, England's master of the precise pass, the thunderbolt shot and flick-over hair.

had failed fitness tests. All attention was now switched to the final Home Championship match against Scotland that would decide which of them would represent Great Britain in the European Nations Cup quarter finals. **Gordon quote**: "I remember this game for the anger of Alf Ramsey at half-time. He would never tolerate complacency, and gave us a rollocking for our casual and careless play. It woke us up and we stepped up our game in the second-half and finally won without ever being at our best."

Match No 40
USSR, Wembley, 6.12.67. Drew 2-2
Banks Knowles Wilson Mullery Sadler   Moore*
Ball 1 Hunt Charlton R. Hurst Peters 1

Highlights: Ray Wilson was given a rare chasing on a snow-carpeted pitch by flying Russian winger Chislenko, who appropriately was also an outstanding ice hockey player. Alan Ball gave England an early lead, but two goals from 'Red Rocket' Chislenko put Russia in command. Bobby Moore and Ray Wilson combined to make an opening for Martin Peters, who headed an equaliser. Tottenham defender Cyril Knowles made an assured debut out of position at right-back. Pshenichnikov proved himself a worthy successor to Lev Yashin in goal with a series of stunning saves as England pressed for victory in the last twenty minutes of a skilled and entertaining match that was a credit to both sides. **Gordon quote:** "This was the only time I ever saw our unflappable left-back Ray Wilson outplayed. 'He was like a bloody Russian rocket,' Ray said later. 'I wish he'd gone to the moon instead of Wembley.' Ray was a great pro and a funny companion. I always found it difficult to imagine him in his later role as an undertaker. He had a dry wit that used to have us in stitches, and I now wonder what he meant when he used to say how good certain players were in the box!"

Match No 41
Scotland, Hampden Park, 24.2.68. Drew 1-1
Banks Newton Wilson Mullery Labone Moore*
Ball Hurst Summerbee Charlton R.   Peters 1

Highlights: England needed a draw to qualify for the European championship quarter-finals, Scotland a win. Martin Peters produced one of his most impressive performances for England, scoring their goal with a superbly controlled swerving shot and going close on three other occasions. John Hughes headed Scotland's equaliser when Gordon Banks slipped on the treacherous surface that was a mixture of mud and ice. Charlie Cooke had a brilliant twenty-minute spell when he ran the England defence dizzy, but the Scottish strikers could not cash in on his creative work. Mike Summerbee made a quietly impressive debut, and played an assist role in the Peters goal that guaranteed England playing Spain in a two-legged Nations Cup quarter-final. **Gordon quote:** 'I was never one for making excuses, but I felt justified in blaming the surface for their equaliser. I pushed off with my right foot for what I anticipated would be a save from a John Hughes header, but I slipped on the mud and missed the ball. Alf went out of his way to sympathise with me."

Match No 42
Spain, Wembley, 3.4.68. England won 1-0
Banks Knowles Wilson Mullery Charlton J. Moore*
Ball Hunt Summerbee Charlton R. 1 Peters

Highlights: Bobby Charlton crashed the ball into the net from a short free-kick taken by Martin Peters to equal the 44-goal England record held by Jimmy Greaves. Spain threatened to snatch a last minute equaliser in this first-leg European championship quarter-final tie, but Banks pulled off a spectacular save from a lightning back heel by Amancio. The Spaniards played a cautious defensive game, putting their faith in a victory in the second-leg in Madrid. **Gordon quote:** "It was a pure reflex save against Amancio. There seemed little danger as he stood with his back to the goal, and he appeared to have over-stepped the ball. But he was just foxing and suddenly with a back flick of his right heel sent the ball skimming towards the far corner of the net. I instinctively leapt to my right to smother the ball. Amancio clapped his hands together in a mixture of applause and frustration. Chelsea goalkeeper Peter Bonetti, who had been sitting on the subs bench, congratulated me on the save. I really appreciated that, coming from one of the game's great shot stoppers. The Cat, as he was known throughout the game, replaced me because I was unavailable for the return match in Spain, and he helped us win 2-1 and so reach the European Nations Cup finals in Italy."

Match No 43
West Germany, Hanover, 1.6.68. England lost 1-0
Banks Newton Knowles Hunter Labone Moore*
Ball Bell Summerbee Hurst Thompson

Highlights: England's unbeaten record against the Germans, which had lasted twelve matches and sixty-seven years, ended when Brian Labone deflected a Franz Beckenbauer shot wide of Gordon Banks eight minutes from the end of this warm-up match before the Nations Cup finals. It was a goal that silenced the jeers of the German spectators who had been barracking their own team as England made and missed a string of chances. **Gordon quote:** "The Germans knew they were very lucky to win this game. I had

Sir Alf Ramsey, the tactical genius who planned and plotted England's World Cup triumph of 1966.

Beckenbauer's shot covered, but Brian Labone stuck out a leg and deflected the ball into the net. This was only our third defeat in our last forty matches, and we headed for the European Nations Cup semi-final against Yugolsavia in Florence in good spirit."

Match No 44
Yugoslavia, Florence, 5.6.68. England lost 1-0
Banks Newton Wilson Mullery Labone   Moore*
Ball   Peters Charlton R.   Hunt   Hunter

Highlights: Dragan Dzajic, Yugoslavia's world-class winger, snatched the goal that won this ill-tempered European Nations Cup semi-final after Bobby Moore had failed to get his head to a high cross five minutes from the end. It was a bruising, angry battle in which the Yugoslavs kicked anything that moved, and in the final moments Alan Mullery became the first player ever sent off while playing for England. He got his marching orders for retaliating after being on the receiving end of a brutal tackle by Trivic. By today's no-contact rules at least two players from either side would have been sent for early baths long before Mullery made his miserable exit. 'It was the worst moment of my career,' he said later. 'I felt as if I had not only let the team down but also my wife and family. The player I kicked out at had been hacking at me throughout the game and I just lost my temper. To be the first England player ever sent off is a record I will hate having to live with.' **Gordon quote:** "Of all the matches I proudly played for England, this is the game I would have to place at No 1 in my chamber of horrors. The Italian press had launched a vicious campaign against us in the build-up to the tournament, accusing us of being a team of cloggers who had kicked our way to the World Cup. They were getting their own back on Alf Ramsey for refusing to give interviews. Alf was a genius of a tactician, but hopeless at press and public relations. The referee must have believed every word he read because he whistled against England virtually every time one of our players even hinted at making a tackle. Meanwhile, he was seeming to be blind to a spate of vicious tackles by the Yugoslavs, and it all led to players on both sides losing their composure and their tempers. It was not a pretty sight."

Match No 45
USSR, Rome, 8.6.68. England won 2-0
Banks Wright Wilson Stiles Labone   Moore*
Hunter Hunt   Charlton R. 1   Hurst 1   Peters

Highlights: Goals from Bobby Charlton and Geoff Hurst lifted England to victory in this play-off for third place in the European championship finals. Nobby Stiles was recalled for his first England match for fourteen months in place of the suspended Alan

Mullery, and played in his trademark tigerish style. The Russians had been deadlocked with Italy after extra-time in a goalless semi-final. Italy went through to the final on an unsatisfactory toss of a coin (even critics of the penalty shoot-out deciders could not accept that this was the right way to settle stalemated matches). Italy then beat Yugoslavia 2-0 in a replay of the final after a 1-1 draw. For Sir Alf Ramsey and his England players the priority now was the defence of their World Cup in Mexico in 1970. **Gordon quote:** "It was great to see Nobby Stiles back in the team, and he silenced the boos of the crowd with a magnificent performance – as usual, hard but fair. Because of what the Italian press had written about him, he was jeered as if he was the biggest villain on earth but by the end of the game even his biggest critics in the crowd were having to admire his dedication and determination."

Match No 46
Romania, Bucharest, 6.11.68. Drew 0-0
Banks Wright (McNab) Newton Mullery Labone Moore*
Ball Hunt Charlton R. Hurst Peters

Highlights: Tommy Wright, who had partnered his Everton team-mate Ray Wilson at full-back against Russia, now had Blackburn's Keith Newton playing with him at left-back. England's World Cup heroes Cohen and Wilson had both had their international careers ended by injuries after playing together in twenty-seven matches. Wright and Newton, who would later continue their partnership at club level with Everton, hardly had time to get to know each other before Wright went off injured in the tenth minute to be replaced by Arsenal's Bob McNab who, despite playing out of position, gave a sound debut performance in a dreary, defence-dominated match. **Gordon quote:** "George Cohen and Ray Wilson were a hard double act to follow. They had been wonderful servants to England, and it was heart breaking to see them both forced into retirement by knee injuries."

Match No 47
Romania, Wembley, 15.1.69. Drew 1-1
Banks Wright McNab Stiles Charlton J. 1 Hunter
Radford Hunt Charlton R.* Hurst Ball

Highlights: A memorable match for the Charlton brothers. Bobby captained the team in injured Bobby Moore's absence in what was his ninetieth international, and big Jack scored England's goal. It was John Radford's first game for England and Roger Hunt's last. Hunt was sick of the criticism being aimed at him during an unsuccessful press campaign to get Jimmy Greaves recalled, and he asked Ramsey not to consider him for any more matches. The media built it into a Hunt-hates-Greaves war, but the truth is that they liked and respected each other. It was just footballing fate that these two exceptional goal scorers reached their footballing peak at the same time. **Gordon quote:** "Roger Hunt never, in my opinion, received the appreciation and credit he deserved. Outside Liverpool – where he was idolized – there were always people comparing him unfavourably with Greavsie. It was unfair on both of them. Jimmy was a natural genius, while Roger had to work harder for his success, but he gave fantastic service to England and was a key man in the team that won the World Cup."

Match No 48
France, Wembley, 12.3.69. England won 5-0
Banks Newton Cooper Mullery Charlton J. Moore*
Lee 1 Bell Hurst 3 Peters O'Grady 1

Highlights: Geoff Hurst was again a hat-trick hero, this time two of his goals against an outclassed French side coming from the penalty spot. Francis Lee scored his first goal for England and Mike O'Grady, recalled after six years in the wilderness, was also on the mark. Terry Cooper was Keith Newton's new left-back partner as Ramsey continued his search for a duo to compare with Cohen and Wilson. It was a relief for Sir Alf Ramsey to find his forwards on the mark after only four goals in the previous six internationals. There were two Wembley milestones. This was England's 100th victory against overseas opponents, and Hurst's goal was the 200th by England at the twin-towered cathedral of English football. **Gordon quote:** "I took careful note of Geoff Hurst's penalty-taking technique. He scored both his penalties by firing the ball with full-blooded power just to the right of the French goalie. I filed it away in my mind for if and when I faced him at club level. Two years later it proved valuable information when I faced Geoff taking penalties in the League Cup semi-final."

Match No 49
Northern Ireland, Windsor Park, 3.5.69. England won 3-1
Banks Newton McNab Mullery Labone Moore*
Ball Lee 1 Charlton R. Hurst 1 Peters 1

Highlights: The scoreline flattered England. Goalkeeper Gordon Banks was under long periods of pressure after Eric McMordie had cancelled out a 39th minute Martin Peters goal. With Newton doing an excellent containing job on George Best, England began to gain command. Goals from Francis Lee and Geoff Hurst wrapped up the game for them but not before Banks had made two splendid saves against the always-dangerous Derek Dougan. Live television cut the attendance to 23,000. **Gordon quote:** "Alf

Ramsey used his long experience as a fine international right-back to give Keith Newton good advice on how to mark George Best. He told him, 'Jockey him … don't let him commit you to making tackles.' Keith kept on his feet against George, and played him just about as well as any full-back could. It was about the least effective I had ever seen Bestie, a true genius of the game."

Match No 50
Scotland, Wembley, 10.5.69. England won 4-1
Banks Newton Cooper Mullery Labone Moore*
Lee Ball Charlton R. Hurst 2 Peters 2

Highlights: The old West Ham double act of Hurst and Peters sunk the Scots with two goals each, the second of Hurst's goals coming from a thunderous penalty that many observers considered the hardest they had ever seen a ball hit from the spot. Colin Stein scored to make it 2-1 at half-time, and the final scoreline was harsh on a Scottish team powerfully driven from midfield by Billy Bremner and Archie Gemmill. The victory put England in just the right mood for their fact-finding tour in preparation for their 1970 World Cup defence. **Gordon quote:** "This was my 50th international, and it was so sweet to help England beat the Scots for the first time under Alf's management. Once again I noted the way Geoff took his penalty. He took no prisoners from the spot."

Match No 51
Uruguay, Montevideo, 8.6.69. England won 2-1
Banks Wright Newton Mullery Labone Moore*
Lee 1 Bell Hurst 1 Ball Peters

Highlights: Gordon Banks, back in the England goal following a round-trip home to England for the funeral of his father, had to be at his best to keep out the Uruguay attack after Francis Lee had scored an early goal. Banks was beaten by a diving header from the exceptional Luis Cubilla, before Hurst collected the winner ten minutes from the end following neat approach work by Ball and Lee. The game was played in the Centenario Stadium, the venue for the first World Cup final in 1930. **Gordon quote:** "This was an emotionally exhausting time for me. My Dad had been ill for some time, but it still came as a nasty shock when Alf took me on one side to tell me that he had died. I had no hesitation in making the round trip to get to the funeral and then back in time for this match against the Uruguayans. It may not have been very professional of me, but nothing would have stopped me saying a last farewell to my Dad, who had always been a source of strength and inspiration to me throughout my career – throughout my life."

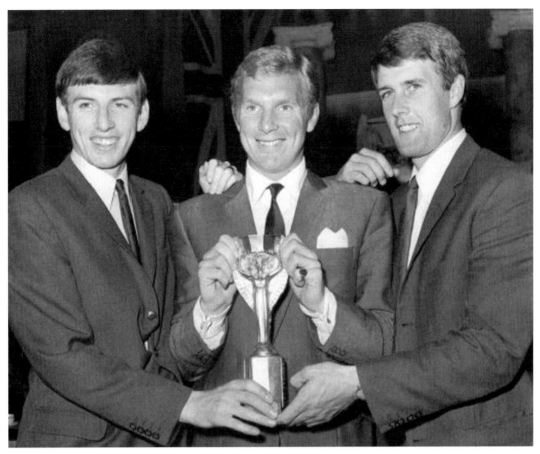

This was the West Ham United grip on the Jules Rimet Trophy in 1966 – Martin Peters (who scored the second goal in the final), captain Bobby Moore and hat-trick hero Geoff Hurst.

Match No 52
Brazil, Rio de Janeiro, 12.6.69. England lost 2-1
Banks Wright   Newton Mullery Labone Moore*
Ball   Bell ₁   Charlton R. Hurst Peters

Highlights: Colin Bell gave England a 1-0 half-time lead and victory hopes were high when Banks saved a penalty from Brazilian skipper Carlos Alberto that briefly silenced the 135,000 crowd in the magnificent Maracana Stadium. Alan Mullery policed Pelé so well that he made hardly any impact on the match, but England tired in the final twenty minutes and they were brought to their knees by late goals from Tostao and Jairzinho (a sign of things to come!). Sir Alf Ramsey said after the match: 'I am proud of every one of our players. We were so close to a deserved victory. I am delighted with our overall performances on this tour, and it will be of great benefit when we come back next year for the World Cup.' **Gordon quote**: "This was my first time on the same pitch as the great Pelé, and Alan Mullery did a magnificent job of marking him and keeping him shut out. It was a memorable match for me because I outfoxed Brazil's skipper Carlos Alberto."

Match No 53
Holland, Wembley, 14.1.70. Drew 0-0
Banks Newton Cooper Peters   Charlton J. Hunter
Lee (Mullery) Bell Jones (Hurst) Charlton R.* Storey-Moore

Highlights: England were slow-handclapped and jeered by their fans who did not appreciate that Holland were an emerging power in world football. The Dutch team included such quality players as Cruyff, Van Hanegem, Krol and Keizer, and England's defenders had to work flat out to hold them. Leeds striker Mick Jones, playing his first international match for four years, was substituted by Geoff Hurst after seventy minutes. Ian Storey-Moore, making his one and only England appearance, had a good-looking headed goal disallowed. The referee blew the final whistle as Bobby Charlton unleashed one of his specials that flew into the net, but too late to count. It was another milestone match for Bobby, who in his ninety-eighth international overtook the Billy Wright record of sixty-seven matches against overseas opposition. **Gordon quote:** "We got the bird from the England fans, who did not understand just how special this emerging Dutch team was as they began to lay the foundation to their 'total football' revolution. Dear old Alf would never hear a word of criticism about his team, and when a Fleet Street reporter asked him what he thought of the slow-handclapping he gave him that famous cold stare of his and replied: 'But surely they were slow handclapping the Dutch team …'"

Match No 54
Belgium, Brussels, 25.2.70. England won 3-1
Banks Wright Cooper Moore* Labone Hughes
Lee Ball 2 Osgood Hurst 1 Peters

Highlights: Alan Ball was rewarded for one of his typically non-stop performances with two goals in appalling conditions in rain-lashed Brussels. Geoff Hurst scored the other goal against a punchless Belgium team which had Paul van Himst as their one world-class player. Chelsea's graceful but unpredictable Peter Osgood made a quietly satisfactory debut in snowy conditions. The game was won by England in midfield, where Ball and Peters and the enthusiastic Emlyn Hughes were outstanding on a quag-mire of a pitch that made every step an effort. **Gordon quote:** "Ballie was an amazing player. He had the energy of two men and could chase defences into panic. His heart was bigger than his head and he was a motivational player who lifted his team-mates with his non-stop effort."

Match No 55
Wales, Ninian Park, 18.4.70. Drew 1-1
Banks   Wright   Hughes   Mullery   Labone   Moore*
Lee 1   Ball   Charlton R.   Hurst   Peters

Highlights: Sir Alf Ramsey was shaping his tactics for the coming defence of the World Cup, and had settled on a 4-4-2 formation with Francis Lee and Geoff Hurst as the two front runners supported from midfield by Alan Mullery, Alan Ball, Bobby Charlton and Martin Peters. There was press criticism of the system after England had struggled to hold Wales, Lee salvaging a draw with a spectacular solo goal after Dick Krzywicki had given the Welsh a well-deserved lead. Sir Alf said later that he was satisfied with the performance. 'Everything we do now is with Mexico in mind,' he said. 'We must adapt the way we play for the conditions we will meet out there.' **Gordon quote:** "We were now shaping our tactics in preparation for Mexico, and Alf had made a subtle switch from the 4-3-3 of 1966 to 4-4-2. There was blind criticism that this was too defensive but Alf knew that in the exhausting high altitude conditions of Mexico we would need strength in depth in midfield."

Match No 56
Northern Ireland, Wembley, 21.4.70. England won 3-1
Banks   Newton (Bell)   Hughes   Mullery   Moore*   Stiles
Coates   Kidd   Charlton R. 1   Hurst 1   Peters 1

Highlights: Bobby Charlton led the team out in his hundredth appearance in an England shirt and celebrated with his forty-eighth goal. Peters, now of Tottenham, and Hurst were also on the mark to give England a comfortable victory. George Best, Charlton's gifted Manchester United clubmate, gave Northern Ireland a rare moment of supremacy when he took advantage of dithering in the England defence to turn a half chance into a goal. Ralph Coates and Brian Kidd had their international careers launched as Alf Ramsey searched for his ideal combination for the World Cup. **Gordon quote**: "For one of the few times, I lost my temper with team-mates in this match. I had a real go at Martin Peters and Emlyn Hughes because they were not positive enough in clearing the ball and allowed George Best time and space in which to pick his spot. I shouted some hurtful things in the heat of the moment and apologized afterwards, but both Emlyn and Martin held up their hands and accepted that I was right to have a go."

Gordon Banks with Peter Bonetti, outstanding goalkeepers who had a mutual respect for each other.

Match No 57
Scotland, Hampden Park, 25.4.70. Drew 0-0
Banks Newton Hughes Stiles Labone Moore*
Thompson (Mullery) Ball Astle Hurst Peters

Highlights: This was England's final game before flying off for the World Cup warm-up games in South America, and the Scots were hell bent on giving them a morale-sapping defeat as a farewell present. England were equally determined not to be beaten and the game became bogged down in a midfield stalemate. A buffeting wind whipped around Hampden and made ball control difficult, robbing the 137,438 spectators of what had been an anticipated classic. The game produced the first goalless draw between Scotland and England since the first ever international football match between them back in 1872. **Gordon quote:** "I remember getting a deserved dressing down from Alf just before this match. I took two hold-alls with me to the team hotel, one containing my boots and match kit and the other my overnight things. Imagine my panic when I opened my bag in the dressing-room to find I had brought the wrong hold-all to the ground. A cab brought my gear to Hampden just minutes before I was due out on the pitch. It upset my pre-match ritual, and I never again left a hotel without checking the contents of my bag."

Match No 58
Colombia, Bogota, 20.5.70. England won 4-0
Banks Newton Cooper Mullery Labone Moore*
Lee Ball 1 Charlton R. 1 Hurst Peters 2

Highlights: England arrived in Bogota after two weeks altitude training in Mexico. Sir Alf Ramsey fielded what he considered his number one World Cup team and two goals from Martin Peters and one each from Bobby Charlton and Alan Ball gave England a comfortable victory at an altitude of 8,600 feet high up in the spectacular Andes mountains. England were a goal up in just ninety seconds from a deft header by Peters, and were rarely troubled by a Colombian side that played a neat passing game but without penalty area punch. This 4-4-2 line-up featured Francis Lee and Geoff Hurst working in tandem up front and supported by a midfield quartet of Alan Mullery, Alan Ball, Bobby Charlton and Martin Peters. Everton skipper Brian Labone had taken over from Jack Charlton at the heart of the defence, and only Gordon Banks and Bobby Moore had survived from the fortress that had been so impressive in the 1966 World Cup finals. **Gordon quote:** "The air was so thin that just a walk up a flight of stairs could leave you breathless. The humidity and heat were stifling, and the outfield players had to learn how to conserve their energy. When I was weighed after the match I found I had lost seven pounds and was down to below thirteen stone for the first time since I had become a professional footballer."

Match No 59
Ecuador, Quito, 24.5.70. England won 2-0
Banks Newton Cooper Mullery Labone Moore*
Lee 1 (Kidd 1) Ball Charlton R. (Sadler) Hurst Peters

Highlights: England literally went up into the clouds for this final warm-up match before the start of their World Cup defence. Quito is more than 9,000 feet above sea level, and the ball swerved around like a boomerang. Francis Lee gave England the lead and was then substituted in the seventieth minute by Brian Kidd, who scored a second goal. Ironically, Kidd had been told he was one of six players not included in the final World Cup squad of twenty-two. **Gordon quote:** "It was during a stop-over in Bogota on the flight back to Mexico that our skipper Bobby Moore was arrested on a trumped-up jewel-theft charge following an allegation that he had stolen a bracelet from a hotel shop. He was held under house arrest for five days before the British ambassador negotiated his release. It would be another two years before his name was finally cleared. Nobody who knew Bobby ever doubted his innocence. How he kept his sanity I will never know. He rejoined us just in time for the start of our World Cup defence …"

MAD dogs and footballers went out in the mid-day sun in Mexico to satisfy the great god of television. To catch peak audiences in Europe, many of the 1970 World Cup matches kicked off in ridiculous heat in a country where – for those not properly acclimatised – the thin air made breathing let alone moving difficult.

Sir Alf Ramsey was meticulous in the build-up to England's defence of the Jules Rimet trophy, won on that never-to-be-forgotten day at the old Wembley on July 30 1966. The squad that arrived in Mexico was perfectly prepared for the high altitude challenge, and in the opinion of many experts it was a stronger combination than had beaten West Germany after extra-time in the 1966 final.

For the record, this was the 22-man squad that arrived at the team's headquarters in Guadalajara, the capital of the state of Jalisco in the western-Pacific area of Mexico:

Jeff Astle (West Bromwich Albion)
Alan Ball (Everton)
Gordon Banks (Stoke City)
Colin Bell (Manchester City)
Peter Bonetti (Chelsea)
Jack Charlton (Leeds United)
Bobby Charlton (Manchester United)
Allan Clarke (Leeds United)
Terry Cooper (Leeds United)
Emlyn Hughes (Liverpool)
Norman Hunter (Leeds United)
Geoff Hurst (West Ham United)
Brian Labone (Everton)
Francis Lee (Manchester City)
Bobby Moore, captain (West Ham United)
Alan Mullery (Tottenham Hotspur)
Keith Newton (Everton)
Peter Osgood (Chelsea)
Martin Peters (West Ham United)
Alex Stepney (Manchester United)
Nobby Stiles (Manchester United)
Tommy Wright (Everton)

So there were eight surviviors from the team that beat West Germany in 1966: Gordon, Ballie, the Charlton brothers, three-goal Geoff, Martin Peters, Nobby Stiles, and, of course, the captain Bobby Moore, who had a mind-blowing adventure on the way to Mexico.

Bobby had been arrested in Colombia on a charge of stealing a diamond bracelet from a shop in the foyer of the England team hotel while in Bogota for a warm-up friendly. Back home in England (hands up those who remember that *Back Home* was the England players' football song that went to No 1 in 1970!) we were flabbergasted by the news.

To get background facts I talked to two people who were out in Mexico, my co-author Norman Giller and my good buddy Jimmy Greaves who had arrived in the most unusual of circumstances. He drove there in the London-to-Mexico World Cup Rally, finishing sixth with his co-driver Tony Fall in a battered Ford Escort. Only a handful of cars from the original field of 71 entries survived the punishing 16,245 mile course.

Norman told me:

‘Under orders from my *Daily Express* editor Derek Marks, I visited all the embassies in Mexico City while Bobby was locked up in Colombia. I found that every country had received complaints over the years from people being held to ransom for jewellery thefts in Bogota that they had not committed. My front-page story in the *Express* was headlined, "Bobby in Bogota Boobytrap." It was read by government officials in London, and they put renewed pressure on the Colombian government to release the England captain.

When Bobby arrived in Mexico to rejoin the England squad after four days under arrest I was among a posse of press photographers and reporters standing on the tarmac at Mexico City airport as his plane from Bogota touched down. Alongside me was the unique Geoffrey Green, Corinthian football correspondent of *The Times* and arguably the greatest football writer of any time. He had a charming habit of using song-lines when he talked, and he always greeted people with phrases like "Younger than springtime …" or "Over the rainbow, baby …" This in a cut-glass Oxbridge accent. In fact, the intellectual Geoffrey was the first person I ever heard say "I'm over the moon" long before it became the cliché crutch of tongue-tied footballers.

As Bobby Moore stepped out from the plane to be met by dazzling flashbulbs, he spotted the tall, willowy figure of Peter O'Toole-lookalike Geoffrey among the hordes at the bottom of the plane disembarkment steps (can you imagine us being allowed on the tarmac today?). Bobby punched a fist into the air and shouted, "Over the rainbow, baby …!"

Foreign reporters, anxious to record Bobby's first words on his return to freedom, scratched their heads as they tried to decipher what the England captain had said.

"Show us the bracelet, Mooro" ... best of mates, Jimmy Greaves and Bobby Moore

The next day Jimmy Greaves arrived in Mexico City at the end of the *Daily Mirror*-sponsored rally. His first concern as he climbed out of his car was for his West Ham team-mate and best pal Bobby Moore. "Mooro wouldn't take a liberty, let alone a bracelet," he said.

I took Jimmy by cab to the home of the British embassy official who was keeping Bobby out of sight of the press pack. Jimmy climbed over the back wall surrounding the garden, and disappeared from view. Hours later he described how he had been caught by the embassy official's wife, given a bollocking and then allowed in to see Bobby.

Jimmy's first words were, "Show us the bracelet, then Mooro." The embassy official's wife overheard and went ashen faced. Her and Greavsie's humour were from different planets.

Greavsie and Mooro – as they were affectionately known throughout the game – sank half a dozen bottles of beer, and Bobby told me later:

"Seeing Jimbo was the best medicine I could have had. We didn't stop laughing from the moment he came through the French windows until he left three hours later. It was just the relaxation I needed. I would not wish my ordeal on my worst enemy."

Jimmy confirmed all this for me, and gave me some extra background:

'This was in my drinking days, of course, and I made up for not having drunk during the rally by getting legless on my arrival in Mexico. I was interviewed by a Swedish journalist while sitting half pissed in an armchair that had somehow got into the hotel swimming pool.

It was before I managed to see Bobby, and I told the journalist that Mooro was as honest as the day is long and there was no way in a million years that he would have stolen anything. I knew Bobby better than anybody. We had travelled the world together, and it was disgraceful the way he had his name dragged through the mud for something he so obviously did not do.

When I got in to see him at the embassy official's home I had Lou Wade, Mooro's then business partner, with me. Lou stood 6ft 7in and wore garish clothes. This particular evening he was wearing bright red trousers, a yellow and green checked jacket, a frilly yellow shirt and a wide, dazzling tie. All eyes were on this technicolor spectacle at the front of the house, where there were dozens of TV and newspaper reporters. With Lou causing a distraction, I climbed over the rear garden wall. I got into the house through some French windows and Mooro almost dropped his lager in surprise when he saw me approachng from the direction of the kitchen.

The wife of the embassy official was furious and ordered me out, insisting that I go through the pantomime of ringing the doorbell before she would officially admit me.

Outside, the television cameras whirred and bewildered journalists looked on open mouthed as I came sheepishly out of the front door only to be let back in one minute later, this time with the outrageous Lou Wade in tow. I think the embassy official's wife was close to fainting when she caught sight of Lou!

The first thing I asked Mooro is what he had done with the bracelet he was supposed to have stolen. That set the tone for the evening and we raided the cocktail cabinet and had a good relaxing drink.

I can think of nobody who could have handled the crisis better than Mooro, and I knew that he personally would have an outstanding World Cup. But I feared for the England team because of the heat and the high altitude.

A couple of years later when Bobby was finally cleared after a full investigation I encouraged him to sue the hotel, but he made the valid point that if he had gone down that road they could have produced a witness from nowhere. "They have already stitched me up once," he said. "I am not going to give them the chance to do it again. I am just happy to have my name cleared."[9]

England were drawn in the toughest of groups, with Romania, Czechoslovakia and mighty Brazil standing between them and a place in the quarter-finals. Their opening game in the finals was against Romania, a team that had collected a reputation for kicking much more than just the ball. You would never have believed that Bobby Moore had been to hell and back as he strode the pitch like a colossus. He led by example, staying calm and controlled as the Romanians unleashed a series of vicious tackles to try to upset the rhythm of the reigning world champions.

I was watching it on television at home and remember leaping in the air when Geoff Hurst continued where he had left off in the 1966 final, scoring the goal that clinched a 1-0 victory. Years later, I was privileged to have Sir Geoff join the A1 Sporting Speakers camp, and I was able to ask him for his memories of that match against Romania:

'There was enormous pressure on us before the match with Romania. We were not particularly loved in Latin America, and got a terrible hammering from the local press after a series of PR bungles. We tried to import our own meat, which was against Mexican law, and brought our own British-made coach. This brought sneering comments that Mexico had got round to discovering the wheel. There was the ridiculous business with Bobby, and Alf was snarling at press conferences instead of trying to win friends. Wherever he went Alf got stick from the local press and he was continually having his 'Argentina are animals' quote after the 1966 quarter-final thrown back at him. It was interpreted as an insult of all Latin Americans.

Apart from the English fans who had managed to make the trip, the crowd were really hostile and the Romanians must have felt as if they were playing at home. Alf had warned us before the game not to get involved in responding to any cyncial stuff from the Romanians. We had a lot of experience against them, and they always resorted to crude tackles when things were not going their way.

The heat on the pitch was just unbelievable, and all we players were losing more than half a stone during the games. You have to pace yourself in the conditions we faced in Mexico, and we played a containing game, and were rarely in any sort of trouble against a Romanian team that was suffering just as much as us in the heat.

My goal halfway through the second-half was not the prettiest I ever scored. An Alan Ball centre was headed on by Francis Lee to me at the far post. Martin Peters was calling for me to pass to him, but I instictively went for a shot from a tight angle, and topped the ball. It spun through the legs of the Romanian goalkeeper and crept over the goal-line. It was bit of a fluke but a goal is a goal is a goal.

At the press conference afterwards Alf got in a muddle and described in detail how Martin had scored the goal. It gave Martin a good laugh, and he claimed it should have been his goal anyway.

The next day Alf took the entire squad to watch Brazil in their opening match against Czechoslovakia. Brazil won 4-1 without ever being really stretched. It was obvious that the Brazilians had class but Bobby Moore summed up our feelings when he said: "We will not give them that sort of freedom to play. The Czechs treated them with far too much respect." The crowd were totally behind the Brazilians, and taunted us when they saw us sitting in the stands. It gave us a taste of what to expect when Brazil were our opponents in the next match ...**'**

Martin Peters, who was described by Sir Alf Ramsey as "a player ten years ahead of his time."

To find out how England made their final preparations for the vital match against Brazil, I turned to Martin Peters, who is a regular member of our A1 Sporting Speakers panel. It was a big time in Martin's life. He had just become British football's first £200,000 footballer in a deal that took him to Tottenham and Jimmy Greaves to West Ham as a makeweight. He recalled:

❛I was still reeling from what was going on in my life. It was stunning for me to make the move to Tottenham with Jimmy coming the other way. You have to remember what Jimmy meant to me. I had idolised him when I was at school. He was almost a god to me. We went to schools only a mile apart and I'd go anywhere to see him play. He was four years older than me, and was my role model. I can still see him now banging in eleven goals – yes, eleven – when his school team beat mine 13-2. And there I was joining Tottenham where he was a legend, and Jimmy moving to West Ham.

I had to get all of this out of my mind and give full concentration to the 1970 World Cup finals. We made a comfortable start against Romania in what on paper was a far from easy opener. I gave Geoff a lot of ribbing for not passing the ball to me when he scored, because I was unmarked and could not have missed.

Alf did his usual thorough preparation job before our match against Brazil. When we watched them against the Czechs we could not believe the room they gave to Pelé. The Czechs were in awe of him and seemed almost honouring him with the freedom of the pitch. That was the game in which Pelé tried his audacious shot from the halfway line that missed the Czech goal by inches. We were determined not to give him breathing time in which to try things like that against us. Alan Mullery was going to mark him for England, and I knew there was no way my new Tottenham team-mate would give him nearly as much space.

We returned to our hotel after the victory over the Czechs and following a nice relaxed evening Alf got down to the business of getting us in the right frame of mind for the second game aganst Brazil. He took us to the local television studios to watch film of our game against Romania and we also watched highlights of the Brazil-Czechoslovakia match, and Alf pointed out where the dangers were.

He warned us not to commit ourselves to reckless tackles and always to try to shut down the space for the likes of Pelé, Rivelino and Tostao. Alf also made us aware of the influence of Gerson, and told us to try to cut out his supply of passes that made the Brazilian attack tick. We spent half an hour discussing the manipulative powers of Gerson, not realising that he would miss the game because of a pulled muscle.

As a former international full-back, Alf had a lot of respect for the flying Jairzinho, and he gave Terry Cooper good advice about keeping him wide to the line and not allowing him to cut in and let loose with his dangerous cross shots.

Our fans at home just could not realise the pressure we were being put under in far-off Mexico. We were being greeted with naked hatred by the Mexican and South American fans, who made up the large majority of spectators. The local press and television looked for every negative thing they could find about us, and painted us as villains for allegedly moaning about their food, their weather, the state of their pitches and stadiums and their fans. Among the scandalous stories put out about us was that the 1966 World Cup had been loaded against the Latin American teams, which was why four European countries made up the last four, and they took every opportunity to dig up the quarter-final against Argentina, even suggesting that the referee who sent off Antonio Rattin was in the pay of the English Football Association.

It was all nonsense, of course, but the Mexicans and Brazilian supporters believed everything they were told about us, and ganged up to make our lives as difficult as possible.

We were staying in the too easily accessible Hilton Hotel. On the eve of the most important game we had played since the 1966 World Cup final there was a concerted effort by a mix of Mexican and Brazilian fans to upset the entire team. Right through the night a cavalcade of cars drove round the hotel with horns beeping. It was all designed to stop the England players from sleeping, and several asked to change their rooms to try to get farther away from the incessant noise.

It had a counter effect to what was intended. It made us stronger as a group and more determined to do our best to keep the World Cup in what was a hostile environment.**'**

In England the country stopped for the match. There were record viewing figures as we all gathered round our television sets for what we saw as a rehearsal for the 1970 World Cup final.

As we tuned in for the build-up to the game at the Jalisco Stadium on June 7, it was obvious the conditions were going to favour Brazil. It was a Sunday afternoon more suited to siesta than soccer. The temperature was a scorching 98 degrees Fahrenheit, familiar to Latin Americans but rarely experienced in England.

The Brazilians scored a huge PR victory in the moments before the kick-off when their reserve players did a lap of the pitch carrying a huge Mexican flag. There were 3,000 England fans in the ground, but outnumbered and outshouted by 72,000 spectators cheering for Brazil.

All these years later, I can recall how sick with nerves I felt as I watched the great Bobby Moore walk to the centre-circle to shake hands with Brazil skipper Carlos Alberto for the coin toss.

What would the next 90 minutes of football produce? Little did I know it would include a moment of magic that nearly forty years later I would be recalling in the form of this special book (Yes, Greavsie, it's a funny old game).

THE match was just ten minutes old and goalless when the master of all strikers – Pelé – came face to face with a genius among goalkeepers – Gordon Banks – in a High Noon duel.

Carlos Alberto, Brazilian right-back and captain, pushed a carefully calculated pass down the right wing into the path of the skilled Jairzinho, who suddenly and dramatically accelerated past Terry Cooper to the by-line. He then stabbed a centre into the goalmouth that seemed to hang invitingly for Pelé, who had instinctively read the situation as only he could. He had got himself perfectly positioned beyond his marker Alan Mullery to meet the ball.

The master climbed above the ball and headed it with ferocious power down – and so he thought – into the net. Mullery later reported that Pelé shouted "Goal!" as the ball flew off his head. So did most spectators in the stadium, including the commentators sending their descriptive phrases around the world to millions of television viewers and radio listeners. In thousands of homes in England we shouted in agony, as we thought we had gone a goal down.

Banks looked rooted on the wrong side of goal but suddenly, with the blurring speed of a panther, sprinted and then dived to his right and somehow managed to get an outstretched hand under the ball to flick it up and away over the bar. Pelé stopped dead in mid-celebration to mourn what had somehow become a missed chance.

This moment of astounding gymnastics from Banks inspired England to give the eventual world champions their hardest match of the tournament, but after a magnificent battle they finally succumbed to a superbly drilled shot by Jairzinho on the hour. He cut in from the right to score after an arrowing Tostao pass and a deft, perfectly delivered ball from Pelé had ripped open the middle of the England defence.

Jeff Astle had a gilt-edged chance to equalise within moments of coming on as a substitute but – yes, even in those heatwave conditions – he was caught cold and shot tamely wide.

Evidence that the England players had given their all is that several of them lost up to ten pounds in weight after running round in the mid-day sun so that the World Cup organisers could satisfy the deadline demands of the great god of world-wide television. The millions tuned into the match will always recall it for having seen one of the saves of the century.

For me, a fifteen-year-old schoolboy, sitting at home in Dorset, it was like the end of the world. I admit to crying as the final whistle signalled that we had lost a game we deserved to win. There was a close-up of Pelé and Bobby Moore cuddling and exchanging shirts. Mooro had been the outstanding player on the pitch, but it was Alan Mullery who had virtually shut Pelé out of the game with a magnificent display of marking. It is Mullers who kicks off our collection of descriptions of the Banks save:

'Gordon had quite rightly gone to the near post to cover Jairzinho's cross. Pelé got just beyond me and met the ball perfectly, hammering it down with his head. As the ball left him he screamed "Goal!" Everybody else in the stadium thought the same thing. Banksie was a blur as he hurled himself back towards the far post. I will never know how he got there, and even more amazing was the fact that he managed not only to reach the ball but to knock it up with his right hand and send it up and over the bar. I thumped him on the back and shouted something like "F****** fantastic!"'

This is how Pelé described the moment that was the talk of football:

'I just couldn't believe it when Gordon stopped my header. It was incredible that he got it and even more incredible that he managed to push the ball over the bar. It was the biggest surprise I have ever had on a football pitch. All these years later I still say it was the greatest save I've ever seen. I have since watched it many times on television and on film at the cinema and I am always astonished that he managed to save it.'

England skipper Bobby Moore, who gave one of the most accomplished individual defensive performances of his life, said:

'I was getting ready to pick the ball out of the net when Gordon appeared from nowhere. He swooped across the goal like Superman and must have set some sort of world speed record getting from his near post to the far post. Was it a bird? Was it a plane? No, it was Banksie! What a pity we lost the game, because Gordon didn't deserve to be on the losing side after making a save like that. It was out of this world.'

Sir Bobby Charlton said:

'It was without any doubt the greatest save I have ever seen. I felt heartbroken for Gordon that he finished on the losing side after an effort like that. In a blinking of an eye he had made the impossible possible. It was the unforgettable

Alan Mullery and Tostao look on as Gordon completes his save in a million.

highlight of one of the finest football matches in which I ever participated. Some time later I saw a film of the full 90 minutes and remember thinking what a wonderful advertisement it was for the Beautiful Game. It was a film you could have used to coach young footballers as to how the game could and should be played. There was everything, all the skills and techniques, the tactical control and, above all, an unbelieveable lesson in how to save by Gordon! If there had been any justice we would have at least got a draw.'

Brian Labone, England and Everton centre-half, was among the players lining up to praise the Banks save in the dressing-room after the match. He said:

'I had my eye on Tostao as Jairzinho crossed the ball from the bye-line. Gordon was at the near post and we were all caught out by the loft that Jairzinho gave the ball. Tostao had made a dummy run towards the near post and I went with him. Gordon had already stationed himself there and I thought he was beaten when the ball sailed past us to Pelé. Alan Mullery just failed to get his head to the ball and Pelé almost hung in the air as he executed a classic header. The ball flew down and on its way into the net when Gordon hurled himself across the goal and diverted it over the bar. It was a phenomenal save, and even some of the Brazilian players joined in the applause.'

A sensational picture of a sensational save. Just a blink of an eye ago Gordon was standing at the near p

Bobby Moore and Brian Labone look on in disbelief

Television commentator David Coleman said:

> 'I had to look at the action replay to convince myself that my eyes had not deceived me. It was the nearest thing I have ever seen on the sports field to a player managing to be in two places at once. One moment Banks was at the near post, and was then suddenly at the far post making a save that defied belief. I instantly desribed it as the save of the World Cup.'

Hugh Johns, commentating for ITV, said:

> 'This was the Save of the Century. Pelé, along with 75,000 spectators, was convinced it was a goal the moment the ball left his head. Every commentator and press box reporter had it marked down as a goal. There was not a soul who believed it could be saved ... except that man Gordon Banks. And I doubt if even he knew how he had done it. You cannot explain miracles. They just happen. I told Gordon later that he should join the Magic Circle.'

In England a new phenomenon had been introduced called 'the World Cup panel.' ITV had four outspoken pundits under the chairmanship of Brian Moore. On this particular night they were Malcolm Allison, Derek Dougan, Pat Crerand and Bob McNab, with Jimmy 'The Beard' Hill always having the last word.

When introducing a stand-alone action replay of the save, Brian told the nation: "You are about to see something you will not believe." They then showed the save over and over again and went to each panellist for his view. These were their reactions dug up from the archives:

Malcolm Allison, at the time Manchester City coach and the most outspoken man in English football:

> 'In years to come we will tell our grandchildren about that save. Pelé headed the ball to perfection, and nine hundred and ninety nine times out of a thousand it would have hit the back of the net. I take my hat off to Banks for making what I consider as good a save as I have ever seen. You cannot teach anybody to make a save like that. It is called natural talent. We are so lucky in this country to have the greatest goalkeepers in the world. There's Banks, Alex Stepney, young Peter Shilton, Peter Bonetti and our big Joe Corrigan at Man City. Gordon gave an example there of English goalkeeping at its best. The Brazilians have some of the worst goalkeepers in the world. They will not have believed what Gordon did.'

Derek Dougan, the witty and opinionated Wolves and Northern Ireland centre-forward and chairman of the Professional Footballers' Association:

‘Don't forget we also have in my countryman Pat Jennings the finest goalkeeper of them all, but I have never seen even Pat equal that save by Banks. There are not words to describe it ... but I will try. Stupendous. Sensational. Unbelieveable. Magical. Astonishing. Astounding. It was all those things. There is no way Pelé could have bettered the direction of his header. He put it in exactly the right spot. Gordon had done the right thing going to the near post when Jairzinho was in possession, and the fact that he made the save at the far post just beggars belief. I played with Gordon at Leicester and have never seen a goalkeeper with faster reflexes. ’

Pat Crerand, Mancheser United mifield maestro and a Scottish international who could make any team tick with his precise passes:

‘I always thought the best save I ever saw was Alex Stepney's against Eusebio late in ordinary time of our European Cup final against Benfica two years ago. If he had been beaten we would have lost the match. But this save by Banks surpasses even that. Gordon was working on instinct, but his speed of thought and movement were superhuman. I think other goalkeepers might have got a hand to it, but to be able to flick it up and away like he did took extraordinary strength of wrist. This save will be shown on television for years to come. ’

Bob McNab, Arsenal left-back who had been one of six players released from the England squad the week before the tournament started (for the record, the others were: Ralph Coates, Brian Kidd, David Sadler, Peter Shilton and Peter Thompson):

‘We have an exceptional goalkeeper at Arsenal in Bob Wilson, but I think he would be honest enough to admit he would not have saved that header from Pelé. I am certain there is no other goalkeeper in the world who could have saved it. Even when I watch these action replays I think the ball is going to go into the net. Pelé's positioning to meet Jairzinho's centre was just right, and one of the few times in the match when he got the better of his marker Alan Mullery. He produced the copybook header, sending it down, and Gordon managed to get his hand under the ball as it bounced up towards the net. He was almost a blur as he moved across the goal. If there has been a better save, then I've not seen it. ’

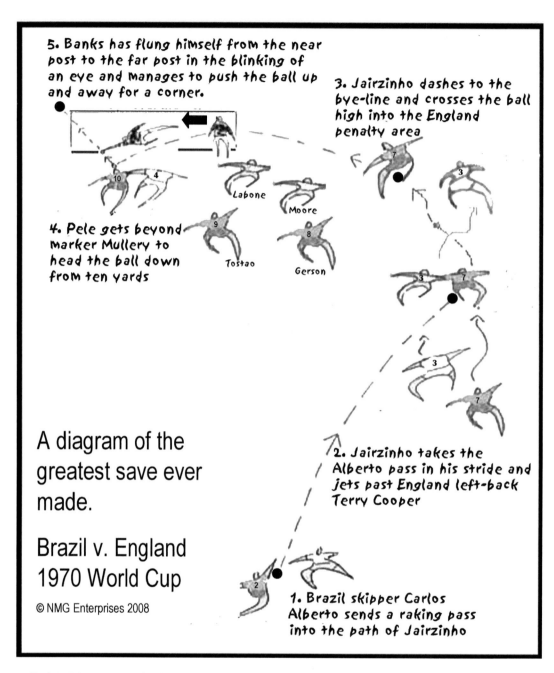

5. Banks has flung himself from the near post to the far post in the blinking of an eye and manages to push the ball up and away for a corner.

3. Jairzinho dashes to the bye-line and crosses the ball high into the England penalty area

4. Pelé gets beyond marker Mullery to head the ball down from ten yards

A diagram of the greatest save ever made.

Brazil v. England 1970 World Cup

© NMG Enterprises 2008

2. Jairzinho takes the Alberto pass in his stride and jets past England left-back Terry Cooper

1. Brazil skipper Carlos Alberto sends a raking pass into the path of Jairzinho

Brian Moore was the hugely respected anchorman of the ITV panel, and a close friend of my co-author Norman Giller, who – along with Bob Wilson – delivered the eulogy at Brian's funeral following his sudden death in 2001. Norman collaborated with Brian on the book telling the story of his life and times *(The Final Score)*, and they discussed the Banks save in detail. Moore, the Master of the Microphone, said:

‘The moment Gordon made the save our backroom boys in the editing room knew that this was something special, and they immediately started to put together a gallery of Gordon's greatest saves. There was one against Uwe Seeler in the 1966 World Cup final that was every bit as good as the one against Pelé, and also a double save in the same match from Overath and the follow-up shot from Emmerich. I went into the editing suite as they were going through the archives, and was able to watch the save against Pelé half a dozen times, including in slo-slo-motion. Everytime I watched it I became more in awe of what Gordon had achieved. As he stationed himself at the near post Jairzinho fired the ball high towards the for post. Pelé meantime was racing into the penalty area with Alan Mullery in close attendance. You would have put your house on Gordon not being able to get across goal in time to save Pelé's header. The fact that he not only got to the far post but also had the strength, speed and skill to push the ball over the bar was the stuff of football legend. I told Jimmy Hill: "In his commentary for the BBC David Coleman called it the save of the World Cup. I think we can prove it was the save of *any* World Cup."’

Bob Wilson, who became a respected television sports presenter after a distinguished goalkeepeing career with Arsenal and Scotland, said:

‘Gordon's save against Pelé was one of those footballing moments that live in the memory for ever. As a fellow goalkeeper, I rated it as good a save as I had seen and the fact that it was achieved by an old mate made it extra special. Gordon and I both started our Football League careers with Chesterfield, a club famous for producing outstanding goalies including the legendary England international Sam Hardy. I used to stand behind the goal watching the young Gordon in action, and then at half-time I would go to the other end of the ground for the same privileged view of an outstanding talent in action. I used to jokingly tell him that he was flashy, but in truth he was incredibly consistent and reliable. Gordon was born with the most natural spring in his step, so lithe and supple. Every movement was poetry in motion and I coveted the qualities that he possessed. Even all these years on I have the David Coleman commentary in my head of that magnificent Brazil-England game ... *"Felix throws the ball out to Carlos Alberto ... a through pass into the path of Jairzinho ... he's past Cooper ...Pelé's at the far post ... Oh! what a save ... Gordon Banks! That has to be the save of the World Cup ... "* It seems like only yesterday, and time has not diminished the sheer brilliance of the save.’

This picture of the ITV World Cup panel comes from a 1970 scrapbook, left to right: Bob McNab, Pat Crerand, Jimmy Hill, Derek Dougan, Brian Moore and the outspoken Malcolm Allison.

Jimmy Hill, before his move across the channels to BBC, always had the last word and pioneered in-depth analysis of football on television. His verdict on the save:

'This was as fine a save as you're ever likely to see. Gordon Banks has proved time and again that he is as good as any goalkeeper in the world, and it is his remarkable reflexes that put him in the master mould. It was a moment of blinding brilliance and owed as much to his instincts as anything. He showed the physical prowess of a gymnast, and this was no fluke save. It is the reward for all the hours I know he puts in training and perfecting his speed of movement and reactions. Pelé was the most surprised person in the ground when the ball failed to find the back of the net. There is nobody in his class as a finisher, but on this occasion he met his master. There have been few, if any, better saves in the entire history of the World Cup.'

For a neutral view of the save we unearthed a quote from the referee of the match, Abraham Klein, taken from an interview he gave to Israeli journalists when retiring from the game. He said:

❛The most memorable match I refereed was Brazil against England in the 1970 World Cup. It was the game all the referees wanted, and I could not believe my luck when I was handed an envelope giving me the responsibility for the match. There was a save made by England goalkeeper Gordon Banks from a header that Pelé that was just unbelievable. In fact I had the whistle to my mouth to signal a goal, and suddenly had to change my decision to awarding Brazil a corner. After the game I made a point of congratulating Mr. Banks on his save. In all my years in the game I did not see a better save. I also got the autographs of Pelé, Bobby Moore and Bobby Charlton. They were all outstanding in the greatest game I ever refereed. There was so much noise in the stadium that I could not make my whistle heard when blowing for full-time. I even let it go on a few minutes overtime because it was such a wonderful game.❜

And, finally, we feature the memory of the man who made the save, the one and only Gordon Banks:

❛I was too involved in what was happening on the pitch to give a second's thought to the save. All my concentration had to be on the coming corner kick. As I completed the save I remember Alan Mullery whacking me on the back, and Mooro smacking my arse, both in "well done" gestures. Only later when I saw it on television did I fully realise that it was a bit special. It was an instinctive save, but if Pelé says it was the greatest he has ever seen, who am I to argue with the king…? Now every time I see a replay of the save I wonder how I got to it. Somehow I managed to make the 'impossible' save.

I hope this doesn't sound arrogant, but I honestly think I made better saves … one against Uwe Seeler in the 1966 World Cup final from a close-range shot and several for Stoke. But what made the save against Pelé stand out is the stage. You could not have a more important setting than the World Cup, and to have made the save against probably the greatest footballer that ever breathed added to the drama of it all. There was also the little matter that the match had a world-wide audience of millions.

Alf had warned me time and again to be alert to Jairzinho's habit of cutting in and shooting at the near post. This is why I positioned myself there as Jairzinho darted past Terry Cooper.

Instead of trying to shoot from what was an impossible angle he crossed the ball, and it went high towards the far post. As I turned, the ball arced over Alan Mullery's head and there was Pelé behind him timing his jump to perfection. He caught the ball with the full meat of his forehead and produced the textbook header, powering it down, which makes it harder to save.

I had never moved so fast in my life to get across the eight yards of the goal. I was propelled by fear and a determination not to let the ball go into our net in what was our most imponrtant game since the 1966 World Cup final.

There was a lot of luck involved, because the ball bounced just right for me to reach it with my right hand. I made a sort of uppercut flick with my outstretched fingers and was relieved to see the ball fly up over the bar for a corner.

Bobby Moore always had something dry to say, and he later told me: "You're getting old Banksie. There was a time when you would have caught it!"

Pelé and I have become good mates over the years, and he always jokes: "I scored more than a thousand goals and people only seem to remember the one that you saved!"

Now, nearly forty years later, I am very proud to be associated with the save. I always think of my football career as the summertime of my life, and that save helps bring back so many wonderful memories.'

Yes, it was a save in a million ... but waiting just around the corner for our hero (and the England team) was a footballing nightmare.

Just for the record and to make sure this book contains a complete breakdown of Gordon's 73 games for England here are summaries of his three World Cup matches in Mexico:

Match No 60
Romania, World Cup, Guadalajara, 2.6.70. England won 1-0
Banks   Newton (Wright)   Cooper   Mullery   Labone   Moore*
Lee (Osgood)   Ball   Charlton R.   Hurst ₁   Peters

Highlights: England started their World Cup defence as they had finished it in 1966, with Geoff Hurst emerging as the goal-scoring hero. His goal in the sixty-fifth minute - the ball going through the legs of the Romanian goalkeeper - was enough to give England a winning send-off. Captain Bobby Moore, back with the squad after his harrowing experience in Colombia, was the outstanding defender on the pitch. It was a satisfactory rather than spectacular start by England against opponents who concentrated solely on defence in a bid to squeeze a draw out of a hard-fought match. **Gordon quote**:"The one worry for us was an injury to right-back Keith Newton, but his Everton clubmate Tommy Wright proved a sound substitute. This was the first time Alf had used substitutes in a World Cup match. They had never been allowed during his club managing career with Ipswich, and so it was all new to him."

Allan Clarke, who coolly scored from the penalty spot in his England debut against Czechoslovakia

Match No 61
Brazil, World Cup, Guadalajara, 7.6.70. England lost 1-0
Banks Wright Cooper Mullery Labone Moore*
Lee (Astle) Ball Charlton R. (Bell) Hurst Peters

Highlights: The moment of astounding gymnastics from Gordon Banks when saving from Pelé's header in the tenth minute inspired England to give the eventual world champions their hardest match of the tournament. But after a magnificent battle they finally succumbed to a superbly drilled shot by Jairzinho on the hour. A lasting memory of the match for all those lucky enough to have witnessed the classic confrontation is of Bobby Moore and Pelé cuddling each other before swapping shirts, two masters of the game recognising each other's genius. **Gordon quote**: "For everybody who played in or saw the game, this match has gone down in the memory as an all-time masterpiece of a game. It was disappointing that we lost, but we had the satisfaction of knowing we had proved ourselves at least the equal of a Brazilian side that history proves was one of the greatest football teams in history. We matched them in every department, and all neutrals agreed that we deserved to come out of the game with at least a draw."

Match 62
Czechoslovakia, World Cup, Guadalajara, 11.6.70. England won 1-0
Banks Newton Cooper Mullery Charlton J. Moore*
Bell Charlton R. (Ball) Astle (Osgood) Clarke ₁ Peters

Highlights: Allan Clarke volunteered for penalty duty in his first England international appearance, and showed an ice-cool temperament as he slotted home a disputed forty-eighth minute spot-kick that clinched a place in the World Cup quarter-finals. It was a stuttering performance by England, but they were always a step ahead of a Czech side that rarely troubled a tight defence under the command of the imperious Bobby Moore. **Gordon quote**: "The only time the Czechs looked like scoring was when a speculative shot from twenty-five yards by right-back Dobias swerved violently in the thin air. I had to go to full stretch to get my hands to it, and I managed to tip it on to the bar. As I turned the ball rebounded into my arms. Comedian Bobby Moore shouted: "Can you go to first slip for the next over."

   Little did any of us then realise that this would be Gordon's final World Cup appearance.

WE had been brought to a peak of excitement and anticipation by England's march through to the quarter-finals. Waiting for them for a showdown in Leon were the old enemy, West Germany. They had come through their group in first place, beating Morocco 2-1, Bulgaria 5-2 and Peru 3-1. All their matches had been in Leon, the 'Leather City' right in the heart of Mexico. For days television and radio were crowded with news and views on the build-up to the match, but the newspapers were silent. A Fleet Street strike had briefly silenced the football writers.

For this schoolboy in far-off Dorset time suddenly stood still as I waited for a repeat of the 1966 World Cup final. There was a fairly unanimous view that England were a stronger side than the one that captured the Jules Rimet trophy. Analysing the match on television, Jimmy Hill told the nation: "The preparation for these finals have been perfect. Alf Ramsey has got the team nicely acclimatised to the conditions, and we have a superior defence that I am confident can nullify the German attack. In Gordon Banks, we have the outstanding goalkeeper in the tournament ..."

Over to Gordon for his heartbreaking story ...

❛On the night before we were due to travel to Leon from Guadalajara I could not sleep for feeling sick. I had to keep dashing to the bathroom to vomit, and I felt as if an army of soldiers was marching in my head as the room kept spinning around. My room-mates Keith Newton and Bobby Charlton were also feeling below par, but not as bad as I was.

Doctor Neil Phillips had done a marvellous job helping us all beat the bugs that can knock you over in the sort of climate Mexico has. We had all been on a daily ration of iron and salt tablets, and I doubt if any British sports team had been better looked after from a medical point of view. But something had got through the Doc's defences to destroy my system.

I felt a little better the next morning after the sort of night I would not have wished on my worse enemy. I could not face breakfast, and made do with plenty of liquid because during the night I had become dehydrated. I pulled myself together and got on the coach for the five-hour drive to Leon. After about an hour I was suddenly having the huge waves of sickness coming over me again, and I started to feel like death warmed up. Our trainer Harold Shepherdson gave me tablets to help control the nausea and I somehow survived the trip without disgracing myself.

I was feeling so weak when we arrived at our hotel that I had to ask my room-mate Alex Stepney to carry my bags for me. Alf advised: "Get yourself to bed, and let's see how you are in the morning."

After spending the next ten hours in bed, I ducked out of the next morning's training session because I was still fragile. Alf provisionally named me in the side to face the Germans, and I attended the team meeting on the morning of the match.

Then, just as Alf was starting to outline our tactics, I felt ill again and reluctantly had to pull out of the game. It was one of the lowest points of my career.

I watched a recording of the quarter-final on a television in my hotel room. It was being screened about an hour behind the game and I was feeling decidely perky when Alan Mullery and Martin Peters put us into a 2-0 lead. Peter Bonetti had taken my place in goal at the last minute and appeared to be coping well with everything the Germans could throw at him.

The second-half had not long started on the replayed version that I was watching when Alex Stepney came walking heavily into the room like a man in mourning.

"What's up with you?" I asked. "You haven't caught my bug, I hope."

He looked at me as if I was mad. "Don't you know?" he said. "We lost."

I laughed because I was sure he was pulling my leg. "Get away with you," I said, pointing at the television. "England would never lose a two-goal lead ..."

Oh yes they would, as we watching it live on television at home in England had discovered to our grief and disbelief. I – stupid boy – cried my bloody eyes out.

So that this is a complete record of those 1970 finals, here are the teams and a brief report on that painful-to-watch quarter-final in Leon:

West Germany: Maier Vogts Fichtel Schnellinger Hottges (Schulz) Beckenbauer Seeler* Overath Libuda (Grabowski) Muller Lohr

England: Bonetti Newton Cooper Mullery Labone Moore*
Lee Ball Charlton R. (Bell) Hurst Peters (Hunter)

Montezuma's revenge had never been harsher, robbing England of the best goalkeeper in the world. Peter Bonetti, who had not played a full competitive match since the end of the previous club season, was called in as emergency deputy following the withdrawal of Banks.

England were in command for sixty nine minutes thanks to goals from Alan Mullery and Martin Peters in stifling conditions that meant much of the play was at walking pace.

Franz Beckenbauer pulled the Germans back into the game with a shot that Bonetti would have saved nine times out of ten. Sir Alf Ramsey immediately sent on Colin Bell as substitute for Bobby Charlton, who was being saved for a semi-final that never came England's way.

German substitute Jurgen Grabowski was running rings round exhausted left-back Terry Cooper, and Ramsey decided on a second substitution, sending on Norman Hunter for Peters in a bid to stiffen the defence. With Charlton and Peters off, it meant England had lost their two most composed players and suddenly they were looking disjointed.

A freak header by Uwe Seeler sent the ball on an arc over the wrong-footed Bonetti to send the game into extra-time just as in the 1966 World Cup final, but this time it was the Germans who came out on top. Geoff Hurst had a goal disallowed, and then Gerd Muller rammed in the winner after Grabowski had beaten Cooper and crossed for Lohr to head the ball down into 'Der Bomber's' path.

England's reign as world champions was over, as was the great international career of Bobby Charlton after a record 106 caps. Several of the England players were in tears, and Sir Alf was shell shocked. He did not believe it possible that any team could come back from two goals down against the England defence. How different it might have been had Gordon Banks been fit, and how different it might have been had Sir Alf not made a mess of his substitutions. He had not used substitutes throughout his club managerial career, and was never comfortable with the system. Now the knives were out for him at home. The Football Association officials he had too often treated with contempt were plotting their revenge.

There was savage criticism of the way Ramsey handled the substitutes. The sight of the legendary Bobby Charlton being called off to be replaced by Colin Bell was a huge psychological boost for the Germans. Beckenbauer later said: "Seeing Bobby walking off the pitch suddenly gave us new belief that we could win the game, with England's best player on the touchline."

Sir Bobby said: "I knew Alf's thinking was to save me for the semi-final, but I was feeling fit and full of energy. I could almost see Franz Beckenbauer's face light up as I was summoned off."

It seemed obvious to most observers that left-back Terry Cooper had been run close to exhaustion by fresh susbstitute Jurgen Grabowski, but when Ramsey decided to make his next susbstitution – a maximum of two were allowed – he pulled off the elegant playmaker Martin Peters and replaced him with the purely destructive Norman 'Bites Yer Legs' Hunter.

Even as a schoolboy watching the game 7,000 miles away in England it seemed clear to me that it was Cooper who needed to be replaced. He looked completely buggered, and Grabowski was running him into the ground.

It was heart-breaking to see Peter Bonetti being beaten by two soft goals that everybody knew Gordon would have saved with ease. But you have to sympathise with Peter, because he went into the game without proper preparation and had not played a competitive match for two months. There were all sorts of rumours flying that he was concerned about his wife being in Mexico without him, and the fact that he was unable to escort her in what was for her a rare trip abroad.

Back to Gordon's recollections:

'I heard some spiteful things said about Peter's performance and that he didn't have his mind on the match because his wife was in Mexico.

I am sure that if Peter could have played the game all over again he would have saved those killer goals from Beckenbauer and Muller. But goalkeepers never get a second chance. They are there to be shot at and any mistakes are magnified a hundred times because they usually mean a goal for the opposition.

There is no way I can or would want to judge how I would have coped with the West German revival after they had looked dead and buried. All I do know is that I rated Peter among the world's top goalkeepers of my era in the game and I am sure he did his absolute best to keep England in the World Cup.

In fairness to him, he did not know until vey late that he was playing against the Germans and there was not the chance for him to go through the thorough mental build-up that goalkeepers need for a game of such importance.'

What about the rumours that Gordon had been 'got at' before the quarter-final against West Germany? He revealed:

'There was an unproven theory that I had been nobbled as part of a Latin American plot to stop England going any further in the World Cup. It was Franny Lee who first put it in my mind. "Bet somebody slipped something in your drink," he said. "It doesn't make sense that you're the only one in the squad who has gone down with a bug." This started to become the talk of the camp, and suddenly I began to wonder if my illness had not just been fate.

When I think back on the ridiculous Bobby Moore jewel-theft charge, the vicious smear campaign against us by the Mexican press, the hostile attitude of the fans and then my mystery illness, you cannot help but begin to wonder if there was something in the theory. All I did know is that England were out of the World Cup. I was sick in more ways than one.'

For Bobby Charlton it was a 106th and final England appearance. He later summed up everybody's thoughts when he said: "I will always wonder what might have been if Gordon had not become ill. We will never ever know."

WEST GERMANY were completely drained by their victory over England, and three days later they were beaten by Italy in an astonshing semi-final that again went to extra-time. The Italians finally won 4-3, five goals coming in the extra-time period when both teams were the victims of fatigue, the furnace heat, the high altitude and the punishing pace of a match that had more twists than an Alfred Hitchcock thriller. Waiting for Italy in the final at the Aztec Stadium on Sunday June 21 in front of an audience of 107,412 spectators and a billion more on television were Pelé-propelled Brazil, who comfortably eliminated Uruguay 3-1 in their semi-final.

Both Brazil and Italy had won the World Cup twice before and the extra incentive in this final was that the winners would keep the Jules Rimet trophy for all time. There was never any real doubt in most minds that it would be Brazil who would capture the prize. Now that England were out, I gave my unconditional support to Brazil and my far-away hero Pelé.

They held a Brazilian carnival in Mexico. The Aztec Stadium was a sea of Brazilian yellow shirts, and the stands looked like huge swaying fields of daffodils. It was difficult to pick out any Italian fans in the crowd, and there was a non-stop sound of drums being beaten to a samba rhythm. It was almost as if they were celebrating victory by Brazil before a ball had been kicked. But those of us who had avidly followed the tournament on late-night television (you could tell us by the bags under our eyes) knew that Italy would not be a pushover. They had attacking players of the quality of Riva, Boninsegna and Domenghini, and a defence infamous for its miserly allowance of goals against.

But Brazil had an attack that ran off the tongue like old friends ... jet-paced Jairzinho, smooth-as-silk Tostao, the one and only Pelé and the muscular, moustachioed Rivelino, and just behind them pulling the strings the vastly under-rated Gerson, who was the invisible man of the team. He made everything click into place without seeming to stamp his authority on the game. Analyse Brazilian goals in the 1970s and you will usually find Gerson's fingerprints (or perhaps that should be footprints) somewhere on the movement eventually taking the ball into the net.

After some nervous opening sparring on a treacherously wet pitch soaked by pre-match thunderstorms Brazil took the lead after eighteen minutes ... and it was That Man Pelé who scored from Rivelino's cross. It was a beautifully judged header not unlike the one saved by Gordon Banks, but Albertosi in the Italian goal was beaten all ends up.

Mario Bertini, the defender trusted with the unenviable job of marking Pelé, said later: "I commented before the game that Pelé is just skin and bone like the rest of us.

Captains Carlos Alberto and Bobby Moore face the cameras before the 1970 World Cup showdown

I now know that he is not. He is a man and a player like no other."

With Mazzola providing a procession of neat passes from his midfield patrol point, Italy started to have more of the play and deserved their equaliser seven minutes before half-time. Clodoaldo, reliability personified as a midfield anchorman, had a rare lapse of concentration when he back-heeled the ball into the path of Boninsegna, who gratefully and gracefully raced away to give Italy a surprise equaliser after goalkeeper Felix had collided with his team-mate Brito. For the one and only time in World Cup 70 the Brazilians looked shaken and disorganised.

But they again took command in the second-half and schemer Gerson turned scorer in the sixty-sixth minute as he rifled in a left-foot cross shot from just outside the penalty area while the Italian defenders stood waiting for him to make a pass that never came.

With the scent of victory in their nostrils, Brazil started to produce the football that has those of a certain age purring with pleasure at the memory. At the peak of their pressure Brazil conjured a third goal, Jairzinho running the ball into the net after Gerson and Pelé had combined to slice open the armour-plated Italian defence.

Italy made the odd substitution of sending on midfield maestro Gianni 'Golden Boy' Rivera for striker Boninsegna six minutes from the end. Many thought Rivera should have started the match, and it was far too late now for him to have any impact. He was like a footballing Canute, unable to do anything to stop the waves of Brazilian attacks that brought a superb fourth and final picture goal from skipper Carlos Alberto. It deserved an oil painting rather than a press photograph.

Clodoaldo laid the foundations with a dribble in midfield past four opponents. He then fed the ball to Rivelino who passed it to Jairzinho. The winger transferred the ball to Pelé who was twenty yards from goal. The crowd drew in its breath expecting a run and a shot from the great man. But Pelé was never ever a selfish player, and he was one of the few who had spotted Carlos Alberto darting from his right-back position down the right touchline. With what was almost nonchalance, Pelé rolled the ball into his captain's path with the precision of a Jack Nicklaus putt. Carlos Alberto took aim and fired in an unstoppable cross shot that bulged the net just behind goalkeeper Albertosi's right-hand post. It was a corker of a goal that put the icing on the cake of Brazil's brilliant performance. This is how Pelé recalled the 1970 World Cup:

❝I like to think that in 1970 we were the Beautiful Team playing the Beautiful Game. It was a bonus for me to play in the tournament because I thought I would never again play in the World Cup after my miserable experience in England in 1966.

People continually ask me if the 1970 champions were the greatest team with which I played. My answer is that they were the best organised team. There were very few weaknesses and we had a fine understanding with each other. But for the team with the greatest individuals I would have to select that side of 1958 with which I made my World Cup debut. We had exceptional footballers such as Garrincha, Vava, Djalma Santos, Didi and, if you don't mind me saying, Pelé.

It is strange but true that in both 1958 and 1970 our hardest games were against England. They held us to a goalless draw in Sweden, and I made my debut in the next match. In 1970 they had a wonderful side including the two Bobbys, Charlton and Moore, who are among my favourite players of all time. And, of course, in goal there was Gordon Banks who made THAT save against me.

I would class Bobby Moore among the very best defenders I ever faced. He was *the* outstanding defender in the 1970 finals. I could outwit most defenders by looking them in the eyes and then sending them the wrong way by going in a different direction to what they expected. But there was no foxing Bobby Moore. He looked at the ball rather than into my eyes, and I could never get him off balance.

He would stand his ground and then make a sudden movement for the ball and win possession with a tackle that was always hard but fair. I found Bobby an English gentleman. A lot of players tried to kick me to stop me getting past them, but Bobby played by the rules. In that photograph taken of us at the end of the match in 1970 I was telling him how great it had been to play against him, and I added that he was no thief after that silly business over the bracelet.

In the final against Italy in 1970 it all came together for Brazil and we played some wonderfully choreographed football. It was one of the most memorable moments of my career when I headed our first goal from Rivelino's exact cross.

To win the Jules Rimet trophy outright was an extraordinary thing for the morale and happiness of the people at home in Brazil, where football means so much. It should not be forgotten that on the way to winning the World Cup we had beaten former champions England, Uruguay and Italy.*

There was a moving moment in the Brazil dressing-room after the 1970 final. It had been well publicised that there had been friction between Pelé and his former World Cup team-mate Mario Zagallo, who had taken over as manager just a few months before the finals. Pelé and Zagallo came face-to-face after the victory and, without a word, ran to each other for a long, tearful embrace. Pelé later presented Zagallo with his prized No 10 shirt.

For the record, these were the players who had the honour of taking part in that majestic match:

Brazil: Felix, Carlos Alberto* 1, Brito, Piazza, Everaldo, Clodoaldo, Gerson 1, Jairzinho 1, Tostao, Pelé 1, Rivelino.

Italy: Albertosi, Cera, Burgnich, Rosato, Facchetti*, Bertini (Juliano) , Domenghini, Mazzola, De Sisti, Boninsegna 1 (Rivera), Riva.

Match No 63
Malta, Valletta, 3.2.71. England won 1-0
Banks   Reaney   Hughes   Mullery* McFarland Hunter
Ball   Chivers   Royle   Harvey   Peters ₁

Highlights: Alan Mullery was skipper in place of Bobby Moore, who had been suspended by his West Ham club following the 'Blackpool Affair' (Bobby along with
West Ham team-mates Jimmy Greaves and Clyde Best had been caught drinking in a
nightclub on the eve of an FA Cup tie they thought was going to be cancelled because
of snow … the match went ahead and West Ham lost). Martin Chivers, Roy McFarland
and Everton team-mates Joe Royle and Colin Harvey made their debuts in a European
championship qualifying match played on an iron-hard pitch that made ball control
a nightmare. Martin Peters scored the only goal after half a dozen chances had been
missed. **Gordon quote:** "This was without doubt the worst pitch I ever played on in
my life. It was grassless and rutted, and while we were training there in the dark the
night before they brought a road roller on to the pitch to try to roll it flat for the match.
I had only one save to make, diving to stop a late shot. When I got up I found my shorts
were torn and my leg grazed and cut. That's how bad the pitch was."

Match No 64
Greece, Wembley, 21.4.71. England won 3-0
Banks Storey Hughes Mullery McFarland Moore*
Lee ₁   Ball (Coates) Chivers ₁   Hurst ₁ Peters

Highlights: Greece arrived for this European championship qualifying match without
any of the their star players from Panathinaikos, who were being saved for a European
Cup semi-final. A superbly struck goal by Martin Chivers was all that separated the
teams at half-time, and it took late headed goals by Geoff Hurst and Francis Lee to
clinch victory and silence the jeers of a frustrated crowd. Peter 'Cold Eyes' Storey got
his first England call-up as reward for his consistent performances for an Arsenal team
on the way to a League and FA Cup double. A hard-tackling midfield ball winner for
the Gunners, he went back to his original position of right-back for his first taste of
international football. **Gordon quote:** "We could have played without a goalkeeper.
The Greeks came only to defend and I did not have a single shot to save."

Match No 65
Malta, Wembley, 12.5.71. England won 5-0
Banks Lawler 1 Cooper Moore* McFarland Hughes
Lee 1 Coates Chivers 2 Clarke 1 Peters (Ball)

Highlights: Allan Clarke scored one penalty and missed another and Martin Chivers netted twice and might have had five goals. Francis Lee was on the mark, and Chris Lawler decorated his debut with a spectacular long-range goal from thirty yards. But it was not enough to please the 36,500 spectators who jeered and slow-handclapped England's performance in this return European championship match. **Gordon quote:** "It was so one-sided that again I did not have a single shot to save, and touched the ball only from back passes aimed at me by team-mates. I found my concentration wandering to such an extent that I picked up the scent of bacon coming from the terraces. I was quoted about this in the newspapers, and a fan contacted me to say he had been eating bacon sandwiches at Wembley during the match!"

Match No 66
Northern Ireland, Windsor Park, 15.5.71. England won 1-0
Banks Madeley Cooper Storey McFarland Moore*
Lee Ball Chivers Clarke 1 Peters

Highlights: George Best had an opportunist goal disallowed after flicking the ball away from Gordon Banks as the England goalkeeper threw it up in preparation for a kicked clearance. Many people considered it a magical piece of skill and impudence by Best, but Scottish referee Alistair Mackenzie decided he had been guilty of dangerously high kicking. Much to the annoyance of Best and the crowd, he awarded England a free-kick. Allan Clarke's winning goal ten minutes from the end brought off-side claims from the Irish defenders who also insisted that Francis Lee had handled the ball before passing to Clarke. It was not Ireland's lucky day. Paul Madeley, Leeds United's versatile defender, came in at right-back as Sir Alf Ramsey continued to search for the perfect blend and balance at full-back. **Gordon quote:** "That little Irish genius Bestie was standing in front of me as I attempted to clear the ball after making a save. I dodged around him and prepared to kick my clearance. As I threw the ball up he hooked it away with an upraised foot. We both raced for it as the ball bounced in the goalmouth, and George just got there a split second in front of me and headed into an empty net. The ref, quite rightly in my opinion, awarded us a free-kick. Bestie blew his top, arguing that the ball had not been in my hands. But the ref ruled that he had been guilty of dangerous kicking, because his foot was up near my head. If he had not made this decision, I would have protested because it would have given attackers licence to put their feet up

Tottenham striker Martin Chivers scored twice against Malta and might have had five goals.

at goalkeepers and so risk serious injuries. In today's game George would have been pulled up earlier for harassing me. There was no greater admirer of Bestie's brilliance than me, but on this occasion his creative genius was out of order."

Match No 67
Scotland, Wembley, 22.5.71. England won 3-1
Banks Lawler Cooper Storey McFarland Moore*
Lee (Clarke) Ball Chivers 2 Hurst Peters 1

Highlights: Martin Peters headed England into the lead before Alan Ball gifted Scotland an equaliser with a suicidal back pass into the path of Hugh Curran. Ball made amends with a storming performance in midfield, and two Martin Chivers goals gave England victory and the home international championship. The defeat was a massive disappointment for Scotland central defender Frank McLintock, who at the same Wembley Stadium two weeks earlier had collected the FA Cup as captain on the day that Arsenal completed the double. **Gordon quote:** "The hordes of Scottish fans in the Wembley crowd cruelly turned their despair on their manager Bobby Brown and kept up a non-stop chant in the last twenty minutes of, "If you hate Bobby Brown clap your hands …" I thought it was a wonderfully warm gesture of Alf Ramsey's at the end to put a comforting arm around Brown's shoulders as they walked to the players' tunnel together. Alf had a lot of critics, but I will always think of him as a warm, sincere and intensely loyal man who was shy and sharp with strangers and who would not suffer fools at all, let alone gladly. He never ever criticized his players in public, saving any harsh words for the privacy of the dressing-room or training ground. What a pity he lacked the communication skills he showed with we players when it came to talking to the media."

Match No 68
Switzerland, Basle, 13.10.71. England won 3-2
Banks Lawler Cooper Mullery McFarland Moore*
Lee Madeley Chivers 1 Hurst 1 (Radford) Peters 1 o.g.

Highlights: Two rare mistakes by Gordon Banks let Switzerland in for equalisers after England had twice taken the lead through goals by Geoff Hurst and Martin Chivers in the first-half of this European championship qualifier. It was just looking as if the Swiss would escape with a draw when a Chivers cross was deflected into the net by defender Weibel for a seventy-ninth minute winner. The victory put England top of their qualifying group. **Gordon quote:** "Alf didn't hold back with his criticism of me for two sloppy goals, one the result of my poor positioning and the second after Bobby

Freda and Terry Baker forge a partnership and friendship with Pelé, along with The King's advisers Peppito and Jesue Marin (below). It is a great coup for A1 Sporting Speakers.

It's a sign of the times as Pelé (watched by Terry Baker, above) and Gordon autograph pictures of THE save that was the talk of the 1970 World Cup. They were at exclusive signing sessions organised by A1 Sporting Speakers.

Gordon holds up the autographed picture of the 1966 World Cup heroes, signed by the surviving team members who won the Jules Rimet Trophy at Wembley Stadium on 30 July 1966. A1 Sporting Speakers work closely with the squad.

Pelé, Tommy Wright and Alan Mullery (No 4) look on as Gordon makes the Save of the Century

Colin Bell (No 8) comes racng back just in time to see Gordon denying Pelé a certain goal

Pelé and Bobby Moore, two footballing legends, swap shirts and words of mutual admiration at the end of the unforgettable 1970 World Cup match in which Brazil beat England 1-0.

he one and only 'Toothless Tiger' Nobby Stiles joins Gordon in an A1 Sporting Speakers signing session

Terry Baker sneaks
into the team pictu.
for a reunion of the
1966 World Cup
heroes, whom he
represents at signi*
projects. The line-
up, back row: Ray
Wilson, Terry, the l*
great Alan Ball, Ja*
Charlton, Nobby S*.
and George Cohen*
front: Gordon Ban*
Martin Peters, Rog*
Hunt, Geoff Hurst.

Look out, Jim, he's
behind you! Nobby
Stiles shadow-mar*
Greavsie in a 1960
Man United-Spurs
match. Both are
prominent member*
of the A1 Sporting
Speakers stable of
stars.

Moore and I had for one of the few times in our all games together got in each other's way. I would have to put this game down as my worst for England, and I deserved Alf's rollocking. Typically, he did it in private."

Match No 69
Greece, Athens, 1.12.71. England won 2-0
Banks Madeley Hughes Bell McFarland Moore*
Lee Ball Chivers 1 Hurst 1 Peters

Highlights: A cannonball shot from Geoff Hurst midway through the first-half put England in charge of a match dominated by the attacking midfield trio of Alan Ball, Colin Bell and Martin Peters. Martin Chivers wrapped up the victory with a last-minute goal to clinch England's place in the quarter-finals of the European championship. Francis Lee twice hit the post, and the final scoreline flattered a Greek team under the management of 1958 Northern Ireland World Cup hero Billy Bingham. Waiting for England in the quarter-finals were Franz Beckenbauer's West German side, and a re-match at Wembley. **Gordon quote:** "We were satisfied with our performance on an uneven pitch, and that chirpy man Billy Bingham told us he thought we had every chance of winning the European championship. But we knew we had a tough test coming up against our old enemy …"

Match No 70
West Germany, Wembley, 29.4.72. England lost 3-1
Banks Madeley Hughes Bell Moore* Hunter
Lee 1 Ball Chivers Hurst (Marsh) Peters

Highlights: Derby manager Brian Clough pulled slightly injured Roy McFarland out of the England squad at the last minute, and Sir Alf Ramsey's gamble of playing Bobby Moore at centre-half was a tactical disaster in this European championship quarter-final. Moore and Norman Hunter were always struggling at the heart of the defence against the dynamic Gerd Muller, who fed off a procession of passes from the gifted Gunter Netzer. Francis Lee cancelled out a twenty-sixth minute goal by Uli Hoeness, and outplayed England clung on until six minutes from the end when Netzer scored from the penalty spot. Moments later Muller made it 3-1 with a devastating shot on the turn. It left England with a mountain to climb in the second leg in Germany. **Gordon quote:** "Alf was rarely wrong with his tactics, but on this occasion he made a mistake in playing Bobby Moore as our main central defender. It was well known throughout the game that if Bobby had a weakness it was his lack of authority in the air. He just could not cope with the thrusting style of the goal machine Gerd Muller."

Rodney Marsh was right in the face of German defender Horst-Dieter Hottges at Wembley

Match No 71
West Germany, Berlin, 13.5.72. Drew 0-0
Banks Madeley Hughes Storey McFarland Moore*
Ball Bell Chivers Marsh (Summerbee) Hunter (Peters)

Highlights: Franz Beckenbauer was outstanding as the German defence shut out England's attack in a match played in a non-stop downpour. The Germans, content to protect their two-goal lead from the first leg, came closest to breaking the deadlock when a 40-yard free-kick from Gunter Netzer smacked against the bar. England, with Norman Hunter and Peter Storey literally making their presence felt, conceded twenty-seven free-kicks and were described by German manager Helmut Schoen as 'brutal'. For Sir Alf Ramsey the 1974 World Cup finals in Germany now became all-important. His enemies at the FA were gathering like vultures. Only four of the 'Old Guard' were left in his squad – Banks, Moore, Ball and Peters. **Gordon quote:** "The game was played in pouring rain in the stadium designed by Hitler. I had a heated exchange in the dressing-room after the match with Peter Storey, who had argued against building the wall that I wanted as Netzer prepared to take a free-kick from thirty yards. His shot smacked against the bar, and I forcibly made the point that if a goalkeeper wants a wall he should have it regardless of what anybody thinks. The goalie has to be the boss of his penalty area."

Match No 72
Wales, Ninian Park, 20.5.72. England won 3-0
Banks Madeley Hughes 1 Storey McFarland Moore*
Summerbee Bell 1 Macdonald Marsh 1 Hunter

Highlights: England cruised to a comfortable victory in a bruising Home Championship match in which Peter Storey and Terry Yorath, two of the hardest men in the League, had a personal feud, with Norman Hunter often joining in on Storey's side. Leading 1-0 from a first-half goal by Emlyn Hughes, England clinched victory with two goals in a minute midway through the second-half. Rodney Marsh scored with a first-time volley from eighteen yards, and then Mike Summerbee laid on the third goal for his Manchester City team-mate Colin Bell. Malcolm Macdonald made a bright debut in the number nine England shirt. **Gordon quote:** "Storey and Yorath took a history of incidents in club matches into the match, and it was ugly to watch as they went for each other with reckless tackles. The feelings spilled over after the final whistle and we had to separate the two warring rivals as they went for each other in the players' tunnel. When I think back to the likes of Storey, Yorath, Hunter, Bremner, Tommy Smith and Chopper Harris I realise it was a real man's game when I was playing."

Match No 73
Scotland, Hampden Park, 27.5.72. England won 1-0
Banks Madeley Hughes Storey McFarland Moore*
Ball 1 Bell Chivers Marsh (Macdonald) Hunter

Highlights: The referee called captains Bobby Moore and Billy McNeill together and ordered them to tell their players to calm things down after forty-six free-kicks had been awarded in the first thirty minutes. An Alan Ball goal in the twenty-eighth minute gave England victory in this daggers-drawn centenary match between the two countries. Peter Storey and Norman Hunter were at the heart of the trouble with their fierce tackling, and this brought out the competitive spirit in the likes of Billy Bremner, Bobby Moncur and Denis Law. For long spells players seemed more intent on kicking each other rather than the ball. Scottish FA President Hugh Nelson described the game as "a disgrace," and made no secret of the fact that he thought England had started it with their retaliate-first approach. Veteran onlookers could not recall a more vicious encounter between the auld enemy, and football was the loser. **Gordon quote:** "Two weeks before this game I had been thrilled to receive the Footballer of the Year award. Everything was going marvellously and I had secretly made up my mind to do everything I could to keep my form so that Alf would *have* to pick me for the 1974 World Cup campaign. If I had known this was going to be my last match for England I could not have asked for a more satisfying finale than a victory over Scotland at Hampden Park ..."

10. The Gordon Banks Story, the Second Half

AFTER the triumphs of the first half of his life, Gordon Banks was suddenly overtaken by tragedy. In just ten seconds of careless driving he wrote off not only his car but a career during which he had established himself as one of the all-time great goalkeepers; some would even say THE greatest ever. In a worldwide poll he came second only to the legendary Lev Yashin as the No 1 goalie of the 20th Century, with the dynamic Dino Zoff back in third place.

But it all ended suddenly, painfully and stupidly on a stretch of rain-soaked Staffordshire road on Sunday October 22 1972. Gordon was on top of his game at the time of his accident that sent shock waves through the world of football.

He was the reigning Footballer of the Year after helping Stoke City win the Football League Cup at Wembley (the only major trophy in their history), and he was holding off a challenge for his England place from his former Leicester City clubmate Peter Shilton.

Now, some thirty-six years later, Gordon – one-eyed Gordon – can look back on that fateful Sunday with a resignation that hides the grief he must have gone through at the time. I can remember crying for the great man when news of his car smash first hit the headlines. This is how he recalls it:

‘The court's verdict at the time was that I was guilty of dangerous driving, and I must admit that I lacked my usual concentration at the wheel as I pulled out to overtake a crawling lorry and a car that was stuck behind it. Sunday lunch was five miles and ten minutes away at my home in Ashley Heath. This was no time for hanging about. My mind was action-replaying the previous day's League match at Anfield when I had lost my temper with the referee for appearing to give Liverpool every advantage.

As I thought about the mouthful I had given him as we came off at the end I didn't see the Austin A60 van coming towards me. Suddenly, too late, I realised I was smack in the path of the van. I braked and tried to steer my powerful Ford Granada back behind the lorry, but I went into a skid on the road made greasy by drizzling rain.

Safety belts were not compulsory then, and I foolishly did not have mine on.

As I smashed into the van I was hurled against the windscreen and knocked out. Glass from the smashed screen lodged in my right eye, and after a series of operations over the next few weeks I was given the news I dreaded. I had lost the sight of my right eye.

It was the lowest point of my life, and I went into a deep depression. I lived for football and suddenly it was all over. No more First Division action. No more England internationals. No more World Cups.

Thankfully, I had trained myself over all my years as an international goalkeeper to think and act positively. I attempted to play again for Stoke, but with limited vision I could not perform to the standards I had set myself.

My goalkeeping strength was in being able to get the right angles to minimise the target for oncoming forwards. It is all about geometry and geography and with one eye I set out to re-educate myself about angles and positioning. I spent hours in lonely training sessions refamiliaring myself with the six-yard box in relation to the position of the goalposts now that I had a restricted view.

My next test was to face shots, and this was when the real heartbreak began. I had adjusted quite well to knowing where to position myself, but what my one eye couldn't judge properly was the *pace* of a shot. I was continually a split-second out with my timing, and shots that I would normally have eaten for breakfast were just slipping past my fingertips.

The deep depression came back as I began to realise that I was never ever going to play to anything like my peak form again. My Stoke City colleagues guessed I was losing my confidence and tried to help me by putting less power and swerve on their shots, but this – friendly and helpful as it was meant – just made me feel worse about myself.

Reluctantly, I started playing in testimonial matches and friendly fixtures, but I was not enjoying it because I had acquired a king-size complex about performing in public in case I made a fool of myself. The mistake I made was judging myself by the standards of Gordon Banks of England.

It was the summer of 1973 – eight months after the crash – when I finally had to concede that my career in the Football League, and with England, was definitely over.[9]

Yes, a lot of people thought it was all over ... but not quite. In an extraordinary twist to the Gordon Banks story, he accepted an offer to restart his career in the United States of America where a huge effort was under way to sell soccer to the American public.

The main promotion line: dreamed up by the high-powered publicists selling the game like soap powder was: "Soccer is a kick in the grass."

Astonishingly, Gordon got his game together to the extent that he was voted the North American Soccer League's 'Most Valuable Goalkeeper,' This is what he told me about goalkeeping life in the United States:

'After a year training the Stoke City youth team, I gradually began to adjust to taking a one-eyed view of the world. My peripheral vision was quite severely restricted, but as I grew accustomed to new angles and to re-focusing on football I started to recover my old touch in goal.

I had mentally accepted the fact that I would never again be able to play as a top-line goalkeeper, but while taking part in kickabout training matches and friendly fixtures it slowly dawned on me that even with one eye I could still do a useful job at the back of a defence.

When I was first approached to play in America I kicked the idea right into touch. There was, I thought, no way they were going to turn me into some sort of circus freak. You now ... *'Roll up, roll up ... and see the world's only one-eyed goalkeeper ...'*

But I was finally convinced that they wanted me for my goalkeeping ability and not for any gimmick purposes. I signed for Fort Lauderdale Strikers in the North American Soccer League and had some of the most extrordinary experiences of my life.

They went to extreme lengths to sell the game in the States, and I was involved in some mind-blowing stunts. I once rode on to the pitch on horseback as a cowboy when we were at home to a team from Dallas, and other forms of transport on to the pitch included a fire engine, a motorbike, a police car, a tank and, the most memorable, an elephant.

Another time I helped five team-mates carry a coffin on to the pitch. Then, with an organist playing suitably mournful music, the lid of the coffin was pushed open from the inside and out jumped our manager Ron Newman dressed as Count Dracula.

"Lauderdale Strikers are coming back from the dead!" it was announced over the loudspeakers. All this because we had just lost two successive matches. I tried to envisage Sir Alf Ramsey taking part in such a stunt, but it was a bridge too far for my imagination.

Sometimes I had to pinch myself to make sure I wasn't dreaming it all. Perhaps I was back in the operaing theatre with my thoughts running wild?

Gordon gets padded up for American football ... but Soccer was his kick in the grass.

But it was all real enough and slowly I adapted to the game of football American-style. It took a lot of getting used to after all my years in English football with its great traditions and old-fashioned approach to projecting the sport.

Soccer was being sold in the States as a family entertainment. They had no hooliganism problems, and they played in weather conditions conducive to family outings. I admired the way clubs went out of their way to make the spectators feel part of the occasion. The most important part, in fact. They were almost pampered from the moment they came into the ground to the second they left. The fans were entertained for an hour before each match, and again during half-time. I saw men wrestling with alligators, tight-rope walking clowns, acrobats, sky-diving displays, motor-cyle stunt jumps, and, inevitably, brash and exciting marching bands accompanied by scantily dressed cheerleaders.

After every game the fans were encouraged to meet the players. The dressing-rooms were open house to the Press and media, and once all the interviews were finished we players mingled with the fans in the club bars or in the car parks where barbecues were being cooked.

The role of the players in America when I was there was different to anything else I had ever experienced. Playing the game was just part of the duty. Each club involved its local community in activities run by the players. We did a lot of coaching, made personal appearances and lectured on soccer at the local schools and colleges.

It was all part of a campaign to get football accepted at grassroots level, and the success of the 1994 World Cup finals in the United States owed a lot of its popularity to the foundation work we players put into selling the game in the 1970s.

The standard when I was playing out there was about the equivalent of England's Second Division. At the end of my first season with Fort Lauderdale Strikers I was voted the North American League's Most Valued Goalkeeper, the equivalent of Player of the Year. That gave me a lot of satisfaction. I knew I was only seventy or so per cent of the player who had won a World Cup medal with England in 1966, but this accolade was a terrific boost to my confidence.

I had all sorts of offers to stay out in the States after my two-year contract was up, but there were several reasons why I headed back to England. For a start, I wanted to get back into the bosom of my family. Also, I knew deep down that I still wanted to be involved in English football.

In my estimation, English Football was then – and remains – the best in the world and I came back from America hoping to be able to play a backroom part in helping it develop ...**'**

Gordon is too much of a gentleman to say it, but he was treated disgracefully by the Establishment on his return to England. It was well publicised that he was back and hungry to get involved with the game he had served so well, but he was shunned. The best offer that came his way was first-team coach to Port Vale down in the Fourth Division, and he later had a spell as manager of non-League Telford United.

What a way to treat a hero. And the great Bobby Moore was getting the same shabby treatment. You did not have to be a scientist to know that Gordon and Bobby would have made wonderful ambassadors for our game, but both were virtually ignored.

They built statues to Bobby at Wembley and West Ham after he had lost a battle with cancer. But where were they when he was alive? He was forced to scrape a living at the soccer outpost of Southend.

Disillusioned, Gordon finally left the football world to set up a promotions company, which briefly got caught up in an overblown scandal about FA Cup final tickets finishing up on the black market. If anybody had bothered to listen, Gordon had a perfectly logical explanation for how this happened, but the Establishment came down on him like a ton of bricks and banned this gentleman of the game from receiving any more tickets for the final. If only they could have been as positive in helping Gordon when he was down and depressed.

I underline the fact that these are my opinions. Gordon would not lower himself to get involved in a slanging match with the people running – I nearly said ruining – our Beautiful Game.

There were people around who continued to recognise his service to football after his career was cruelly cut short by at least six years. He was an inaugural inductee to the English Football Hall of Fame in 2002, and was awarded an honorary doctorate from Keele University in 2006. The award was not only for his football achievements, but for his quiet work to help those less fortunate than himself. He was so touched by the plight of patients when asked to present a cheque to a cancer sufferer that he started raising money for a children's cancer ward in Stoke. The cash he raised has gone towards the development of a special examinations room on the ward, a play area and vital equipment.

It was with reluctance that in 2001 Gordon sold his World Cup winners' medal and the cap awarded for that memorable match. It was one of the hardest decisions he ever had to make, because they meant so much to him. But it should be remembered that

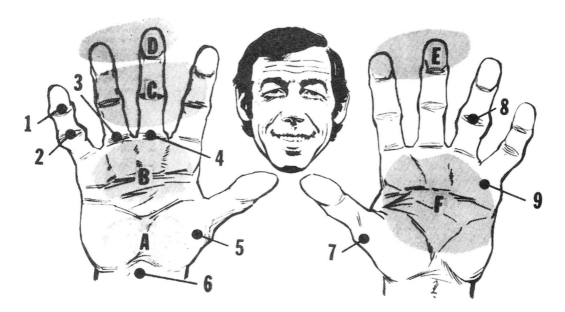

This graphic showing the injuries Gordon collected during his goalkeeping career was presented to him by the world famous sports artist Paul Trevillion, and has a prominent place in his scrapbook. It illustrates how Gordon suffered for his art. His catalogue of injuries included: the right little finger on the right hand broken at the top (1), and the middle joints fractured (2); dislocations to the third finger (3), middle finger dislocated and broken (4); a broken and dislocated right thumb (5); a fractured wrist (6); a torn and dislocated left thumb (7); a break in the third finger of his left hand (8); and a mysterious knuckle injury (9), which has left him missing a knuckle that disppeared during a match when he was trampled on in the goalmouth. The letters A-B-C-D-E-and-F show the key points of Gordon's hands that he used for making vital saves

he earned less than £100 a week for much of his career. He is from the generation of professional footballers who were were comfortably off while playing, but never ever mega-rich like today's superstars.

In 2001 Gordon sold his World Cup Winners medal at Christie's auction house in London. The medal sold for £124,750 easily exceeding the initial estimate of £90,000. Banks said the decision to sell was difficult - the 4-2 cup final victory over West Germany at Wembley was the greatest day of his career. But the former Leicester and Stoke City 'keeper wanted to save his children the burden of deciding what to do with the medal after his death. The proceeds of the medal were divided between them.

Gordon's international cap from the 1970 Brazil match was also sold in the same auction. It fetched £27,025. His cap awarded for that unforgettable game was bought for £8,225 by TV personality and Stoke City fan Nick Hancock.

While Gordon is an honorary Staffordshire man, he is proud of his origins as a Yorkshireman from Sheffield. In May 2006 he was the first person to be honoured with a bronze plaque cemented into the pavement in front of Sheffield Town Hall on the 'Sheffield Walk of Fame.' Sons of Sheffield who have followed him include actor Sean Bean, singers Jarvis Cocker and Joe Cocker, athlete Lord Sebastian Coe, Monty Python comedian and presenter Michael Palin, and master rock climber Joe Simpson. The first woman to be honoured is Britain's pioneering astronaut Helen Sharman.

Gordon said:

'To be the first honoured in this way fills me with pride. Once a Sheffield man always a Sheffield man. I just wish my Dad was alive to see me get this acclaim. He was Sheffield through and through and would have been so proud. I was born and brought up in Tinsley with a steel works at the end of the road. You can't get more Sheffield than that.

I started my football career with Tinsley schoolboys and then played for Sheffield Boys, so I have unbreakable links with the city where I started out on my adventure as a goalkeeper.'

The bronze pavement plaque is star shaped and set in a circle with a blue background. Inscribed are the words: *SHEFFIELD LEGEND GORDON BANKS OBE, FOOTBALLER.*

I would have made it read: *FOOTBALLER AND GENTLEMAN.*

L IKE Gordon Banks, Pelé started the second half of his footballing life playing in the United States. He joined New York Cosmos in 1975 and in three seasons in the North American Soccer League added to his legend as a god of the game. He went out the way he came in – as a winner, helping the Cosmos win the North American Soccer League Championship and drawing record crowds wherever he played. Here are his answers to twenty questions, based on the years following the 1970 World Cup finals …

How did you come to play in the United States?

'I had virtually retired from playing major football when in 1975 I was approached by a former English football journalist called Clive Toye, who had become general manager of New York Cosmos. He was very persuasive in talking me out of retirement, even getting Dr Henry Kissinger to meet me and to fill me with enthusiasm as to how I could spread the message of the Beautiful Game to one of the world's most powerful countries. You could say they made me a generous offer that I could not refuse, and I enjoyed this unexpected new lease of football life.

As long as I live I will never forget the final match of my career on October 1 1977. New York Cosmos organised a friendly against the club of my heart, Santos. We played in front of a capacity crowd at the New York Giants stadium in a match that was televised around the world. I spoke to the crowd just before the kick-off and asked them to say the word 'love' with me three times. Love-Love-Love echoed around the world. All my time in the game, and I had never known an atmosphere quite like this.'

For which team did you play in that final match?

'I played the first-half for Cosmos and the second-half for Santos, and I managed to score the final goal of my career with a direct free-kick before half-time. In a ceremony during the interval my Cosmos No 10 shirt was retired, and in what was a very emotional moment for me I presented it to my father, who was brought on to the pitch by Cosmos captain Werner Roth.

Cosmos won the match 2-1, and at the final whistle I did a lap of the pitch carrying an American flag in one hand and a Brazilian flag in the other. My Cosmos team-mates then got hold of me and carried me on their shoulders. It was all so wonderful and I

Pelé in the No 10 New York Cosmos shirt that was retired after his emotion-charged final game

admit to crying tears of joy and also sadness because my career was definitely over.

I felt very satisfied in that I had done what had been asked of me, and I had helped win over a lot of new fans to the Beatutiful Game.'

Did your experience in the United States make you wish you had played club football outside Brazil when you were at your peak?

'Not at all. I had the greatest time possible playing for Santos. We travelled the world giving exhibitions, and for many years we were the No 1 club in Brazil, winning all the domestic competitions. They were very exciting days for me, and my heart was always with the club. Let me stress that I was very proud to play for Santos throughout my career, and it was an honour to get the chance to have those wind-down seasons with the Cosmos.'

What are your memories of your final appearance for Brazil?

'It was against Yugoslavia in Rio on July 18 1971. We drew 2-2, and my legs were telling me that the time was right to hang up my international boots. It was my 97th game for Brazil and I finished with 93 goals. I wore the Brazilian shirt just once more, in an exhibition match against Flamengo in 1976. Pulling on the Brazilian shirt always made me feel ten foot tall.'

You finished with a remarkable total of 1281 goals in 1363 games.

'That is what I am told by the experts who know these things. I was too busy scoring the goals to count them! I used to leave the adding up to others. What I do know is that there is no thrill to beat that of scoring a goal. I got as much pleasure from my last goal as my first.'

How difficult was it for you when you first retired?

'I had no problems because I had achieved all I wanted to on the football pitch. Ever since my last game I have been extremely busy with my commercial and charity work, and I have watched games in every corner of the globe. Much of my time has been spent helping unfortunate children, and that has given me tremendous satisfaction. To see a young boy's face light up when he has a football at his feet is great reward for me when I am involved in my charity work. It makes all that I try to do worthwhile. I am heartbroken by the amount of poverty and hardship there is in the world, and football is one way of lifting the spirits.'

You have been loaded down with honours since retiring in 1977. Which has meant most to you?

'I don't like to single them out, and I am just grateful to have what I achieved on the football pitch recognised. One presentation I found very moving was when I was given the Laureus World Sports Lifetime Achievement Award in Monaco in 2000. What made it extra special is that it was presented to me by Nelson Mandela, who is one of my great heroes. It is engraved on my heart what he said before presenting the magnificent trophy to me ... "Sport has the power to change the world. It has the power to inspire. It has the power to unite people in a way that little else does. Sport can awaken hope where there was previously only despair." That is exactly how I think of all sport and, in particular, the Beautiful Game of football.'

Being named Athlete of the Century by the International Olympics Committee must have been a pleasant surprise. Just to remind our reader – because I know you'll be too modest to say – the four giants of sport who finished behind you were Muhammad Ali, Carl Lewis, Michael Jordan and Mark Spitz.

'It surprised me because I was the only one of those who did not compete in an Olympics. If I have one regret about my career it is that I did not get to play in an Olympic Games, the greatest sporting event on earth. In my day professional sportsmen were not allowed to compete. To find myself getting the vote ahead of the like of legends like Muhammad Ali, Carl Lewis, Michael Jordan and Mark Spitz makes me feel very humble and grateful.'

What price do you put on loyalty in football?

'I am sad to say it is something going out of the game. There is a river of money in the game at the moment, and some players are in danger of drowning in it. I sometimes lie awake at night and wonder why Pelé is still so popular and, to be honest, I don't know. Maybe it is because I was identified with one club and one team, not like so many of today's players. There are a lot of good players around now but they go to one club, score a few goals, kiss the club badge and then they're off to another club where they do the same. Fans don't like that and so I think it will be hard for a lot of the present-day stars to be remembered for so long. They do not show the same loyalty as the footballers from my generation. Just think of England players like the Charlton brothers and Bobby Moore, who stayed with one club for many years. I am very proud of my long service to Santos, and today's footballers should think more about the loyalty they owe to their club and their fans.'

Yet another honour came your way when you shared the FIFA Footballer of the Century Award with Maradona. How big is the rivalry between you and Diego?

❝The rivalry between Maradona and myself is not of our making. There will always be debates about which sportsman is the greatest, but it is difficult to compare players from different generations. Maradona and I are not great friends but I admired him as a player. I was honoured to receive 72.5 per cent of the votes from the Fifa 'Football Family,' with Di Stefano second and Maradona third. Diego got more than 50 per cent of the vote on the Fifa website, and so it was decided to share the award between us.

It is more than thirty years since I played competitive football, and I am so grateful to still be remembered for what I achieved on the football pitch – as I was so lucky to find fame as a player.❞

Were you disappointed when Maradona did not stay to see you receive your award at the ceremony in Rome?

❝I was going to call Maradona up on to the stage to stand beside me, and I was surprised at his decision to leave the hall after he had received his trophy. But Maradona has to do what Maradona has to do. The same goes for Pelé. He has his way of doing things, and you have to accept that you cannot please all of the people all of the time.❞

The general view in Britain is that George Best was one of the few players who could be mentioned in the same breath as you and Maradona.

❝No question, George was an exceptionally talented player. I used to tell him that he was a South American. "Europeans cannot play the way you do," I used to say as a joke. He had Latin skills. He chose to lead a life syle that would not have suited me. But, as with Maradona, George did things his way, and it was not for me to criticise. He was a wonderful footballer, and that is how I will always think of him.❞

You had a spell as Sports Minister of Brazil. How difficult was that?

❝It was never easy. I accepted the position of Sports Minister because the President called me and said that he needed my help. What I did was my duty as a man who loves his homeland. I wanted to organise and moralise football and other sports in Brazil. There was no prouder international footballer than Pelé. Everybody knows, and I have said a lot of times that we had the best teams and players but outside of that we didn't have good laws. We didn't have good administration. It's unfortunate that I had to say this but it was best to face facts Everybody knew that Brazil had a lot of problems.

Pelé receives the 2007 Fifa Presidential Lifetime Achievement Award from Sir Bobby Charlton

When I was approached by the President almost every club was near bankruptcy. I had to try to help because football and sport gave me everything that I have in my life. I don't want to see anyone kill this game. I am not a politician and I don't have a political party. I just did my best to support the sport and that was the reason we fought for new laws. I wanted to make a law to punish the presidents of clubs who don't use the money properly and then I became the big enemy. Everybody said, "Oh Pelé doesn't know anything about football." It was an interesting time in my life!'

How do you see the power base of football in the future?

'The 2010 World Cup finals in South Africa are going to be fascinating. In my opinion it is only a question of time before an African team wins the World Cup, and then European and Latin American countries will find their status as the best in the world being challenged. I have been to Africa to see the progress being made across that great continent. Countries like Nigeria, Cameroon and Egypt are making rapid strides, and in my visits to the Far East I have seen some remarkably talented young players. The Beautiful Game is alive and kicking across the world, and we must keep doing all we can to improve it at grassroots level.'

What responsibility do you think today's millionaire footballers have?

'Today's highly paid players must recognise they owe it to the game that has brought them fame and fortune to help and encourage the next generation. It must not be all take, take, take. I think football is a sport which brings people together as well as instilling discipline. The game has a big responsibility to society. It can be used to take kids from the streets and away from drugs. You can look to Japan, Africa, China and other parts of the world and see great players but what is more important is how football has developed these men in their personal life. As such it is the type of sport which should be passed down to each generation of children.'

You provide action to go with your words because it is well known you do an enormous amount for charity, particularly where under-privileged children are concerned.

'I do my best to give something back and I am more than happy to lend the name of Pelé to such things as UNICEF and other charities that look after needy children and those caught in the poverty trap. I feel that Pelé has a responsibility to use his celebrity status to help those in need. I went to China and the Far East recently and there were hundreds of little children shouting my name outside my hotel. It was really unbelievable, and I thank God for what football has given me.'

The King with a leather-panelled ball, the type he played with in his first two World Cup finals of 1958 and 1962. The photograph comes from Pelé's personal scrapbook.

How do you think David Beckham will settle to playing in the United States?

❝I have a lot of time for David, and think he is a fine player. He is very good at public relations, and his fame – along with that of his wife – has transcended football. He is not a natural goalscorer, and I am not sure the American public realise that. I think he needs to have better players around him at Los Angeles Galaxy if he is to have the chance of making the best possible impact. I was not a one-man team at the Cosmos. They surrounded me with fine footballers, and this is why we were able to win the championship.❞

You met David in America in unusual circumstances?

❝Yes, I was invited to a charity function in New York, and was surprised by an announcement that I was to be given a lifetime achievement award. I was very pleased to find that they had flown David in to make the presentation. He was kind enough to refer to Pelé as the greatest sportsman of all time. That was very flattering coming from a fine ambassador for England and for football.❞

A completely different and very trivial question ... was that spectacular bicycle kick goal you scored in the film* Escape to Victory *instinctive or scripted?

❝It was in the script, and the famous director John Huston got me to perform it more than a dozens times, and guess what – he used the very first take. That was a really enjoyable experience, particularly as my good friend Bobby Moore was among the footballers who took part. Sylvester Stallone was a charming man, but knew little about soccer. He kept on about wanting to score the winning goal. We had to tell him that as the goalkeeper he was there to save the ball not to shoot at goal.❞

If you had your time over again, would you do anything differently?

❝No, no, no. I would not change a thing. I have been blessed. Pelé, the little boy from Tres Coracoes. has had a charmed life. Of course there have been down times, but you need these to appreciate the up times. I owe everything to the Beautiful Game. I travel all around the world and people still call Pelé! Pelé! Pelé! wherever I go ... but no one remembers Edson. That is me. The real me. Edson is the person who has the feelings, who has the family, who works hard, and Pelé is the idol. Pelé doesn't die. Pelé is going to go on for ever. But Edson is a normal person who is going to die one day. I was recently told that in the Bible in Hebrew Pelé means 'miracle.' Now isn't that something? Yes, Pelé ... the Miracle Man .❞

Pelé, with author Terry Baker (above), always wore his heart on his sleeve when playing (right) and was never frightened to show his emotions. There were many tears during his career, usually of triumph.

BANKS v. PELÉ: The Save that Shook the World

12. Pelé and Me: How I came to represent a legend

THIS book and my partnership with Pelé is the stuff of fairy tales. The story deserves a place here because it allows me the opportunity to give a unique insight into the greatest footballer who ever pulled on a pair of boots. I deliberately use that phrase because we are talking about somebody who was so poor as a kid that his parents could barely afford shoes for his feet let alone football boots.

It is from this background of poverty that Pelé has risen to the status of not only the greatest footballer but also one of the best known people in the history of the world. What makes it mind-boggling for me is that along the way in his great adventure he has become a treasured part of my life.

I am often asked how I – "a Dork from Dorset" – have managed to become the UK representative for the prized signature of the legend that is Pelé. Excuse my trumpet blowing, but it was my *honesty* that first of all earned me Pelé's trust and what has grown into a mutual firm and lasting friendship.

As a purveyor of sporting memorabilia, I operate with my wife and business partner, Freda, in what is, sadly, often a shady world. There are swindlers out there who cheat and connive to get people to part with money for items that are – at best – plagiarised and – at worst – forged. When we set up our A1 Sporting Memorabilia company we vowed that every item we sold would be the genuine article. As a collector myself, I did not want our customers to have the heartbreak of finding that their cherished mementos were counterfeit.

Pelé has always been a target for the sharks who infest the periphery of the sporting world, and he has had several painful and costly experiences where people he trusted have cheated and deceived him. So he was naturally suspicious when a mutual friend, David Holland, brought us together for a couple of signing sessions that I had organised.

These went well and Pelé and his advisers were sufficiently impressed to allow us a third session that involved the sale of 1500 Pelé-endorsed pieces. Unbeknown to Freda and me, Pelé's friend and business manager – a Brazilian called Peppito – decided to count the items. He found the numbers were exactly as we had said, and the monies that he and Pelé received in return were correct to the nearest penny.

They realised that we were running an honourable company, and were happy to come on board when we put forward a proposal for a lucrative worldwide deal. We have a contract that runs until 2012, and hopefully we will operate beyond that because in representing Pelé we are working with not only a sporting god but a man who has become a very special friend to both Freda and myself.

A key man in getting us established with the Pelé team is a Spanish agent contact, Jesus Marin, to whom we owe so much. He is another who operates on the principle of honesty at all times, and believes in our motto, "Trust is a must." He has opened the doors for us to work on exclusive projects with the likes of Maradona, Torres, Cristiano Ronaldo, the Brazilian master Ronaldo and Figo. Marin is so well thought of in the Latin American world of football that he can talk to any of the major players on a mutual trust basis.

But Pelé is still The King. It is more than thirty years since he kicked a ball in competitive football, yet he remains a superstar with an aura around him that can only be matched by presidents, royalty and The Pope.

Pelé is from the generation that can remember John Lennon getting into trouble for calling The Beatles more popular than Jesus. I am not going down that road, but what I will say is that Pelé is known in every corner of the world, from Alaska to Zambia and every alphabetical stop off in between.

The first time I met him I was as excited as a kid at Christmas. In my mind's eye I was going to meet a true sporting giant, and the image I had in my head built him up as a colossus. So I was surprised, as a six footer, to be looking down at him. He stands five foot eight, and even in his sixties has a young man's build that reminds you immediately of the Pelé of his peak years. Those were the days when he had the physique and spring of a gymnast and the strength and speed of a panther. .

He has shaken a million hands during his life time, but still managed to squeeze mine with a warmth and sincerity that signalled that this was a true champion without a shred of arrogance. Freda was with me and was immediately charmed by Pelé's hug and kiss on the cheek, acting as naturally as if we were old friends.

The first thing you notice with him is that he talks about Pelé in the third person, and he asked that I should call him Edson. "Pelé is the legend," he said. "Edson is the man that I am. I try to be the best possible ambassador for Pelé, but when it comes to my private life I prefer to think of myself as Edson. That makes me able to relax and not have to give of myself all the time."

When you look into his liquid brown eyes you see a man of affection and good humour. He laughs easily and is clearly comfortable with himself and the life he has created away from the football pitch. Pelé in his sixties is contented and trying to give as much back to the world as he can.

One of the major things that helped him agree to work in harness with our company is our association with the Murry Foundation. This was set up by British businessman Adam Murry, a conservationist and one of the most caring and inspirational people I have ever met. He channels his enormous energy into raising money for aids-infected orphans in South Africa and Nepal, and somehow also finds the time to pour extra

Signing day ... Freda and Terry Baker make the A1 Sporting Speakers union with Pelé official.

effort into helping animal welfare charities. It is a remarkable show of devotion beyond the call of duty by somebody who puts action where his mouth is.

I told Pelé that one of our ideas was to raffle shirts autographed by him with the proceeds going to the Murry Foundation to help the orphanage in Limpopo. It was the clincher. "That is something close to my heart," he said. "Pelé will do anything to help needy and deprived children."

When I told him that we would be raffling the signed shirts at the Jimmy Greaves road shows that we promote his wonderful face lit up like a beacon, with a smile on which you could warm your hands.

"Jimmy!" he said. "One of my favourite English footballers. He scored many beautiful goals."

Suddenly I did not just like Pelé. I *loved* him! As anybody who knows me will testify, Greavsie is my all-time hero. I played football at local level for twenty-three seasons always dreaming of scoring Jimmy-style goals. Unfortunately I was more Jimmy Cricket than Jimmy Greaves.

Beyond my wildest dreams I eventually became Jimmy's agent, and we are so close that he has part of my business as a shareholder. To find that Pelé thought so highly of him as a player cemented my desire and determination to work with The King.

When Pelé continually hears English people talking about the Gordon Banks save, he

Pelé puts the world's most sought-after footballer autograph on to a Brazilian shirt, ready for an A1 Sporting Speakers raffle to boost the Murry Foundation children's charity.

pretends to be annoyed. "All the goals I scored and they talk about one that I missed," he says. He quickly breaks into his famous grin and adds that he thinks that the save deserves special attention.

Our company works closely with the 1966 World Cup winning team, sadly now down to just nine survivors following the too-early deaths of skipper Bobby Moore and Alan Ball. Gordon was the first of the team that I met, and we hit it off immediately. I bored him silly going on and on about my memories of his Save of the Century, and when I told him I was going to write a book about it he looked at me as if I was mad. Maybe I am, but it's a nice madness because I am intoxicated by sporting nostalgia.

The more I meet and mix with Pelé the more I like him. I have never known anybody match the response he gets when he greets fans at autograph-signing sessions. He makes everybody for whom he signs feel special and as if the privilege of him signing is his rather than theirs.

His aura is such that you can almost imagine a saint-like halo over his head, and I have seen people so in awe of him that they have been close to fainting. But he always puts them at their ease, and manages to make it seem like it is the first time he has heard it when they say: "You are the greatest footballer ever."

There are no prima donna antics from Pelé, and he is enormously industrious and enthusiastic, taking a world-wide business schedule in his stride. He is also generous to a fault. On my birthday in 2008 he presented me with a superb engraved glass plaque with 'Pelé thanks you' inscribed on it in Portuguese. That is one collectors' item that I will never sell.

Pelé's favourite English word is "beautiful." I sat with him and his manager Peppito watching a DVD of 300 of his greatest goals on a 60-inch TV screen in his hotel suite. One goal, from the early 1960s with a lumpen leather ball, came after he had nutmegged three players and then delicately dinked the ball over the diving goalkeeper.

"Beautiful," said Pelé, as if seeing the goal for the first time and being scored by somebody else.

The next goal, he punched the air as he watched himself heading the ball over one defender, then another, and then over the goalkeeper. It was poetry in motion.

"Pelé scored some beautiful goals," he said.

Pelé – Edson Arantes Do Nascimento – is a beautiful person, and it is a privilege for Freda and I to work with him and have him as a friend.

Yes, beautiful.

13. A Statue Stokes the Memories

THE immortal Pelé and the goliath of goalkeepers Gordon Banks came face-to-face again in the summer of 2008, although this time not in rivalry but in friendship. They got together at Stoke City's Britannia Stadium, where Pelé performed the honours at the unveiling of a bronze statue of Gordon.

Helping out at the ceremony was Archbishop Desmond Tutu, who praised both Pelé and Banks for always being good role models to the thousands of young footballers in his native South Africa.

The statue was the brainchild of award-winning Irish author Don Mullan, who wrote an inspiring autobiography called *The Hero Who Could Fly*. The thrust of the book is how Mullan hero worshipped Banks from when he first saw him helping England win the World Cup in 1966. The moving story then follows the subsequent forty years of Mullan's life with constant references to what he saw as a mirror image of the experiences of Gordon, culminating with a one-on-one interview with the man he describes as the world's greatest goalkeeper.

Mullan said: "I still proudly retain a 500-page scrapbook as a testimony to the inspiration this supreme athlete had on my formative years. As a dyslexic child, crippled with self-doubt and low self-esteem, it was through that scrapbook I learned to read and write. That's one of the reasons why I retain such an affection for Gordon Banks to this day. If Pelé is the god of strikers, then Gordon is the god of goalkeepers." Proving he is a man of compassion and benevolence, Mullan is donating royalties from the book to the Dyslexia Association of Ireland.

It was Mullan who was the driving force behind getting the money together to erect the statue to his hero, and local sculptor Andrew Edwards created a masterpiece showing Gordon holding aloft the Jules Rimet trophy after the 1966 World Cup triumph. The statue now stands at the Britannia Ground along with that of another Stoke City legend, Sir Stanley Matthews.

Gordon said:

❝I was overwhelmed by the decision to erect a statue to me at Stoke. There is no higher honour for a person than to have a statue built while still alive. Don Mullan is a remarkable character, and when I inscribed his book I dedicated it to "My greatest fan." He kept an amazing scrapbook on all the things I achieved in football, and used my experiences to motivate himself. He told me that *he* was my greatest save because I saved him from going down the wrong road during 'The Troubles' in Ireland.

Thirty-eight years after THAT save, Gordon and Pelé come face to face at the Stoke statue unveiling

Don is a great humanitarian, and through his world-wide work for peace became friendly with Archbishop Tutu, which explains his involvement with the statue unveiling.

It was a wonderful gesture by Pelé to agree to travel to Stoke for the ceremony. He took great delight in reminding me that he had played at the old Victoria Ground in Stoke with Santos in a friendly back in 1969. He grinned like a Cheshire cat as he recalled that Santos won 3-2 and he scored two of the goals against me.

We gave dozens of interviews, and everybody asked us about the save I made against him in Mexico in 1970. Here is a man who scored more than a thousand goals, and – in England – all anybody was interested in was a goal that he missed.

Typical of Pelé, he took it in good spirit. He is not only the greatest footballer of my lifetime, but also a nice guy. We have forged a good friendship over the years, and he remains a fine ambassador for the game. I guess I am always going to be remembered for THAT save, but Pelé will go down in history for his thousand-plus goals. He is a living legend and I am thrilled and proud to have my name linked with his.⁹

While Gordon and Pelé were together in Stoke, a story broke in the newspapers that Fifa President Sepp Blatter had said modern footballers were being treated like slaves. This followed Manchester United's refusal to let Cristiano Ronaldo go to Real Madrid.

Blatter provoked anger at Old Trafford and ridicule throughout football when he declared that a disaffected Ronaldo should be free to pursue a transfer to Real Madrid rather than be kept to the £120,000-a-week contract that he signed less than 18 months earlier. Ronaldo suggested that the sport's most powerful figure was right.

"I agree with the statements of the president," Ronaldo told TVI, the Portuguese television channel, when asked about the "slavery" comments. "What he said is correct. You know what I said, what I want and what I would like. Now I have to wait and see what happens."

Ronaldo got no sympathy from Banks or Pelé. Gordon said:

‘It is nonsense to call the modern top footballers slaves. When I started out as a professional with Chesterfield I was earning £17 a week, and Stanley Matthews and Tom Finney were earning the same. Now *that* was soccer slavery. I wonder if Ronaldo realises that he earns in just one week more than I picked up in wages throughout my career. Good luck to him I say, but don't go crying that he is being treated as a slave. Footballers should honour their contracts, otherwise the whole game will become a farce. How can a manager have a team-building plan if the moment a player gets a better offer from another club he insists on leaving. Can you imagine what Pelé would have earned a week if he was at his peak today? I would say £200,000 plus, and even then he

The unveiling at Stoke in the summer of 2008, with Archbishop Tutu, Gordon, Pelé and the Statue

would be underpaid. If a player has just signed a new contract then he should respect his manager and the club supporters by seeing it through. It's stupid. I don't understand what the problem is. Ronaldo plays for a team that has just won the European Cup and the Premier League. He plays for his country. What more does he want?'

Pelé was as outspoken on the subject as Gordon:

'You are a slave if you work without a contract or you don't get paid. If you have a contract then in any job you have to finish the contract. I think that when a player has honured his contract, then he should be free to go wherever he wants to go. The money paid to international footballers today is astronomical, and I think that if they sign a contract they should see it through The soccer slaves were those players in my early days who had no contracts, yet were still denied the chance of leaving a club.'

Now to a man with a neutral view on the Banks/Pelé debate ... Greavsie!

FOR a balanced view of Banks and Pelé I turned to a man who played against each of them, and who just happens to be one of my best friends. Enter James Peter Greaves, my role model as a player when I was growing up and now the most prominent and popular member of the A1 Sporting Speakers team.

Greavsie, of course, has a strong opinion on just about everything. He does not always talk sense but he is never ever less than entertaining with his views. I can say that sort of thing about him because we have each other's full respect and support.

It was Jimmy more than anybody who encouraged me to make an international success of my business, and he had sufficient faith in my entrepreneurial skills to become a shareholder in my company. He saw close up that I was a man to be trusted in a world where there are too many people looking for easy pickings with what is often faked and forged material.

It has been my privilege to promote Greavsie in a road show series that has been running for more than ten years. Anybody who has seen it will, I know, agree when I say that he has developed into as good a stand-up comedian as any in the land. The secret of Jimmy's success as the greatest goal scorer England has ever produced was his timing in the penalty area, when he instinctively knew when to unbalance a defender and then slip the ball past the goalkeeper. I loved the way Jimmy always used to pass the ball into the net rather than the wham-bang stuff. Now he has transferred that same timing and delivery to the stage with his comedy routine.

I have brought him to these pages to give his expert analysis of Banks and Pelé, but first I just had to get his slant on the "soccer slave" controversy. This is what Jimmy had to say in his intimitable style:

'I hear they are going to film a remake of *Spartacus* with Cristiano Ronaldo in the Kirk Douglas role as the rebel slave, and Alex Ferguson playing the Laurence Olivier part. I don't want to spoil it for you, but it ends with Ronaldo getting melted down by Fergie's hairdryer treatment. What a load of balls from Blatter. If Ronaldo is a slave on his hundred and twenty grand a week wages then what did that make of the likes of Stanley Matthews, Tom Finney, Nat Lofthouse and Billy Wright, who used to have to get by on twenty quid a week. I know times have changed, but that does not mean we have to lose our senses. Ethics come into this ... and I am not talking Ethics Girl here. There is a moral code of conduct that demands when you sign a contract you honour it. Simple as that. The game will quickly nosedive into a crisis if players start walking out on contracts because they had found greener fields. I don't want to do the "in my day" whine, but it is a fact that loyalty meant something when I was playing. It makes me want to throw up when I see players running to the fans kissing and holding the club badge on their shirt after scoring, knowing full well that they will be off at the first whiff of a few extra quid bunged their way. There is a restlessness among fans over the amount of money players are taking out of the game, which has led to ridiculous ticket prices. Any more of that stupid sort of "slave" talk from the likes of Blatter and they could find those all-seater stadiums with a lot fewer bums on the seats.❜

I have helped Jimmy off his high horse, and explained that he is here to give his view of Gordon Banks and Pelé. We have agreed that the best way to paint a Greavsie portrait of them is to dip into his *Football's Great Heroes and Entertainers* book. Published by Hodder Stoughton, it is the best football book I have read in years. Yes, I am biased because of my association with Jimmy, but the book gives a fascinating insight into the finest players of Jimmy's lifetime. Greavsie wrote it in harness with his long-time pal Norman Giller, and I have their permission as copyright holders to reproduce the chapters on Banks and Pelé.

We kick off with Jimmy's view of Gordon, and we join Greavsie as he is discussing the topic of Banks v. Peter Shilton ...:

❛THE toughest job I had compiling my file of most unforgettable footballers was choosing between Gordon Banks and Peter Shilton as the greatest of all England goalkeepers. The restrictions put on me by my demanding Editor meant there was not room for both of them.

There was always a little of the Master and Apprentice about Banksie and Shilts. Peter had grown up in the shadow of Gordon at Leicester, learning his trade by watching Banks in action in the first-team.

He had learned his lessons so well that when Gordon returned from the glory of helping England win the World Cup in 1966 the Leicester directors decided they could afford to let him move on to Stoke, because in the young Shilton they had a ready-made replacement (note added by Jimmy: If you wanted evidence of soccer slavery there it was ... Leicester decided they could off load Gordon despite his success in the 1966 World Cup. He was not given an option of staying. On yer bike!).

Shilts developed into a magnificent goalkeeper. The arguments will always continue as to whether he became even better than Banks. I finally came down on Gordon's side because of a save that was made and one that was missed.

The one that was made, of course, was when Banks denied Pelé with the famous 'Save of the Century' during the 1970 World Cup against Brazil.

Every time I see it replayed on television I am convinced Pelé is going to score!

Peter Shilton has a word in the ear of Gordon Banks, whom he succeeded at club and country level

Gordon just had no right to get across his goal to fingertip the header over the bar. I had gone to Mexico the unorthodox way, racing with my co-driver Tony Fall in a Ford Escort as we finished sixth in the World Cup Rally.

By the time I left Mexico – bound for a holiday in the Caribbean – Banks was the talk of the World Cup because of that save.

And the save that got away? This involved Peter Shilton in the 1974 World Cup qualifier against Poland at Wembley. Norman Hunter, the most feared tackler in English football, mistimed a challenge out on the right touchline and the ball was transferred to unmarked Polish striker Domarski. His low shot went under the diving Shilton and into the net for a goal that ended England's World Cup life and also virtually finished the reign of England manager Alf Ramsey.

I am convinced that Banksie would have stopped that shot from Domarski. For him it would have been a bread-and-butter save.

So on that evidence I have selected Gordon as the number one England goalkeeper, just a fingernail ahead of Shilts, who went on to make a record 125 appearances for England.

Gordon would have got many more than his 73 caps but for the car smash that robbed him of the sight of his right eye in the autumn of 1972, just a few months after he had been voted Footballer of the Year. Even with only one eye he managed to get himself voted the 'Most Valuable Goalkeeper' in the United States soccer circus after he had failed to get back into League football because of his handicap.

His record with England was phenomenal. He let in just 57 goals in his 73 appearances, a miserly average of just 0.78 goals per game. And he kept a remarkable 35 clean sheets, and was never on the losing side for a sequence of 23 matches between 1964 and 1967, which embraced the 1966 World Cup when he went unbeaten right up to the Eusebio penalty in the semi-final.

As somebody who played against the world's greatest goalkeepers (with Russia's Lev Yashin easily the best of them all) I always had tremendous respect for Gordon. He was the finest of positional players, and his knowledge of angles so good that he left no openings for an advancing striker. Most goalkeepers I faced, I could unbalance them with dummy movements but Gordon always firmly stood his ground. He would be on his feet catching the ball, while lesser goalkeepers would have been diving full stretch to make a save. There was nobody to touch him for coolness and composure, and I used to wonder if he had ice in his veins.

What people don't realise is how hard Gordon worked to perfect his art. There was no more conscientious trainer at our England squad sessions, and Alf Ramsey used to have to order him to stop because the team coach was waiting. I know that he also worked equally hard during club training sessions.

He played at a time when there were no specialised goalkeeper coaches. This meant that goalkeepers would just get a few shots after training and that was it for most of them. But Gordon would go back and have extra sessions, working on sharpening his relfexes and catching ability. He used to go for every shot in practice sessions, even if they were going wide. He developed a habit of never giving up on anything.

The save against Pelé was not luck. It was the pay-off for all that training. Most goalkeepers would have waved goodbye to the ball as it went into the net, but because of all his training Gordon was programmed to go for it.

Most goalkeepers are remembered for their mistakes rather than their saves. But Gordon goes down into football folklore for his saves. Pelé was the one that stands out above all others because of the World Cup stage and the fact that it was made against the phenomenal Pelé. But I speak from experience when I say that Gordon made equally as good saves if not better in many League and international matches.

He would dive and catch shots heading for the top corner while most modern 'keepers tip them over or around the woodwork. Gordon also used to catch the kind of crosses that too many goalies today punch clear. Take it from me, there is not a goalkeeper around today in his class.

I wonder how differently everything would have turned out if he had not missed the 1970 World Cup quarter-final against West Germany? He was lying in bed back at the England hotel shivering and feverish while his last-minute replacement Peter Bonetti – playing his first competitive game in two months – was making a mess of two saves that let the Germans in for a 3-2 victory after trailing 2-0.

To this day Gordon remains convinced that somebody nobbled one of his drinks. Nobody else in the squad was ill, and he had been studious in selecting what to eat and drink in a country notorious for Montezuma's Revenge.

Whenever Gordon and I get back together and reminisce on all our good times together we have a giggle over a goal I scored against him when he was playing for Leicester against Tottenham at White Hart Lane.

It was one of the the craziest goals ever allowed. Spurs had been awarded a penalty on a wet and churned-up pitch. Gordon needed to wipe his hands before facing the penalty and went into the back of the net to find some grass that was not muddy. As he was bending down I – for a joke – side-footed the ball into the other corner of the net. I don't know who was more amazed – Gordon or me – when the ref signalled a goal, but I do know who was more angry.

What made it worse for Gordon was instead of telling the ref he was wrong even his own team-mates were falling about laughing. He chased the referee to the centre-circle and all he got for his trouble was a booking for "ungentlemanly conduct."

Ah, happy days.

What I do know for sure is that when Gordon was between the posts in international matches the England defence was as safe as the Banks of England.

Before moving on with the Greaves view of Pelé, I simply had to find a way to get a reciprical assessment of Greavsie by Gordon Banks. We decided to dive between the covers of his excellent first autobiography *Banks of England* and reproduce a riveting interview he had with Jimmy back in 1980:

❛We had not seen each other for a couple of years and I was expecting the worst after all the harrowing stories I had heard and read about his drink problem. But as he came towards me, moving through the crowded hotel foyer with his familiar balance and economy of effort, I was pleasantly surprised. Jimmy Greaves looked a million dollars.

I had found it hard to believe when he had confessed publicly to being an alcoholic. He had certainly liked his drink in the days when we were England team-mates, but there were players with bigger consumption who had not suffered the nightmare Jimmy had lived through.

As we shook hands with a warmth that suddenly evaporated time and cemented our old friendship we took instant stock of each other. Jimmy wasted no time in getting his sharp Cockney wit to work.

"Just think, Gordon," he said, "since we last played for England together you've become one-eyed and I've become pie-eyed …!"

It was the old Greavsie smiling up at me. Mischievous, impish. A loveable little sod. I wanted to cuddle this loveable man who had given me and millions of football fans so much pleasure and fun over the years.

We were together in a London hotel to talk over old times. I had decided I needed help to revive old memories for my book, and who better, I thought, than Jimmy Greaves who just happened to be one of the greatest things on two feet during my playing career. We had shared so much together both on and off the pitch during the high summer of our playing days.

Now, with a tape-recorder between us, we looked back on the good old days and – sad to say – some not-so-good times …

❛GORDON: "The first time we were together, you bugger, you made me look a right bloody idiot!"

GREAVSIE: "That must have been about 1959 or '60. You had been called up to the England Under-23 squad for the first time."

GORDON: "That's right. We were training at Stamford Bridge and the Press photographers wanted an action shot of me for their files. I asked you to kick the ball to me so that I could make a save. As you approached the ball you dipped your left shoulder and I dived to my right as you slipped the ball into the other corner of the net. The photographers fell about laughing."

GREAVSIE: "That was twenty years ago. *Twenty* years. It seems like only yesterday. I remember that we had two nicknames for you. One was Fernandel because you looked so much like the rubber-faced French comedian. The other was Sugar. You were always impersonating that entertainer who pretended to be drunk. What was his name …?

GORDON: "Freddie Frinton. He used to sing *Sugar in the Morning* with a bent cigarette in his mouth and his top hat over his eyes."

GREAVSIE: "You used to have us in fits taking him off and staggering about as if you were drunk out of your head. So we called you Sugar. It might have been more appropriate if I'd done the drunk act!"

GORDON: "Actually, Jim, I admire the way you've stood up and faced your problem. It took a lot of courage admitting to the world you were an alcoholic."

GREAVSIE: "It was the only way I could beat the illness. I knew that with everybody's eyes on me my pride would help me conquer the problem. When I was asked to write an autobiography (*This One's On Me*) I decided to hang out my skeleton for public viewing. I used the book as a psychiatrist's couch and it did me the world of good."

GORDON: "I really used to envy you, did you know that, Jim? You seemed to have everything going for you. I admired the way you were able to cut off from your playing career to concentrate on building up a successful business. Everything seemed to come so easily to you on the football field and I thought all was perfect with your businesses and your marriage."

GREAVSIE: "I drank it all away. It got so that the booze became like a monster. To be honest, I'm lucky to be alive. But then, you've hardly had roses all the way since we last played together."

GORDON: "You can say that again. But, like you, I've had to come to terms with it. Out of the wreckage, we can salvage the self-satisfaction that we have both been able to help others because of the nightmares we have experienced. I'm sure your book has given hope to a lot of people with the drink problem. Likewise, I have been able to give encouragement to many victims of accidents who have lost an eye. Particularly youngsters. Many parents have asked me to write to children who have lost the sight of an eye to tell them they can still lead ordinary lives."

GREAVSIE: "Something I've learned from the hell I've been through is that you can achieve anything you want provided you are single-minded about it."

GORDON: "Exactly. I made up my mind I was going to play again and I did. Admittedly it wasn't in top-grade football, but at least I got another couple of seasons in when everybody had given me up as finished."

GREAVSIE: "I could have wept for you when I heard about your car smash. In fact I went on a bender when I read about it. I was close to rock bottom with my drinking

From Gordon's personal scrapbook, his 1980 interview with bubble-haired Greavsie

at the time and remember wondering why life had to be so cruel. You still had so much to give to the game. Goalkeeping is such an easy job that you all go on playing until it's time to collect your old age pension.

GORDON: "Very funny, Greavsie. You and I both know that it's the hardest of all jobs in football. Certainly in my time we used to get knocked to bits. But now 'keepers get the protection from referees that they deserve. But you're right in saying that I still had plenty more to give. I was looking forward to several more years at the top when I had my accident. That was obviously a terrible period in both our lives. I came pretty close to breaking down, but I got myself sorted out in America. It was just a question of getting away from domestic pressures for a while so that I could think everything through. Ursula was strong enough to cope with it and to understand that

I was going through torture after the car crash. She and my kids were smashing, and we soon got our family unit back on track. It's been wonderful to be part of watching my children grow up. They give me so much pleasure."

GREAVSIE: "Well all I hope, Gordon, is that you let this tape go into the book verbatim. and tell it as it is. I'm sure people will admire you for the way you have managed to hold everything together despite all the problems. And I know what you mean by the enjoyment you get from being with your kids. Now that I've kicked the bottle I spend all my spare time at home with Irene and the kids, and we get on marvellously together. I call them kids! Lynn, my eldest daughter, has just got married."

GORDON: "Robert, my eldest, is talking about marriage. God, Jim, we could be grandfathers the next time we meet …"

We took a rest from our taping session to share a pot of tea. Joker Jim couldn't resist a gag at his own expense. "At least it's cheaper drinking with me these days, Gordon," he said. "A couple of years ago this reunion would have cost you a bottle of vodka!"

As Jimmy poured the tea, my mind was weighing up what he had said about "telling it as it is". How much should a sportsman strip himself for his public? I went through real torment in the months after the crash, and it was extremely tough on Ursula. Both of us could have capitalised by accepting big-money offers to tell our stories. But it was just not our way. We both believe that people in the public eye deserve their privacy.

Our marriage was strong enough to survive the sort of strains and stresses that have broken many others. Some rubbish found its way into the newspapers but the poison of publicity generated by the tabloid press could not break the bond of love between my family and myself, and once I had completed my contract in the United States I could not get back quickly enough to them.

My thoughts were broken by the sight of Jimmy almost choking over his teacup with laughter. "What have you remembered?" I asked, switching the tape recorder back on …

GREAVSIE: "Do you recall asking my advice about a transfer in 1967 when Leicester put you up for sale? There were two clubs in for you."

GORDON: "That's right, Liverpool and Stoke. I asked you which one you would select."

GREAVSIE: "It's just come back to me what I said to you at the time. My advice was that you should go to Stoke because Liverpool were a finished force. With foresight like that I should have been a BBC weather forecaster."

GORDON: "That's right, you big pillock. Liverpool were such a finished force that they have since won every bloody thing in sight. Still, I've got no regrets about the move I made. Stoke were a great club to be with. They could play some cracking football and socially I would have to say they were *the* top club in the country. You would have had a ball with us, Jimmy."

GREAVSIE: Yes, you had a good drinking school there. I've had lots of good nights out with you and my old mate George Eastham."

GORDON: "George was with us in the squad that night in 1964 when we nipped out for a drink in the West End the night before flying out for a match in Portugal."

GREAVSIE: "Alf (Ramsey) went potty. We thought we'd got away with it when we crept to our hotel rooms at about two o'clock in the morning without being spotted. But trainer Harold Shepherdson had been to our rooms and put our passports on each of our beds. Let's think now. Who were the other players who went on the razzle with us?"

GORDON: "Apart from George, you and me there was Bobby Charlton, Ray Wilson, Budgie Byrne …"

GREAVSIE: "And don't forget our leader Bobby Moore, the man with the hollow legs. He could drink us all under the table, and then dance on it. Mooro and I were always getting each other in trouble with our love for a bevy."

GORDON: "What was the name of that bar we were drinking at?"

GREAVSIE: "The Beachcomber. They had all those exotic drinks, remember? We got stuck into a drink called a Zombie. It was a rum-based drink with a real kick."

GORDON: "That was the place with alligators in the tank. Ray Wilson kept lobbing chunks of ice out of the ice bucket at them."

GREAVSIE: "Nobody said a dicky bird to us the next morning, but when we got to Lisbon for our last training session Alf said in that exaggerated posh voice of his, "I think there are seven gentlemen who wish to see me …"

GORDON: "Alf was fuming. He left us in no doubt that he would never again tolerate us breaking curfews. He said he would have sent us all home if he'd had enough players in the squad. And he would have done as well. Alf was the most loyal bloke walking this earth if you gave him one hundred per cent, but anything less and he could cut you dead."

GREAVSIE: "A myth has been allowed to grow about Alf and me. People think we hated each other, when in fact we got on quite well. He could hit the old G and Ts when he was relaxed, and we had several good drinking sessions. Once switched off, he could be very humorous in a dry way, and had a warmth that unfortunately for him he failed to show in public."

GORDON: "Thank goodness, we won that match in Portugal. He picked all seven of we so-called rebels and we won 4-3 in an epic game."

GREAVSIE: "Two of the AWOL men, Budgie Byrne and Bobby Charlton scored the goals. Budgie helped himself to the sweetest of hat-tricks. Alf allowed himself quite a few G-and-Ts that night."

John 'Budgie' Byrne, who scored the sweetest of hat-tricks for England in Portugal in 1964.

GORDON: "We all felt for you when Alf left you out of the 1966 World Cup final team. You didn't say much, but we all knew you were sick."

GREAVSIE: "What could I say? The team had played magnificently against Portugal in the semi-final when I was nursing an injury. Alf had to decide whether to change the team and it was quite understandable when he stuck with a winning side. It was the worst thing that happened to me in my career, missing that final. I got well sozzled that night, and nipped off with my wife Irene for a holiday in the West Indies. The story got around that I had snubbed Alf and the after-match dinner, but I have always avoided those sort of things. I didn't want to become the story. England's victory deserved all the headlines. Anyway, Gordon, that's enough about me. This is supposed to be *your* book. I've got some statistics here that will interest you. According to the record books I played twenty-three League games against you and scored thirteen goals."

GORDON: "That should be fourteen goals. D'you remember that fantastic shot of yours on the turn at Leicester when you were in your early days with Spurs? I didn't get a sniff of the ball as it flashed into the net. It was right on half-time and we thought the ref had whistled for a goal, but then he said he'd blown for half-time and refused to allow the goal. All you Spurs players went berserk, and no wonder, because it was a belter of a goal."

GREAVSIE: "Here are some more statistics, Gordon, which incidentally come from my well researched book. Ends commercial! You and I played together in twenty matches for England between 1963 and 1967, and we were on the losing side only three times."

GORDON: "Our first defeat was against Scotland in our first game together. That bugger Jim Baxter took control of the game and scored both their goals I thought he was going to become the greatest Scottish footballer of all time, but he didn't maintain his standards."

GREAVSIE: "It's no secret that Baxter had my trouble. He preferred a glass in his hand to a ball at his feet. But what a player when he was at his peak! He was as smooth as silk and all style and skill. They murdered us in midfield where they had Dave Mackay and John White as well as Slim Jim Baxter. The only midfield trio to match them was the one we had in the Spurs side of the time – Danny Blanchflower, Mackay and White."

GORDON: "They were a bit special. Just my luck to come up against them in my international debut."

GREAVSIE: "I thought your international career was finished the next month. Do you remember, we played Brazil?"

GORDON: "Of course, I bloody remember. How could I forget that free-kick of Pepe's? It did a circular tour of the penalty area before going past me into the net."

GREAVSIE: "I never saw Alf get so boiled up over anything. He kept saying over and over again that he had warned you to watch out for that bender. In fact he went on so much about it that in the end every time he mentioned it we would fall about laughing behind his back and poke faces at you."

GORDON: "I still insist that no ball has ever bent as much as that one. It would have taken Superman to save it. Alf wouldn't have it, though. "

GREAVSIE: "Let's be honest, Gordon, you were positioned *behind* the wall instead of to the right of it."

GORDON: "Now don't you start, Greavsie. Even now I can hear Alf saying that in my sleep. I wondered if he would drop me for it, but I kept my place for the first tour match against Czechoslovakia."

GREAVSIE: "That was the game when Alf told us we had to get back to the hotel immediately after the game. I was elected spokesman and had to ask if it would be all right for us to go out for a quiet drink before going back. He gave that piercing look of his and said: 'If you must have a drink you can go back to the f***** hotel and have it."

GORDON: "Alf didn't swear very often, but when he did you knew he meant what he was saying. As I remember it, we *did* go straight back to the hotel that night and Alf and all the officials joined us in a big party to celebrate what had been a great 4-2 victory."

GREAVSIE: "Everybody felt like death the next morning and we had to fly to East Germany. It was a diabolical flight because we had to go through the Berlin corridor at about 3,000 feet and the plane was pitching about like a rowing boat in a storm. I was sitting with Bobby Moore and he said all straight-faced, 'We'll be all right because we've got the England doctor to look after us.' He pointed across the aisle and there was Doc Bass (Dr Alan Bass) laid flat out with sweat pouring off him and looking as green as the Wembley turf. It was a mixture of a hangover and the flight. Mooro called out, 'Is there a doctor on board for the doctor …'?"

GORDON: "Wasn't it in East Germany that Alf took us all to the pictures to see what he said would be an English film?"

GREAVSIE: "It was an English-made war film and Alf said it would be in English with German subtitles."

GORDON: "That's right. When the film started we could not believe our ears. The English actors were talking with dubbed-in German voices. We started having a moan at Harold Shep who kept saying, 'In about five or ten minutes' time they start speaking in English.' When they did start speaking in another language it was Russian and they put up sub-titles in German. With that we all got up *en bloc* and walked out of the cinema."

GREAVSIE: Talking of doing things *en bloc*, d'you remember when we were sitting on the touchline watching Brazil play Argentina in Sao Paulo in 1964? The crowd started pelting us with rubbish and Alf gave the shortest tactical talk of his life, 'Run, lads.'"

GORDON: "I was sitting next to Alf and his actual words after a juicy apple core had splattered against his back were: 'I don't know abut you, gentlemen, but I'm f***** off!'"

GREAVSIE: "Do you realise, Gordon, that we were on the losing side in our first and last matches together for England and each time it was against the Scots."

GORDON: "The second time was in 1967. We lost 3-2 at Wembley. It was our first defeat since the World Cup and the Scots had the cheek to claim they were the world champions."

GREAVSIE: "I've got painful memories of that match. I got a knock on an ankle that put me out for two weeks. Jack Charlton broke a toe and moved up to centre-forward and Ray Wilson was a hobbling passenger for most of the game. I got some terrible stick in the Press for my performance, but if they had seen the state of my ankle after the game I think they would have been more sympathetic."

GORDON: "I could never understand why Alf didn't recall you after that match. He said a couple of years later that you had *asked* not to be selected."

GREAVSIE: "Alf had that all wrong. I would loved to have got my England place back, but Alf had misunderstood a conversation we once had. He had been getting into the habit of calling me up for training with the squad and then not picking me for the match. You know me, Gordon, I was hardly the world's greatest trainer. I'm the bloke who once got fined by Spurs for taking a lift on a milkfloat during a cross country fitness run. Anyway, I told Alf that unless I was going to play I preferred to give the training get-togethers a miss. He interpreted that as meaning I didn't want to play for England any more."

We stopped talking while Jimmy ordered another pot of tea. "I'm hooked on this stuff now," he said. "I drink gallons of tea and coffee, but at least when I wake up the next morning I don't have a hangover and I know exactly what I did the previous day."

You could not tell by looking at him the hell he had been through. He was elegantly dressed and appeared prosperous. Since we'd last played together he had grown a thick, Mexican-style moustache and his hair was well groomed in the modern bubble-cut fashion. I noticed that he smoked heavily, but even in his playing days with England he had liked a cigarette or pipe.

People who had not been lucky enough to have seen him at his peak missed the pleasure of watching a genius at work. I always used to enjoy playing against him because it was such a challenge, and if you were ever beaten by him (which I often was) then at least you had the consolation of knowing a master had put the ball past you.

We continually chatted to each other during games and Jimmy used to tell me exactly where he was going to place his shots. Of course he was bluffing and he would have me diving the wrong way.

As he sat there, teapot in hand, I wondered what his modern-day transfer value would be if Trevor Francis could fetch the first million-pounds fee. It seemed a good point at which to switch the tape recorder back on …

GORDON: "If Trevor Francis is worth a million, Jim, I reckon you would have been worth at least twice that at your peak."

GREAVSIE: "Careful, Gordon. People will read that and think we have formed a mutual-admiration society. Funnily enough, I was just going to say to you if Phil Parkes is worth half a million then your value would be somewhere in excess of three million. I don't mean that as a slight on Phil, because he's an excellent goalkeeper, but I have never seen anybody to match you for class and consistency."

GORDON: "This is getting embarrassing. Let's change the subject. Would you like to be playing in today's game or were you happy to have had your peak when you did?"

GREAVSIE: "Obviously I would like the money they are earning now, but I would not want to swap eras. I think you and I were lucky to have played when we did. I am sure the game was more enjoyable for players and spectators, particularly in the late 1950s and early 1960s."

GORDON: "I agree with you. Goalkeepers got little or no protection from the referee when I first came into the game, and the likes of Bobby Smith and Nat Lofthouse thought nothing of trying to batter you into the net. But it was accepted as part and parcel of the game and you just took it in your stride. Now I think if anything goalkeepers are over protected and consequently they are not learning the physical aspect of the game. It's definitely not as entertaining for spectators to watch."

GREAVSIE: "The last time I played with you, Gordon, was in a Goaldiggers match for the Playing Fields Fund. It was some time after your accident and Jimmy Hill had arranged the game against a team of European All Stars at Birmingham. Bobby Robson was playing in midfield and you – if you'll pardon the expression – were having a blinder, stopping everything that came at you. Bobby turned to me and said: 'If Banksie is one-eyed then all I can say is that the First Division has a load of blind goalkeepers.' After the match he told me he was going to try to sign you for Ipswich, but nothing came of it."

GORDON: "That's the story of my life since the accident. Promises, promises. I got really disillusioned trying to get back into the game. Clubs just didn't want to know me. I don't know if they think I've lost the power to think as well as to see out of one eye, but some clubs didn't even have the decency to reply to my job applications."

GREAVSIE: "It's astonishing how many of that 1966 World Cup squad are now out of the game. Ronnie Springett and Peter Bonetti were the other two goalkeepers in the squad. They are both out. The full-backs were George Cohen, Ray Wilson, Jimmy Armfield and Gerry Byrne. They're all out."

GORDON: "Even Mooro is out of the game. It's madness. Surely the Football Association could employ him in some capacity. All that knowledge going to waste. I would have jumped at the chance to take over the England youth team after Brian Clough and Peter Taylor said they were no longer interested. But I didn't get a look-in."

GREAVSIE: "Nobby and Jackie are managers, but they are the only two unless you count Geoff Hurst, who's involved with the England team. So out of twenty-two players, thirteen of them are no longer connected with the game at top level. Ron Flowers, Roger Hunt, John Connelly, Terry Paine, George Eastham and even Bobby Charlton are not involved in the League scene."

GORDON: "Only Norman Hunter, Ballie, Martin Peters and Ian Callaghan are still playing in the League. I wonder if any of them will get the chance to manage or coach a top club? Or have they got disillusionment to come like so many others who were in that 1966 squad?"

GREAVSIE: "I've never wanted to get involved in the game as a manager. There are too many pressures for my liking. You are answerable to too many people, most of whom don't know what day it is. You have to satisfy not only your players and interfering directors but also the fans and the media. If you're lucky, you might find a few minutes each day for your family. That's not for me. It would be enough to drive me to drink."

GORDON: "Then how do you see the future, Jim? I love being involved in football and want to try to give back all the things that I have learned about the game. How can you live without it?"

GREAVSIE: "Things are opening up for me in the media. I have a column in The Sun and I am starting to get a lot of work in front of the television cameras. That's the way I want to go … telling footballers and managers what they are doing wrong without any of the responsibility of having to put it right!"

As I watched Jimmy walk jauntily away through the crowded hotel foyer, weaving easily past people as if they were not there, the years melted away and I could see a little white-shirted imp conjuring his way through defences for goals that had even the opposition applauding in appreciation. Jimmy Greaves. They don't make them like him anymore.

It's astonishing to realise that this interview comes from 1980, and so many of the opinions Gordon and Greavsie held then hold up today. The thought of Jimmy with a bubble perm is about as funny as it gets.

Now we turn to the off-beat Greavsie view of Pelé from his *Heroes and Entertainers* book. You will never have read an assessment of The Master quite like it ...

'LET me tell you about the twenty minutes I once spent in the company of one Edson Arantes do Nascimento, better known to you perhaps as Pelé. Well, I say 'spent in his company'. In truth, I spent the twenty minutes chasing his arse.

It was during a four-team tournament in Rio de Janeiro to celebrate the 50th anniversary of the Brazilian FA back in 1964. The other teams taking part were Argentina and Portugal. We, England that is, got the short straw and were drawn to play reigning world champions Brazil in the opening match in front of 150,000 screaming fans at the magnificent Maracana Stadium.

Our manager Alf Ramsey came up with this cunning plan designed to paralyse Pelé, in what was his peak period as the greatest player on the planet. 'We will stop the ball getting to him,' he said simply in the pre-match tactics talk.

Then – turning to his 'hard-tackling' inside-forwards – he added: 'Jim (little old me) and George ('Matchstick Man' Eastham), I want you to drop back whenever necessary, and help Gordon (Milne) and Bobby (Moore) to cut out the passes meant for him.'

'Anything you say, Alf,' I agreed. It seemed a good idea on paper, but would it work on the pitch? Stop the ball getting to Pelé. Even the Master couldn't play without the ball. Nice one, Alf.

The plan worked to perfection for the first 40 minutes, but then just before half-time a frustrated Pelé at last got possession and threaded the ball through to a young newcomer called Rinaldo, who whipped the ball first time past our goalkeeper Tony Waiters. *Brazil 1, England 0.*

Despite this late set-back, we felt satisfied with our first-half performance and Alf demanded more of the same in the second-half. 'You're every bit as good as they are,' he said, with that steely eyed confidence we were to get to know so well on the way to the 1966 World Cup finals. 'Just keep working, and remember – *don't let Pelé have the ball.*'

This was the equivalent of saying 'don't let Louis Armstrong sing' ... 'don't let Neil Armstrong walk on the moon' ... 'don't let Lance Armstrong ride his bike.' But it *was* a good plan.

It got even better early in the second-half when I pounced on a loose ball in the Brazilian penalty area and stuffed it into the back of their net. Suddenly in the Maracana you could have heard a pin or a pun drop, and it was England who were laughing.

Alf on the touchline bench grinned like the cat that had got the cream, and waved his fists to call for more of the same.

The game was now more than an hour old. *Brazil 1, England 1*. Budgie Byrne and I put shots inches wide, and goalkeeper Gilmar had to become an acrobat to tip a

Pelé with the Jules Rimet trophy he helped Brazil win outright with victories in 1958, 1962 and 1970.

George Eastham shot on to the bar. Pelé was nowhere to be seen. Alf's cunning plan was working like a dream ... and it was England who were dreaming of a victory.

Then, like a black panther coming out of a sleep, Pelé roared into the game as if he had been deliberately sitting it out while he weighed up what we had in our ammunition box.

First, with me chasing his arse and failing to stop the ball reaching him, he went this way, that way and then – after making a pretence at shooting – passed the ball again to Rinaldo, whose whiplash left foot shot gave our goalie Tony Waiters no chance. *Brazil 2, England 1*.

'Who the f*** is this Rinaldo?' George Cohen gasped, doing his best to mark and contain a player none of us had ever heard of.

Moments later I had a shot scrambled off the Brazilian goal-line. The ball was cleared to Pelé, who set off on a magical carpet ride through the England defence. He ran fully 40 yards with the ball at his feet, going past tackles as nonchalantly as if he was knocking aside daisies. He looked up and picked his spot before beating Tony Waiters all ends up with a fiercely hit right foot shot. Poor old Tony, a Blackpool beach lifeguard in his spare time, was in danger of drowning. *Brazil 3, England 1.*

We had forgotten Plan A. *Don't let Pelé have the ball.*

Now the Maracana was a madhouse. Ever heard 150,000 Brazilians screeching their heads off? It's like standing on the runway at Heathrow. Bobby Moore, who was in danger of getting a sunburned tongue from chasing Pelé, shouted something to me, but all I could see was his lips moving. He later revealed he was saying, 'Come back and help us mark f***** Pelé.'

Within two minutes of this third goal, Tony Waiters was picking the ball out of his net again. Pelé, of course, was the instigator. George Cohen was protesting to the referee about two Brazilian players being in offside positions when Pelé pushed a pass into the path of Julinho. The flag should have gone up as he slotted the ball wide of Waiters. But perhaps the linesman didn't fancy upsetting the frenzied fans baying behind him. In his shoes I wouldn't have been brave enough to raise the offside flag. *Brazil 4, England 1.*

In fifteen minutes of sheer brilliance, Pelé had turned the game on its head. And he still hadn't finished. I was again chasing that arse of his (what muscular buttocks, almost animal-like) when Bobby Moore ran across his path and conceded a free-kick a yard outside the box. Pelé dummied as if to take the free-kick, and then Dias ran in alongside him and chipped the ball wide of a despairing dive by Waiters, who would much preferred at that moment to be diving off Blackpool beach. *Brazil 5, England 1.*

We just could not believe what had happened to us as the referee blew the final whistle. No, that's silly. We *did* know what had happened to us. Pelé had happened to us. We had let him have the bloody ball.

I can honestly say that the football he produced in those final twenty minutes was the greatest I had ever witnessed in my life from an individual. I knew I had seen something special that, one day, I could tell my grandchildren about. That day is now, and the memory of it still sings in my head. While it hurt at the time, the pain has long gone and the beauty of it is what remains. I know that on that afternoon in the Maracana Stadium in Brazil I had been in the presence of sheer genius.

For that twenty minutes of magic alone I would have Pelé top of my all-time list of great footballers. But he did manage a thing or two besides, like scoring 1,216 goals in 1,254 matches from his debut at the age of fifteen until his first retirement on October 2 1974, 21 days short of his 34th birthday.

His peak year for goals was 1958 when he scored the little matter of 139 times, including two classic goals in the World Cup final when we first became aware of the developing legend that was Pelé. He went on to collect 12 goals in four World Cup final tournaments, and he remains the only player to have been a member of three World Cup winning teams (1958/62/70), although he missed the final stages of the 1962 tournament because of a pulled muscle. European clubs queued to try to buy him but the Brazilian government, fearing street riots, declared him a National Treasure so that he could not be taken abroad.

Born on the poverty line in Tres Coracoes in the same year as me, 1940, he came under the influence of former Brazilian World Cup player Waldemar de Brito while playing for his local team Noroeste. De Brito, realising he had unearthed a diamond, whisked him off to Santos in Sao Paulo, where he made a scoring first-team debut at the age of fifteen. A year later, at sixteeen, he was in the Brazilian international team, and the following year became at seventeen the then youngest ever World Cup debutant. The rest, as they say, is history.

Pelé was no angel, by the way, despite his carefully cultivated public persona. There was quite a bit of devil in him. Let me tell a story to illustrate just how competitive he could be:

After the match in which he took us apart in Rio, we flew up to Såo Paulo to watch the second match of the 'mini-World Cup' between Brazil and Argentina, and I can say hand-on-heart that I have never witnessed scenes like it. Because there were no seats left in the stand, the entire England party – including players, journalists and officials – were assigned to touchline benches that were just two yards from the pitch and eight or so yards from the fenced-in capacity crowd. It was far too close for comfort.

As soon as we sat down the spectators spotted us and set up a deafening chant of *'Cinco-Uma!'* – Portuguese for five-one – and a derisive reminder of our defeat in Rio (when we foolishly let Pelé have the ball). Born joker Budgie Byrne could not resist the bait and stood up on the bench and started conducting the fans like the man in the white suit before the old Wembley Cup finals. The Brazilians loved it and started

A kiss from The King as Pelé responds to the affection coming his way from Stoke City fans.

chanting in time to Budgie's waving arms.

Budgie's choir switched their attention to cheering the Brazilian team when they came out on the pitch, and they lit up the night sky by firing three-stage firework rockets high above the stadium. Then we had fireworks of a different kind on the pitch.

Right from the first whistle Argentinian hatchet-man defender Messiano made it clear that his one intention was to stop Pelé from playing. He was not only going to stop him having the ball, but was also determined to give him a good kicking. It was a duel that underlined the naked hatred between Brazil and Argentina.

Messiano kicked Pelé at every opportunity, tripped him, spat at him, wrestled him to the floor and pulled his shirt anytime he seemed likely to get past him. Finally, after about thirty minutes of this almost criminal assault, the devil came out of Pelé as he completely lost his temper. Right in front of us on the touchline bench, he took a running jump at Messiano and butted him full in the face. It made Zinedine Zidane's head-butt in the 2006 World Cup final seem like a harmless kiss.

The Argentinian was carried off with his broken nose splattered across his face, and – incredibly – the Swiss referee allowed Pelé to play on. He knew that if he had ordered him off there would have been crowd riots.

The calculated, cynical fouling by the Argentinians had knocked all the rhythm and style out of the Brazlians, and the stadium became as quiet as a morgue when two minutes from the end the player substituting for the flattened Messiano scored his second goal of the match to make it 3-0 to Argentina.

Budgie Byrne unwisely chose this moment to do an insane thing. He stood on the bench again to face the fans and, holding up three fingers, invited them to join in a chant of 'Three-Zero ...' It was the worst joke of Budgie's life. Suddenly bricks and fireworks rained down from the terraces as the fans turned their disappointment on us. They would have much preferred to reach the detested Argentinians but we were nearer targets.

The usually impassive Alf Ramsey took one look at the avalanche of rubble, rubbish and rockets coming our way and gave his shortest ever tactical talk. 'Run for it lads ...'

Luckily the final whistle had blown and we made a mad dash for the safety of the centre-circle. Villain Budgie Byrne then turned hero as his quick wits finally got us off the pitch in one piece. As the fans began to scream blue murder despite the intimidating presence of armed police, Budgie shouted the wise instruction: 'Grab yourself a Brazilian player.'

He then seized goalkeeper Gilmar lovingly by the arm and walked him off the pitch, knowing full well that no fans would try to harm one of their idols. We all followed Budgie's lead and went off arm-in-arm with bewildered Brazilian players.

You may think we were over-reacting, but uppermost in the minds of everybody in the stadium was the fact that just ten days earlier 301 people had been killed in a riot at the national stadium in Peru where Argentina had been the opponents.

I think the way Argentina had played against Brazil that night – brutally and with deliberate violence aforethought – stayed imprinted on Alf Ramsey's mind and was one of the reasons he made his infamous 'animals' outburst against them after the 1966 World Cup quarter-final.

Pelé, of course, got mercilessly kicked out of the 1966 World Cup, but got his old appetite back in time to steer the greatest of all the Brazilian teams to the 1970 World Cup triumph. He played on for four more years before announcing that his fantastic career was over.

In 1975 former *Daily Express* football writer Clive Toye, then general manager of New York Cosmos, persuaded Pelé to make a comeback in the North American Soccer League. He made a final final farewell appearance against his old club Santos in New Jersey before a sell-out 60,000 crowd on October 1 1977. It was Pelé's one thousand, three hundred and sixty-third match and he naturally marked it with a goal to bring his career total to 1,281.

But I prefer to think in terms of flesh and blood rather than facts and figures, and what I can say with complete authority and without a glance at the record books is that Pelé was the greatest footballer ever to grace a football pitch.

I know, because I once chased his arse.**'**

THE argument as to who's the greatest footballer is a favourite subject in bars and clubs throughout the world. My co-author Norman Giller cashed in on the fascination by creating a series for ITV in the 1980s called, yes you've guessed it, *Who's the Greatest!*

The pilot programme featured George Best against Kevin Keegan for the title of the greatest British forward. Michael Parkinson represented Best, and Liverpool comedian Tom O'Connor spoke up for Keegan. They put their case to a 12-man jury, and each was allowed to call two expert witnesses. Parky summoned Pat Jennings and Ian St John, while Tom called Mike Channon and Trevor Brooking.

Judge Brian Moore then asked the jury to consider their verdict, and shocked the nation by voting Keegan the greater player by eleven votes to one! Parky said: "If that's British justice, please God never let me have to face a jury in a real court!"

It was later revealed that the jury had been put together by a man who used to run a Kevin Keegan fan club. I remember watching the programme and agreed with the Jimmy Greaves opinion. He said that Keegan, great player that he may have been, was "not fit to lace either George Best's boots or his drinks!"

A second series of *Who's the Greatest* was lined up in which Pelé was matched against Maradona, but it was shelved following the sad passing of Brian Moore on the night that England beat Germany 5-1 in Munich.

Pelé v. Maradona remains the hottest debate in world football, and even a Fifa-organised vote for the Footballer of the Century in the early part of the New Millennium could not end the argument. In fact it stoked up the red-hot coals of controversy.

Maradona walked out of a Fifa awards ceremony in Rome before Pelé got up on stage to receive recognition as one of the two greatest players of the 20th century. In what appeared to be a clear snub, Maradona left the gala event early after collecting his own prize as the best player of the century as voted by fans on Fifa's official web site.

When Pelé took the stage to accept a parallel prize based on votes by Fifa officials, journalists and coaches, he was faced with Maradona's empty front row seat. With his usual great dignity, Pelé would not get drawn into criticising Maradona for his appalling manners, and made do with saying he was disappointed his rival was not there. He had planned to call him up on stage to share the applause and the spotlight with him.

It was, so many thought, a dispute of Fifa's own making. They should never have thrown the debate open to a web-only vote because most of the generation who grew up watching the genius of Pele are not tuned into the internet. Pele topped a poll of

FIFA's "Football Family." He captured 72.75% of the votes to 9.75% for Argentine Alfredo Di Stefano, with Maradona back in third place with just 6%.

Maradona took the web-based vote with 53.60%, to only 18.53% for Pele. Okay, I am biased because I am a Pelé disciple, but this vote was clearly nonsensical.

The volatile Argentine, who flew in from Buenos Aires for the ceremony, dedicated his victory to his compatriots, his wife, Cuban leader Fidel Castro and "all the footballers of the world whom I respect with all my soul." Asked who he would have chosen as the century's greatest player, Maradona said he would have selected Alfredo Di Stefano, the Argentinian-born general of the great Real Madrid side of the 1950s and 1960s.

Maradona added, almost reluctantly: "But I would also concede there is a case to be made for such players as Platini, Pelé, Cruyff and Rivaldo."

Pelé was then called up to receive his award, and that was the signal for Maradona to make his exit. It cast a cloud over what should have been a memorable occasion, with both Pelé and Maradona getting the acclaim they deserved.

The stand-off between the two footballing giants came after weeks of animosity over the terms of the Fifa awards, which triggered fierce debate between Argentines and Brazilians during the build-up to the ceremony. In the UK it may have seemed a storm in a tea cup (or a World Cup!), but you have to take into account that football is a religion in Brazil and Argentina, and there was huge national pride at stake.

World soccer's governing body initially planned to name just one Player of the Century and it was quickly clear that Maradona was racing away with the on-line vote.

That outraged Brazilians – arguing that the terms of the web-based vote were unfairly weighed against their hero. They claimed the Argentine Football Federation had led a concerted campaign to swing the vote Maradona's way.

Fifa, anxious to defuse the controversy, then announced on their web site the award would be for a "player of the decade." They then moved the goalposts again and said the change was simply due to a typing error." It should have read decades rather than decade," a Fifa spokesman said, implying the terms of the vote never changed.

For the record, Pele played in four World Cups including two finals, both of which he won. Maradona also played in four including one losing final and the one of 1986, when his Hand of God goal followed by the 'Goal of the Century' sank England in the quarter-finals.

To add to the uniqueness of this book, we are giving you the chance to judge for yourself *Who's the Greatest*. First, we give a biog-by-biog breakdown of the Top 20 forwards as they finished in a wide cross-secion of Footballer of the 20th Century polls (and don't blame us if your favourites are missing ... for instance, we are choked that there's no Greavsie). We present them alphabetically in file form, and leave it to you to place them in 1-2-3 order (you will find the official finishing list tucked away on page 172.). See if you agree with it.

DENNIS BERGKAMP

Born: 10 May 1969
Place of birth: Amsterdam, Holland
Full name: Dennis Nicolaas Maria Bergkamp
Clubs: Ajax (1986-93) 228 gmes, 116 goals
Inter-Milan (1993-95) 68 games, 21 goals
Arsenal (1995-2006) 393 games, 106 goals
Scored 243 goals in 669 league games
International record: 79 matches for Holland, 37 goals

DENNIS BERGKAMP was born to play football. His father idolized Denis Law and named his son after his hero (forgetting to subtract an 'n'!). Bergkamp played mostly as a support striker, where his tactical awareness and deft passes made him a great exponent of the game from the 'hole'. Many, particularly Arsenal fans, consider him one of the greatest ever Premier League footballers, and in 2007 he became the first Dutch player to be inducted into the English Football Hall of Fame. Dennis would have played many more matches, but for his refusal to fly anywhere following a bad flight experience early in his career. He was a maker as well as a taker of goals, most of which were of the spectacular variety.

EXPERT WITNESS QUOTE:

Don Howe: •Dennis had superb vision, and excellent technique. He could bring a ball under control in the blinking of an eye and then quickly use it to the best advantage of the team. There has rarely been a better support striker, and he had the mark of a great player in that he always seemed to have more time to do things. He never looked rushed.•

GEORGE BEST

Born: 22 May 1946 Died 25 November 2005
Place of birth: Belfast, Northern Ireland
Clubs: Manchester United (1963-71) 361 League games, 138 goals
Later clubs: Dunstable Town, Stockport County, Cork Celtic, Los Angeles Aztecs, Fulham, Fort Lauderdale Strikers, Hibernian, San Jose Earthquakes, Bournemouth, Brisbane Lions, Tobermore United
Total goals in League games: 240 in 526 games
International record: 37 games for Northern Ireland, 9 goals

GEORGE BEST never got to play on the World Cup stage, but his skill, speed, sensational dribbling (and, it has to be said, his life style) guaranteed him world fame. In the year he helped Man United win the European Cup he was also voted European Footballer of the Year. He was a beautifully balanced winger whose game combined acceleration, equal control with either foot, the ability to out-pace and out-think defenders, and a striker's instinct. After a long ban, he once scored six FA Cup goals against Northampton in his comeback match. He missed more games than he played for Northern Ireland. In his native Belfast they have a saying: 'Maradona good, Pelé better, George Best.' If only he could have passed a pub like he passed the football!

EXPERT WITNESS QUOTE:

Pat Crerand: ʻGenius is an over-used word in football, but it perfectly suited George. He had fantastic ball control, was lightning fast with the ball at his feet, and was as brave as a lion. He can definitely be mentioned in the same breath as Pelé and Maradona. Best by name, Best by ability.ʼ

BOBBY CHARLTON

Born:11 October 1937
Place of birth: Ashington, North Humberland
Clubs: Manchester United (1954-73)
606 League games, 199 goals
Preston (1973-74) 38 League games, 8 goals
Waterford United (1975) 31 games, 18 goals
International record: 106 games for England, 49 goals
Holds the goal scoring record for both Man United and England.

BOBBY CHARLTON, knighted for his services to football, was voted European Footballer of the Year in 1966, the same year his passes and goals helped lift England to the World Cup triumph at Wembley. He started out as a powerful winger, then became a thunder-shooting inside-forward before developing into a deep-lying centre-forward who pulled the strings of the United and England attacks. He was always a gentleman of the game and went through his entire career without having his name taken. He held the Man United appearances record at 758 games, until Ryan Giggs overtook it in 2008. A survivor of the Munich air crash, he captained the 1968 Man United European Cup-winning team, and he remains England's top marksman.

EXPERT WITNESS QUOTE:

Franz Beckenbauer: *Bobby Charlton was and remains a great ambassador for our game. He was a beautifully skilled player, and a sportsman of the highest calibre. I always felt privileged to be on the same pitch as Bobby. He is respected throughout the world of football.*

JOHAN CRUYFF

Born: 25 April 1947   Dutch name: Hendrik Johannes Cruijff
Place of birth: Amsterdam, Holland
Clubs: Ajax (1964-73) 240 games, 190 goals
Barcelona (1973-78) 143 games, 48 goals
Other clubs: LA Aztecs (1979-80), Washington Diplomats (1980-81), Lavante (1981), Ajax again (1981-83), Feyenoord (1983-84)
Total league games 521, 293 goals
International record: 48 games for Holland, 33 goals

JOHAN CRUYFF was the chief exponent of the Total football style of football with which Holland revolutionsed the game, and he was the total footballer. He could do everything and anything, creating goals, scoring them and directing play from all corners of the pitch. He was named European Footballer of the Year three times (1971, 1973, 1974), a record jointly held with Michel Platini and Marco van Basten. After his retirement in 1984, Cruyff became a successful coach/ manager at Ajax and later Barcelona. His inventive style of football motivated a generation of young footballers, all of them trying to copy the famous 'Cruyff Turn' in which he confused defenders by turning 180 degrees while dragging the ball with him.

EXPERT WITNESS QUOTE:

Bobby Robson: 'There is one word that sums up Johan Cruyff, the player – majestic. He was years ahead of his time, and played exquisite football that made even the opposition purr. I followed him as coach at Barcelona, and I had to live in his long shadow. He is without doubt a footballing legend.'

FOOTBALLER OF THE CENTURY FILE

KENNY DALGLISH

Born:4 March 1951   Full name: Kenneth Mathieson Dalglish
Place of birth: Dalmarnock, Glasgow, Scotland
Clubs: Celtic (1969-77)
Scored 112 goals in 204 Scottish League games
Liverpool (1977-90)
Scored 118 'old' First Division goals in 355 games
Won nine major trophies with Celtic, and 20 with Liverpool
International record: 102 games for Scotland, 30 goals

KENNY DALGLISH was a prolific goalscorer throughout his career, first with Celtic and then Liverpool. He was the first to score 100 goals in both the English and Scottish leagues, and was voted the Player Who Shook The Kop. He was continually a thought and a deed ahead of defenders in the penalty area, and had deadly accurate finishing powers. Dalglish also enjoyed success as a club manager, and is one of only three people to have won the English League (Old Division one pre-1993, and the current FA Premier League) as a manager with two different clubs – Liverpool and Blackburn. He was FWA Footballer of the Year twice (1979 and 1983), and PFA Players' Player of the Year in 1983. Dalglish was the first Scot to win 100 caps.

EXPERT WITNESS QUOTE:

Ian Rush: 'Kenny was a joy to play with. He always put the team first, and helped me to a lot of my goals by his positioning and passing. He was never ever greedy, yet scored many goals himself simply by being in the right place at the right time. He was the thinking man's striker .'

FOOTBALLER OF THE CENTURY FILE

ALFREDO Di STEFANO

Born: 4 July 1926   Full name: Alfredo S. di Stefano Laulhé
Place of birth: Buenos Aires, Argentina
Major club: Real Madrid (1953-64) 212 goals in 286 Spanish League games
Other clubs: River Plate (1943-49), Huracan, loan (1946-47), Millonarios (1949-53), Espanyol (1964-66)
Total goals: 377 in 521 games
International record: 6 goals in 6 games for Argentina (1947), four games for Colombia (1949), 23 goals in 31 games for Spain (1957-61)

ALFREDO DI STEFANO will always be associated with the magnificent Real Madrid of the late 1950s and early 1960s that won the European Cup for its first five years. He was the general of the side, and linking in a prolific partnership with Ferenc Puskas. Nicknamed in his early days Saeta Rubia ("Blond Arrow"), he was almost arrogant on the ball, showing a marathon runner's stamina, tactical versatility, and – above all – great vision. He could play anywhere on the pitch, and some give him credit for being the first total footballer ahead of Cruyff. Born to a family of Italian immigrants, 'have-boots-will-travel' Di Stefano had a maternal Irish grandmother and played international football for Argentina, Colombia and Spain.

EXPERT WITNESS QUOTE:

George Graham: *I was at Hampden the night Di Stefano orchestrated that great Real Madrid victory over Eintracht. He was everything I'd heard about him – stylish, deceptively fast and gliding over the turf, and directing all the movements. He was The Maestro.*

EUSÉBIO

Born:25 January 1942. Full name: Eusébio da Silva Ferreira
Place of birth: Lourenço Marques, Mozambique
Major club: Benfica (1960-75) 317 goals in 301 Portuguese League games
Other clubs: Sporting Lourenço Marques (1957-60), Rhode Island Oceaneers (1975), Boston Minutemen (1975), Monterrey (1975-76), Beira-Mar (1976-77), Toronto Metros-Croatia (1976), Las Vegas Quicksilver (1976), New Jersey Americans (1977-78).
Total goals: 343 in 372 league games
International record: 41 goals in 64 matches for Portugal (1961-1973)

EUSEBIO was the first great player to come out of Africa, and he was the talk of the game when he established himself as top marksman in the 1966 World Cup finals with nine goals (four of which were scored against North Korea in the quarter-final at Goodison after Portugal had gone 3-0 behind). He was elected European Footballer of the Year in 1965. Eusebio was one of the few players in the history of the game to average more than a goal a game. Including cup matches, he totalled 727 goals in 715 matches. in 1968 he was the first winner of the Golden Boot Award as Europe's leading scorer, a feat he repeated five years later. His goals helped Benfica end Real Madrid's domination of the European Cup in 1962.

EXPERT WITNESS QUOTE:

Bobby Charlton: *Eusebio was a dangerous player at all times because of his explosive right foot shot. He was extremely powerful on the ball. We were very lucky that we had one of the greatest of all markers in Nobby Stiles to keep a tight rein on him in the 1966 World Cup and the 1968 European Cup final. *

TOM FINNEY

Born: 5 April 1922
Place of birth: Preston, Lancashire
Club: Preston North End (1946-60)
He played one European Cup tie for Lisburn Distillery in 1963
Total goals: 187 in 433 Football League games
International record: 30 goals in 76 matches for England (1946-58)
Footballer of the Year 1954 and 1957
Knighted 1998

TOM FINNEY was capped in four different forward positions for England, and was devastating no matter what the number of his shirt. Amazingly, throughout his career he was a part-time professional. He concentrated on building up his plumbing business, hence his nickname the Preston Plumber. Tom was a one-club loyalist, winning just a Second Division championship medal and an FA Cup runners-up medal with them (1954). Throughout his career he was at the centre of a Matthews v. Finney controversy. Stanley was the public favourite, but most pros considered Finney the more potent player. When the selectors, after much dithering, played them together in the same attack in 1947 they beat Portugal 10-0 in Lisbon!

EXPERT WITNESS QUOTE:

Tommy Docherty: 'I had the honour of playing behind Tom at Preston and can confirm that he was the greatest thing on two feet. He was two footed, quick enough to catch pigeons, brave and honest, and able to play in any attacking position. If there has been a better all-round forward then I've not seen him.'

GARRINCHA

Born:28 October 1933. Full name: Manoel Francisco dos Santos
Place of birth: Pau Grande, Rio de Janeiro, Brazil
Died 19 January 1983, Rio de Janeiro
Major club: Botafogo (1953-65)
Scored 232 goals in 581 League games for Botafogo
Other clubs: Corinthians (1966), Portuguesa Santista (1967), Atletico Junior (1968), Flamengo (1968-69), Olaria (1972)
International record: 12 goals in 50 matches for Brazil (1955-66)

GARRINCHA ('Little Bird') was a freak of nature. Born with one leg shorter than the other and with two left feet, he became one of the most gifted footballers ever to play the game. A free spirit on and off the pitch, the Brazilian coaches had nightmares trying to get him to confirm to team tactics. It took a petition from senior players to get him selected for his World Cup debut at the same time as Pelé in 1958. Four years later he was the player of the tournament when Brazil retained the Jules Rimet trophy. He was only ever once on the losing side in 50 international matches, and that was in his final appearance in the 1966 World Cup finals after Pelé had been kicked out. He and Pelé were never on a losing side in 39 matches.

EXPERT WITNESS QUOTE:

Jimmy Greaves: 'I was in the England team Garrincha destroyed in the 1962 World Cup quarter-final. He was a footballing genius. He scored with a thumping header and then a swerving shot from 20 yards that spun like a Shane Warne leg-break. He was like Stanley Matthews on speed. '

DIEGO MARADONA

Born: 30 October 1960 Full name: Diego Armando Maradona
Place of birth: Buenos Aires, Argentina
Clubs: Argentinos Juniors (1976-81), Boca Juniors (1981-82 and 1995-97),
Barcelona (1982-84), Napoli (1984-91), Sevilla (1992-93), Newell's (1993)
Total league goals: 311 in 590 matches
Scored 116 goals in 166 league games for Argentinos Juniors
Scored 115 goals in 259 Serie A matches for Napoli
International record: 34 goals in 91 matches for Argentina (1977-94)

MARADONA played in four World Cups, leading Argentina to the 1986 triumph and also collecting the Golden Ball award as the tournament's best player. He scored both goals in the 2-1 victory over England in the quarter-final. The first goal was fisted into the net (He called it the "Hand of God goal"), while the second goal followed a spectacular 60-yard dance past six England players, later voted "The Goal of the Century." Running parallel with his stunning football performances was a reckless off-the-pitch lifestyle that made him notorious for drug offences. Rebel-without-a-pause Maradona was suspended in 1991 after a failed doping test for cocaine in Italy, and then again for ephedrine during the 1994 World Cup. He is a living legend.

EXPERT WITNESS QUOTE:

Peter Shilton: ⁶I could not forgive him for his handled goal, but his second goal proved that he was the finest controller of the ball in the game. When going at full pace and with the ball at his feet, there have been few players in history to equal his skill. In one-on-one situations he was just unstoppable.⁹

STANLEY MATTHEWS

Born: 1 February 1915
Place of birth: Hanley, Staffordshire
Died 23 February 2000, Stoke on Trent
Clubs: Stoke City (1932-47) 262 League games, 51 goals
Blackpool (1957-61) 380 League games, 17 goals
Stoke City (1961-65) 59 League games, 3 goals
Total League games 701, 71 goals
International record: 11 goals in 54 matches for England (1934-57), plus three goals in eight wartime internationals (1939-45)

STANLEY MATTHEWS remains one of the most famous footballers ever. The 'Wizard of Dribble' was the first footballer knighted and the first given the honour while still playing. He was a pioneer in the honours world, the first European Footballer of the Year and the first FWA Footballer of the Year. Matthews, the son of a boxer (Jack Matthews, the Fighting Barber of Hanley) was possibly the finest dribbler ever. A teetotaller and vegetarian, he kept fit enough to play at the top level until he was 50, the oldest player to perform in the top division. He teased and tantalised a procession of full backs with his right wing runs, and memorably got his only major club medal when combining with three-goal Stan Mortensen to win the 1953 FA Cup final.

EXPERT WITNESS QUOTE:

Jimmy Armfield: 'I played with Stanley at Blackpool and was in awe of his astonishing skill. Even in his 40s he could produce acceleration and uncanny dribbling skill to make fools of the best full-backs. He will be remembered for as long as the game is played. That's what you call fame.'

GERD MÜLLER

Born: 3 November 1945 Full name: Gerhard Müller
Place of birth: Nördlingen, Germany
Clubs: TSV 1861 Nördlingen (1963-64) 51 goals in 32 League matches
Bayern Munich (1964-79) 398 goals, 453 matches
Fort Lauderdale Strikers (1979-81)
Total league goals: 489 goals in 565 matches
International record: 68 goals in 62 matches for West Germany (1966-74)
His 14 goals in World Cup finals matches was a record overtaken by Ronaldo

GERD MÜLLER justified his "Der Bomber' nickname by blitzing defences with more explosive results than any other striker in World Cup history. Including qualifying matches, he scored 19 goals in the 1970 series, with ten in the finals. His contribution to West Germany's triumph in 1974 was four goals, and he had a record finals aggregate of 14. He was just as prolific in club football with Bayern Munich, and he gathered 68 goals in 74 European cup games. In international football he averaged more than a goal a game, and while favouring his right foot was nearly as powerful and accurate with his left. He had a low centre of gravity, and used his powerful thighs to produce gymnastic spring in the penalty area for many headed goals.

EXPERT WITNESS QUOTE:

Martin Peters: ʻHe made the hardest job of all – scoring goals – seem easy. Muller looked as wide as he was tall, and defenders used to bounce off him while trying to get the ball. He had excellent close control, and for such a stocky man was surprisingly strong in the air. His shots on the turn were dynamic.ʼ

PELÉ

Born:23 October 1940
Full name: Edson Arantes do Nascimento
Place of birth: Tres Coracoes, Brazil
Clubs: Santos (1956-74) 412 League games, 470 goals
New York Cosmos (1975-77) 64 games, 37 goals
Total goals in all competitions: 1281 goals in 1363 matches
International record: 77 goals in 92 matches for Brazil (1957-71)
Only player to collect three World Cup winners' medals (1958-62-70)

PELÉ was simply phenomenal and was in no way flattered by his nickname, The King. His astonishing collection of 1,281 goals is lasting proof that he was (arguably) the greatest footballer on the planet. He would strike for goal like a cobra, from all angles and at the most unexpected moments. We mere mortals would see a wall of defenders between him and the goal. Pelé would see openings that were beyond our vision. It was nothing unusual for him to beat four, five or more defenders on sudden raids that would end with the ball nestling in the back of the net and a procession of opponents on their backsides. Relatively small (5ft 8in), he had the spring of a gymnast, the speed of an Olympic sprinter and power in both feet.

EXPERT WITNESS QUOTE:

Alan Mullery: 'I considered it an honour to play against him, and I managed to keep him relatively quiet. He was the player who had it all, speed, skill, the ability to shoot with either foot, amazing ball control and heading power. He used to deliberately play the ball off defenders' shins. The man was magical. '

MICHEL PLATINI

Born: 21 June 1955
Place of birth: Joeuf, France
Clubs: Nancy (1972-79) 181 league games, 98 goals
Saint-Étienne (1979-82) 58 goals in 104 games
Juventus (1982-87) 68 goals in 147 games
Total league goals: 224 goals in 432 games
International record: 41 goals in 72 matches for France (1976-87)
Currently President of UEFA

MICHEL PLATINI was the stylish director-general of the French team that won the 1984 European Championship, a tournament in which he was top marksman and voted the best player. A goal-scoring pass master, he finished top scorer in Serie A for three consecutive seasons (1982-85), and won a hat-trick of European Footballer of the Year awards (1983-85). Along with Alain Giresse, Luis Fernández and Jean Tigana, Platini made up the "carré magique" ("magic square"), the quartet of top-quality midfield players forming the heart of the French team throughout the 1980s. A deadly free-kick specialist, he showed the authority on the field that was later to serve him well when he became the all-powerful President of UEFA.

EXPERT WITNESS QUOTE:

Glenn Hoddle: 'He had great peripheral vision, and could pass the ball through the eye of a needle. While essentially a playmaker, Platini was never frightened of taking on the responsibility of going for goal, and many of his goals were scored from outside the penalty area with stunning accuracy.'

FERENC PUSKAS

Born: 2 April 1927
Hungarian name: Ferenc Purczeld Biró
Place of birth: Budapest, Hungary
Died 17 November 2006
Clubs: Kispest 1943-49)177 League games, 187 goals
Honved (1949-55) 164 games, 165 goals
Real Madrid (1958-66) 182 games, 157 goals
International record: 84 goals in 85 matches for Hungary (1945-56)
Four matches, no goals for Spain (1961-62)

PUSKAS had a left foot with which he could unlock a safe door, and sufficient power to dynamite it open. Known as the Galloping Major (his rank with Army team Honved), he dictated play for the magnificent Hungarian team of the 1950s that went 29 games without defeat, including 6-3 and 7-1 victories over England. Following the Hungarian uprising and the Russian invasion of 1956, Puskas joined Real Madrid and struck up a stunning partnership with Alfredo di Stefano. He was top Spanish league goalscorer four times in five years. Puskas collected a gold medal in the 1952 Olympics with the 'Magical Magyar' team that had its unbeaten run ended by Germany in the 1954 World Cup final, when Puskas was carrying an injury.

EXPERT WITNESS QUOTE:

Malcolm Allison: 'I was in the crowd at Wembley watching the Hungarians, who arrived as if from another planet. Their football was light years ahead of anything we were playing, and Puskas was their chief magician with a left foot that was like a wand. He played poor Billy Wright off the park. '

MARCO VAN BASTEN

Born: 31 October 1964 Full name: Marcel "Marco" Van Basten
Place of birth: Utrecht, Holland
Clubs: Ajax 133 league games, 128 goals
AC Milan (1987-93) 147 Serie A games, 90 goals
Total league goals: 218 goals in 280 games
International record: 24 goals in 58 matches for Holland 1983-92
Has managed the Dutch national team and Ajax
Fifa World Player of the Year 1992

VAN BASTEN was one of the most dynamic finishers of all time. A Van Basten goal was usually a thing of beauty, power and explosiveness. He still had much to give to the game when injury forced a premature retirement at 29. He had tactical awareness and was a spectacular striker of the ball. After switching to AC Milan from Ajax, he was voted European Footballer of the Year three times and was elected FIFA World Player of the Year in 1992. Overcoming an ankle injury that finally forced his retirement, Van Basten was in sensational form in Euro 1988. He scored a hat-trick against England, the winner against West Germany in the semi-final and netted a fantastic volley against the Soviet Union in the final to clinch a 2-0 win.

EXPERT WITNESS QUOTE:

Bryan Robson: *Van Basten was unstoppable in Euro 1988. We – England – were on a par with Holland and fancying our chances until Van Basten produced a hat-trick from three chances. If you want to know just how good a finisher he was, try to watch his cracking volley against the Russians in the final. *

RONALDO

Born: 22 September 1976
Full name: Ronaldo Luis Nazário de Lima
Place of birth: Rio de Janeiro, Brazil
Clubs: Cruzeiro (1993-94), PSV Eindhoven (1994-96), Barcelona (1996-97),
Inter Milan (1997-2002), Real Madrid (2002-07), AC Milan (2007-)
Total league goals to date: 228 goals in 307 games
International record: 74 goals in 112 matches for Brazil (1994-2008)

RONALDO is the only one of our top 20 who is still currently playing. Remember that this is a list made up of 20th Century soccer giants, and Ronaldo was voted Fifa World Footballer of the Year in 1996, 1997 and again in 2002, when he helped Brazil win the World Cup after an off-key show in the 1998 final. His 15 goals in World Cup finals took him past Müller's "unbeatable" record. Ronaldo has all the qualities of the perfect striker: power, speed, courage, good control, instinctive positional sense and the ability to shoot with either foot. He has been nicknamed 'The Phenomenon,' and while there have been some down moments in his career this is more than made up for by his awesome performances in more than 100 internationals for Brazil.

EXPERT WITNESS QUOTE:

David Beckham: *When he was in the right mood, Ronaldo could take apart any defence. I would have hated being a defender trying to man mark him, because he has the pace and the power to go past anybody. I've seen him score goals that other players would consider impossible. *

GEORGE WEAH

Born: 1 October 1966
Place of birth: Monrovia, Liberia
Full name: George Tawlon Oppong Ousman Weah
Major clubs: AS Monaco (1988-1992), Paris Saint-Germain (1992-1995),
AC Milan (1995-2000, Chelsea (2000), Manchester City (2000), Olympique
Marseille (2000-01).
Scored 135 goals in 345 major league games
International record: 60 matches for Liberia, 22 goals

GEORGE WEAH is a god in his native Liberia, where he first started his football career. He had to move to Europe to get world recognition, and spent 14 years playing for clubs in France, Italy and England. He was close to being a spent force by the time he got to the Premier League with Chelsea and Manchester City, but still produced flashes of the magic that in 1995 brought him the unique treble of FIFA World Player of the Year, European Footballer of the Year, and African Footballer of the Year. He was later voted African Player of the Century. Weah has since become an outspoken humanitarian and a prominent politician in Liberia, where he was a beaten candidate in the 2005 Liberian presidential election.

EXPERT WITNESS QUOTE:

Arsene Wenger: 'At his peak, George was up there with Pelé. He had everything, speed, skill, the intuitive ability to read the game and finishing accuracy. I worked closely with him in his formative years in France, and at his best I can tell you that he was simply magnificent.'

ZICO

Born: 3 March 1953
Full nme: Arthur Antunes Coimbra
Place of birth: Rio de Janeiro, Brazil
Major club: Flamengo (1971-83 and 1985-89) 551 games, 333 goals
Other clubs: Udinese (1983-85), Sumitomo Metals (1991-92), Kashima Antlers (1992-94)
Total league goals: 399 goals in 653 games
International record: 68 goals in 88 matches for Brazil (1976-88)

ZICO, often referred to as the White Pelé, was a silkily smooth dribbler and a polished finisher. One of his particular specialities was as a free kick specialist who put tremendous spin and bend on the ball. A gifted attacking midfielder, he played for Brazil in the 1978, 1982 and 1986 World Cups., but without the satisfaction of lifting the trophy. Many consider Zico the best player never to have been a World Cup winner. He is a legend at Flamengo where, in all competitions, he scored a club record 508 goals in 731 games. As a coach, he guided Japan to the 2006 World Cup finals, and the Japanese showed their appreciation by building a statue to him at the Kashima Stadium. Like his idol Pelé, he had a spell as Brazilian Minister for Sport.

EXPERT WITNESS QUOTE:

John Wark: *Zico was a real class act in the 1982 World Cup finals. He had a deceptive change of pace which made it difficult to get a tackle in, and his body swerves were bewildering. He scored a fabulous free-kick against us (Scotland) just when we thought we were getting on top. *

ZINEDINE ZIDANE

Born: 23 June 1972
Place of birth: Marseille, France
Full name: Zinedine Yazid Zidane
Clubs: Cannes (1988-92) 61 league games, 6 goals
Girodins Bordeaux (1992-96) 135 games, 28 goals
Juventus (1996-2001) 151 games, 24 goals
Real Madrid (2001-06) 155 games, 37 goals
Scored 95 goals in 502 league games
International record: 108 matches for France, 31 goals

ZINEDINE ZIDANE, known to his team-mates as Zizou, will always sadly be remembered for his head-butt that got him sent off in the 2006 World Cup final against Italy. He deserves to go down in history as one of the most creative improvisors ever to set foot on a football pitch. Zidane never ever did things the conventional way, and could slice through the deepest defences with close control, shielding the ball and making it look as if it was tied to his boots. He virtually won the World Cup for France single handed in 1998, and he was just as influential in helping them capture the European championship two years later. He shares with Ronaldo the distinction of being voted Fifa World Cup Player of the Year three times (1998, 2000 and 2003).

THE TOP 20 in 1-2-3 order

1. PELÉ
2. MARADONA
3. ALFREDO Di STEFANO
4. JOHAN CRUYFF
5. GEORGE BEST
6. MICHEL PLATINI
7. STANLEY MATTHEWS
8. EUSEBIO
9. FERENC PUSKAS
10. GERD MÜLLER
11. BOBBY CHARLTON
12. ZINEDINE ZIDANE
13. RONALDO
14. GARRINCHA
15. MARCO VAN BASTEN
16. ZICO
17. TOM FINNEY
18. GEORGE WEAH
19. DENNIS BERGKAMP
20. KENNY DALGLISH

EXPERT WITNESS QUOTE:

Thierry Henry: *When Zizou was in the French team it made all our lives much easier. He is a guy you can always count on, the one who will take control. He is a born leader, and a born genius of a footballer. I have seen him make the impossible possible with clever use of the ball and darting, feinting runs.*

So much for the goalscorers, now what about the goal stoppers – the goalkeepers who have the job of protecting the net against all-comers. My friend Gordon Banks assures me that goalkeeping can be the most demanding and soul-destroying role in football. A goalkeeper's errors are there for all to see, because they invariably register on the scoresheet. An outfield player can get away with a mistake or two, but for the poor old goalie there is no hiding place.

The top 'keepers not only have to show rapid reflexes, catching ability and an understanding of positioning and angles but also courage for when they are called on to dive at the feet of oncoming attackers.

One of the great mysteries of the modern game is: "Where have all the British goalkeepers gone?" When I was a kid growing up and first falling in love with the game, our goalkeepers were considered the best in the world. Now a succession of England managers have struggled to find a safe pair of hands at the back of the defence. The Premier League is almost exclusive to foreign goalkeepers.

The likes of Gordon Banks and Peter Shilton were famous for the overtime work they put into their training, and I wonder if today's young goalkeepers have the same sort of dedication and determination to succeed.

Gordon is interesting on the subject:

*When I was a young goalkeeper with Chesterfield and then Leicester City I always used to work overtime on my shot stopping practice, and making sure I was perfecting my angles. And even when I was established as England's goalkeeper I continued to work hard to make sure I was on top of my game. You only get out what you put in, and I wonder if English goalkeepers today are prepared to really sweat for their success.

I remember that when Peter Shilton followed me at Leicester and then in the Stoke and England teams he was always a fitness fanatic, and worked even harder than me to make sure he got everything perfect.

When I first came into the game goalkeepers got little protection from the referees and you used to have to be ready to take a battering. Now, if anything, they are over-protected, and I cannot understand why this does not encourage young players to specialise in goalkeeping ... particulary when you see the huge financial rewards that are on offer.*

Completely off the cuff, I would name the following as the top 20 British goalkeepers in post-war football:

Gordon Banks (England, Leicester City and Stoke City)
Peter Shilton (England, Leicester, Stoke, Nottm Forest, Southampton, Derby)
Pat Jennings (Nothern Ireland, Watford, Tottenham, Arsenal)
Frank Swift (England, Manchester City)
Bert Williams (England, Wolves)
Jack Kelsey (Wales, Arsenal)
Ray Clemence (England, Liverpool, Tottenham)
Neville Southall (Wales, Everton)
Bob Wilson (Scotland, Arsenal)
David Seaman (England, Arsenal)
Peter Bonetti (England, Chelsea)
Alex Stepney (England, Manchester United)
Ronnie Simpson (Scotland, Newcastle United, Celtic)
Ron Springett (England, Sheffield Wednesday, QPR)
Tommy Younger (Scotland, Hibernian, Liverpool)
Harry Gregg (Northern Ireland, Manchester United)
Ted Ditchburn (England, Tottenham)
Gary Sprake (Wales, Leeds United, Birmingham City)
Joe Corrigan (England, Manchester City)
George Farm (Scotland, Blackpool)

They just rolled off the tongue, but it is difficult to bring outstanding modern British goalkeepers to mind. I wonder what YOU think.

A player not included in my list is Bert Trautmann, the famous German prisoner-of-war who stayed in England after his release and became a legend at the back of the Manchester City defence.

I did not have the pleasure of seeing him play, but plenty of old pros have told me he was in the class of another foreigner who became a Manchester hero ... the Great Dane Peter Schmeichel, certainly one of the finest goalkeepers to have played in the Premier League.

Thanks to a cross-section of polls conducted on the internet, I am able to give extra breadth to this all-encompassing book by publishing the following list of the greatest goalkeepers of the twentieth century. My congratulations to Gordon for representing England so prominently. If it had been down to me, I would have had him at number one!

GOALKEEPER OF THE CENTURY FILE

1. LEV YASHIN U.S.S.R.

Born Moscow, 22 October 1929
Died Moscow, 20 March 1990
Club: Moscow Dynamo 1949-71
Honours: 5 Soviet Union League championships, 3 Soviet Union Cups
League games 326. International appearances: 78 (1954-67)
European Footballer of the Year 1963
European Nations Cup 1960. Olympic gold medal 1956

Expert Eyewitness – **Denis Law**: ‘I was Yashin's team-mate when the Rest of the World played England at Wembley in 1963. He was already a legend in the game, and we all discovered why as he pulled off a series of unbelievable saves, particularly from Greavsie. The Man In Black, as he was called, had telescopic arms, and seemed to cover the whole goal like a giant octopus.’

2. GORDON BANKS England

Born Sheffield, 30 December 1937
Major clubs: Leicester City 1959-66, Stoke City 1966-72
Other clubs: Chesterfield, Cleveland Stokers, St Patrick's Athletic, Fort Lauderdale Strikers
League games 562. International appearances: 73 (1963-72)
World Cup winner 1966
FWA Footballer of the Year 1972

Expert Eyewitness – **Jack Charlton**: ‘To have Gordon playing behind us made we England defenders feel confident. He had a poise and compusure about him that spread through the defence. I am convinced England would have gone through to the semi-finals of the World Cup in 1970 if he had not gone down with that illness. He was the one player we could not afford to lose.’

Put your hands together for one of the all-time great goalkeepers, Sepp Maier

3. DINO ZOFF Italy
Born Mariano del Friuli, 28 February 1942
    Major clubs: Napoli 1967-72, Juventus 1972-83
    Other clubs: Udinese, Mantova
    League games 642
    6 Serie A championships, 2 Italian Cups
    UEFA Cup winner 1977
    International appearances: 112 (1968-83)
    Euro 68 winner, World Cup winner 1982
    Voted Best Goalkeeper in the 1982 World Cup

Expert Eyewitness – **Enzo Bearzot**, 1982 Italy coach: ‘He was a level-headed goalkeeper, capable of staying calm during the toughest and the most exhilarating moments. He always held back both out of modesty and respect for his opponents. At the end of the Brazil match, he came over to give me a kiss on the cheek, without saying a single word. For me, that fleeting moment was the most intense of the entire World Cup.’

4. SEPP MAIER West Germany
    Born Metten, Germany, 28 February 1944
    Club: Bayern Munich
    League games 536
    International appearances: 95 (1966-79)
    4 Bundesliga championships, 4 German Cups
    3 European Cups, 1 UEFA Cup
    Euro 72 winner, World Cup winner 1974

Expert Eyewitness – **Franz Beckenbauer**, his Bayern and national team captain: ‘Our supporters called him "Die Katze von Anzing" (the cat from Anzing), and he really was like a big cat in the goal. Those gloves he wore made him look like a giant for any forward attempting to shoot, and he was always very brave and stood his ground. He had excellent reflexes, and managed to make very difficult saves appear to be quite easy. ’

5. RICARDO ZAMORA Spain

Born Barcelona, 21 January 1901
    Died Barcelona 15 September 1978
    Clubs: Barcelona (1919-22), Espanyol (1922-30), Real Madrid (1930-36),
    Olympique Gymnaste Club de Nice (1936-38)
    League games 450+
    International appearances: 46 (1920-36) 13 Catalan (1920-30)
    Olympic silver medallist 1920
    Seven Spanish/Catalan league titles
    Eight domestic cups

Expert Eyewitness – **Jack Greenwell**, Durham-born manager who coached Zamora at Barcelona: •He revolutionised goalkeeping by his positioning, and willingness to accept that he was in charge of the penalty area and often beyond. It was nothing for him to bring the ball out with his feet and launch counter attacks. He was ridiculously brave, and pulled off so many spectacular saves that other players as well as fans called him '*El Divino*.' •

6. JOSÉ LUIS CHILAVERT Paraguay

    Born Luque, Paraguay 27 July 1965
    Major clubs: San Lorenzo de Almagro (1984-88), Real Zaragoza (1988-91),
    Vélez Sársfield (1991-2000), RC Strasbourg (2000-02), Penarol (2003-04)
    League games 539, 29 goals
    International appearances: 74 (1989-2003), 8 goals
    12 Leagues and Cups in Paraguay, Argentina, Uruguay and France
    Voted World Goalkeeper of the Year 1995, 1997, 1998

Expert Eyewitness – **John Motson** •If there was a vote for the world's most entertaining player Chilavert would be a certain contender. He was a free-kick and penalty specialist, and several times scored with free-kicks from his own half! He was the first goalkeeper to score a hat-trick in a major match, all from the penalty spot. Chilavert was temperamental and unpredictable, but when on form was a magnificent goalkeeper.•

7. PETER SCHMEICHEL Denmark

Born Gladsaxe, 18 November 1963
Clubs: Gladsaxe (1981-83), Hvidovre (1984-86), Brondby (1987-91), Man U (1991-99), Sp. Portugal (1999-2001), A. Villa (2001-02), Man City (2002-03)
League games: 645 (10 goals)
International appearances: 129 (1987-2001), 1 goal
4 Danish league titles, 1 Danish Cup, 1 Portuguese league title
5 Premier League titles, 3 FA Cups, 1 Football League Cup
1 European Champions League
Voted World's Best Goalkeeper 1992 and 1993

Expert Eyewitness – **Bob Wilson**: *Schmeichel had the ability to fill his goalmouth with a rare presence, and he was very visible and audible leaving nobody in any doubt as to who was the boss of his territory. He had excellent hands, was as brave as they come and time and again came to Manchester United's rescue with his lightning-reflex saves. His positioning was faultless, and I would say he was just about the perfect goalkeeper.*

8. PETER SHILTON England

Born Leicester, 18 September 1949
Major clubs: Leicester City (1966-74), Stoke City (1974-77), Nottingham Forest (1977-82), Southampton (1982-87), Derby (1987-92), Plymouth (1992-95)
League games: 1005 (1966-97), 1 goal
International appearances: 125 (1970-90)
1 League title, 1 FA Cup runners-up, 1 First Division title
2 European Cups
PFA Player of the Year 1978

Expert Eyewitness –Sir Bobby Robson: *Peter had everything you look for in a goalkeeper – safe hands, composure under pressue, quick reactions, courage and good positional sense. There have been few better England goalkeepers in the history of the game, and he always served his country with pride and dedication. Nottingham Forest won back-to-back European Cups mainly because of his powerful presence at the back of the defence.*

9. GILMAR Brazil
Born Sao Paulo 22 August 1930
Major clubs: Corinthians (1951-61), Santos (1961-69)
League games: 500+ (1951-69)
International appearances: 103 (1958-69)
8 State championships, 5 National titles
2 domestic cups, 2 inter-continental cups
2 World Cups (1958 and 1962)
First goalkeeper to collect two World Cup winners' medals
Elected Best Brazilian Goalkeeper of the 20th Century

Expert Eyewitness – **Pelé**: *I played with Gilmar many many times for Brazil and also with Santos. He was an amazing goalkeeper, who would pounce like a panther and save the ball when you were convinced it was on its way into the net. Gilmar had a calming effect on our defence, and he was particularly outstanding in the 1958 finals when I first played. Being ten years older than me, he went out of his way to make me feel at home in the team.*

10. PAT JENNINGS Northern Ireland
Born Newry, 12 June 1945
Clubs: Watford (1963-64), Tottenham (1964-77), Arsenal (1977-85)
International appearances: 119 (1964-86)
League games: 757, 1 goal
2 FA Cups, 2 Football League Cups
1 UEFA Cup
FWA Footballer of the Year 1973
PFA Players' Player of the Year 1976

Expert Eyewitness – **Terry Neill**: *Big Pat, with his big hands and big heart, was a colossus for club and country. As good as he was with his hands, he had the sense to perfect kicked clearances and he was the best at saving with his feet. Time and again he turned games with a decisive save. He was modesty personified, but had lots to shout about. With those shovel hands of his, he was – day in, day out – the most consistent 'keeper I ever saw.*

Pat Jennings uses his feet to halt countryman George Best in a Spurs v Man United match

GOALKEEPER OF THE CENTURY FILE

Just for the record, these were the other goalkeepers on the Top 50 list of the poll conducted by the International Federation of Football History and Statistics:

11	Frantisek Plánicka	Czechoslovakia
12	Amadeo Raúl Carrizo	Argentina
13	Ladislao Mazurkiewicz	Uruguay
14	Ubaldo Matildo Fillol	Argentina
15	Antonio Carbajal	México
16	Jean-Marie Pfaff	Belgium
17	Rinat Dasaev	U.S.S.R.
18	Gyula Grosics	Hungary
19	Thomas Ravelli	Sweden
20	Walter Zenga	Italy
21	Vladimir Beara	Yugoslavia
22	Michel Preud'homme	Belgium
23	Harald Schumacher	West Germany
24	Rudolf Hiden	Austria
25	Ivo Viktor	Czechoslovakia
26	Frank Swift	England
27	Hugo Orlando Gatti	Argentina
28	Jorge Campos	México
29	Edwin van der Sar	Holland
30	Roque Gaston Máspoli	Uruguay
31	Thomas N'Kono	Cameroon
32	José René Higuita	Colombia
33	Joseph Antonio Bell	Cameroon
34	Andoni Zubizarreta	Spain
35	Émerson Leão	Brazil
36	Jan Tomaszewski	Poland
37	J-F van Breukelen	Netherlands
38	Walter Zeman	Austria
39	Mohammed Al-Deayea	Saudi Arabia
40	Giampiero Combi	Italy
41	Naser Hejazi	Iran
42	Neville Southall	Wales
43	Badou Zaki	Morocco
44	Andreas Köpke	Germany
45	Ronnie Hellström	Sweden
46	Jürgen Croy	East Germany
47	Sadok Attouga	Tunisia
48	Alberto Costa Pereira	Portugal
49	Bruce Grobbelaar	Zimbabwe
50	Ronnie Simpson	Scotland

GOALKEEPER OF THE CENTURY FILE

I find it hard to believe there was a greater goalkeeper than Gordon Banks, but Lev Yashin received huge world-wide support in the polls. To get a proper view of Yashin I wanted the verdict of somebody who played against him. I did not have to look far. Jimmy Greaves and Yashin had one of the most exciting duels in Wembley history. This is Greavsie's memory of the occasion, taken from his splendid book *Football's Great Heroes and Entertainers*:

❛LEV YASHIN is the legendary goalkeeper who once almost broke my heart on a football pitch. I promise I am not exaggerating when I say that but for him I would have scored four first-half goals for England against the Rest of the World at Wembley in 1963.

Just to confirm that I am not dreaming this, I looked up a report of the game by the distinguished *Times* reporter Geoffrey Green:

> *'The first-half provided a match within a match, Russia's legendary "Man in Black" goalkeeper Lev Yashin against England's finest goal poacher Jimmy Greaves. Four times Greaves, the Artful Dodger of the penalty area, worked his way into goal scoring positions. Four times we were convinced he was going to score, and four times the human spider that is Yashin denied him with saves that were at one and the same time spectacular yet made to look simple by this master custodian. Sporting Greaves led the applause when Yashin was called off to be substituted by Yugoslavian goalkeeper Soskic. Secretly, the Tottenham goal machine must have been praising the football Gods that the 'Iron Curtain' that Yashin had dropped on his goal had been removed ... It was Greaves who fittingly snatched the late winning goal for England when he beat Soskic with a typical rapier finish after a thunderbolt shot from Bobby Charlton had been beaten out just moments after the Tottenham executioner had struck a shot against the post. You can bet all the vodka in Russia that Yashin, reduced to a spectator on the touchline bench, would have saved the Greaves goal.'*

Yes, that was the way it was, and perfectly described by the doyen of football writers who became a personal friend of mine. Geoffrey told me in later years that Yashin that day at Wembley had been 'out of this world.' One of the more lurid newspaper headlines read: 'Yashin leaves Greaves Gnashing'.

I am not telling this story to pat myself on the back, but to illustrate the incredible goalkeeping ability and agility of the Russian giant. Standing 6ft 3in and with telescopic arms that seemed as long as his legs, he used to cover the goal like a huge black octopus.

I remember that one shot of mine in the first-half was, so I thought, a certainty for the back of the net until Yashin raised a mighty Russian fist and punched it away with all the power of Henry Cooper landing a hook on Cassius Clay's jaw (as he had in the same Wembley Stadium four months earlier!). I fell into his arms to congratulate him, and he gave me a big Russian bear hug and laughed out loud.

It was Lev's performance at Wembley – with the cream of European soccer reporters looking on – that clinched for him the title of European Footballer of the Year. He remains the only goalkeeper ever to have won the award.

Yashin and I often bumped into each other after that match in testimonial games (the Stanley Matthews farewell stands out in my memory), and he always greeted me with that same Russian bear hug. This was all during the supposed 'Cold War', but there was nobody as warm with his greeting and feelings than the towering Lev Yashin.

Amazingly, football was his second-string sport and he was ready to give up the game in 1953 because he could not see a way of progress at club and country level. The goalkeeping job at Moscow Dynamo and with Russia (or the Soviet Union as they were then known) was in the safe hands of Alexei 'Tiger' Khomich, who was then as big an idol as Yashin was to become.

Lev was about to switch full-time to his first love of ice hockey after helping his Moscow team win the Russian championship when Khomich announced his retirement. The Olympic title was as much prized for 'Iron Curtain' countries as the World Cup, and Yashin was made a 'Russian Hero of Sport' after a succession of stunning performances to clinch the gold medal at Melbourne in 1956. While all this was going on, Ferenc Puskas and his Hungarian team-mates were defecting because of the Russian invasion of Budapest. It's a funny old world.

For the next three World Cup campaigns Yashin was the undisputed number one No 1 and he was a major force in helping Russia through to the finals of 1958, 1962 and 1966. He travelled as a distinguished reserve to the 1970 finals in Mexico. They reached three World Cup quarter-finals with Yashin as their last line of defence, and the nearest Russia got to winning the tournament was in England in 1966. Yashin and his team-mates were beaten 2-1 by West Germany in the semi-final, and lost the third-place play-off to Portugal 2-1.

Lev performed heroics between the posts in the semi-final at Goodison Park after Russia had been reduced to nine men, with one player sent off and another hobbling off in what was more of a war than a football match.

GOALKEEPER OF THE CENTURY FILE

Lev Yashin, the master goalkeeper, saves at the feet of Greavsie, the master goalscorer

Thanks largely to Yashin's goalkeeping brilliance, the Soviet Union had been the first winners of the European Nations' Cup in 1960 (a tournament that took two years to complete, and is now better known as the Euro championship). Russia beat Yugoslavia 2-1 after extra-time in the final in Paris, and it was Yashin who was first to get his huge hands on the trophy.

How about this for anybody who collects trivial statistics: During his twenty-two year career Yashin saved no fewer than 151 penalties! In his 78 international matches he conceded just 70 goals.

With facts and figures like that in his defence, how could I fail to have him in my Top 51 list ahead of exceptional foreign-born goalkeepers of the calibre of Bert Trautmann, Peter Schmeichel, Fabian Barthez and Petr Cech.

Once asked the secret of his success, Yashin said: 'The trick is to have a smoke to calm your nerves, then toss back a strong drink to tone your muscles.' It was advice he was later asked not to repeat because it sent out the wrong message to young footballers. Perhaps I was one of those who read it!

On his retirement, Yashin became the national goalkeeping coach while employed by the Sports Ministry, with the honorary title of Colonel. He was also briefly team manager, but did not enjoy the responsibility. 'Goalkeeping is the only thing I know,' he said.

Like so many old pros, he was so lost without the day-to-day regime of training that he turned to the bottle and became hooked on vodka. His last years were torturous. He had just managed to beat his alcoholism when he had a leg amputated following complications to an old knee injury. Lev finally succumbed to cancer in 1990, aged just sixty, and was given a State funeral as a Russian 'Master of Sport.' He had been awarded the Order of Lenin, Russia's top medal that usually went to cosmonauts and army generals. In an unofficial poll he came second only to spaceman Yuri Gagarin as 'the greatest Russian hero.' He beat Gordon Banks by a fingertip in the Fifa-organised vote for the 'Goakeeper of the Twentieth Century' accolade. A bronze statue was unveiled in his memory outside the Moscow Dynamo stadium.

The last time I saw Lev was just a year before he died, when he came to London as a surprise final guest on Billy Wright's *This Is Your Life* tribute programme.

He was the colour of parchment and obviously seriously ill, but he was determined not to miss a final meeting with Billy, his old adversary from the days of the floodlit thrillers at Molineux, when Moscow Dynamo were among the Wolves victims.

Asked about his proudest moment in football, Lev picked out that match at Wembley when he made four stupendous saves against me. It was also a game that I will always recall with pride, because I know I had come second to one of the greatest goalkeepers ever to take his place between the posts.'

In that *This Is Your Life programme,* an emotional Billy Wright told viewers: 'I feel so privileged that this great footballer and sportsman has come all the way from Moscow to pay tribute to me. Through all the nonsense of Cold Wars and political tensions, Lev and I have remained good friends, and I have no hesitation in saying that he is the finest overseas goalkeeper I played against in my 105 international matches for England. He has always represented both football and himself in the best possible light, and was never less than gracious in victory or defeat.'

Lev Yashin and Billy Wright. They don't make them like that anymore.

EXTRA-TIME, First Half

As a sports fanatic since I was knee-high to a football, I have always been irritated at the way statistics are presented in books. They are usually dismissed as filler items in the smallest possible type. This means that crucial facts are often missed by the reader because they are tucked away, almost out of sight. Gordon Banks and Pelé deserve better than that. With the help of my co-author Norman Giller and his sports statistician son, Michael, I offer you the following mind-blowing facts and figures that do justice to the careers of two masters of the football, Banks and Pelé ...

THE EARLY YEARS

●Gordon was born in Ferrars Road, Tinsley, Sheffield, South Yorkshire, on 30 December 1937. His father was a steelworker, and he had three older brothers – John, David and Michael.

●He first played football at Tinsley County School, where he was put in goal because he was the tallest. Gordon was selected to play for Sheffield Schools Under-15s.

●When he could afford it, he watched Sheffield Wednesday at Hillsborough and United at Bramall Lane. His idol was Manchester City goalkeeper Bert Trautmann, the ex-German Prisoner of War.

●When he was 13, his family moved to Catcliffe, a village outside Rotherham, where his father opened a small betting shop in the days when they were illegal. There was a family tragedy when his eldest brother, John, was beaten up while being robbed of the betting shop takings. He later died of his injuries.

THE EARLY YEARS

●Gordon left school at 15, and got a job as a coalbagger and delivery man with a local coal merchant. He later became an apprentice brick layer.

●His first game in senior football was with local league team Millspaugh. He had gone straight from the coalyard to watch as a spectator, but was invited to play in goal when their 'keeper failed to show up. In his debut he wore his coalman's trousers.

●He moved up to a higher level with Romarsh Welfare, but was dumped back to Millspaugh when he let in 15 goals in his first two games.

●Chesterfield spotted him and he helped their youth team reach the 1956 FA Youth Cup final. They were beaten 4-3 by the Busby Babes, including Bobby Charlton.

●He became a full-time professional with Chesterfield on £17 a week after finishing his Army National Service in 1958.

From Gordon's newspaper cuttings book, two of his earliest teams – Sheffield Boys Under 15s (above) and the Chesterfield side that reached the 1956 FA Youth Cup final (below).

THE CLUB CAREER

●Gordon played in 510 Football League matches, all but twenty-three of them with Chesterfield in the First Division. Leicester City bought him for £7,000 in 1959, and he joined Stoke City for £52,000 in 1967.

●His appearances in League games:

Chesterfield	23 (1958-59)
Leicester City	293 (1959-66)
Stoke City	194 (1967-72)

●Club honours:

Chesterfield	FA Youth Cup runners-up (1956)
Leicester City	FA Cup runners-up (1961)
	FA Cup runners-up (1963)
	League Cup winners (1964)
	League Cup runners-up (1965)
Stoke City	League Cup winners (1972)

THE CLUB CAREER

●Following the 1972 car crash that cost him the sight of his right eye, Gordon played for two seasons in the North American Soccer League. He had previously played briefly in the United States in 1967 during the English close season.

Cleveland Stokers	12 (1967)
St. Patrick's Athletic	1 (1977)
Fort Lauderdale Strikers	39 (1977-78)

●Personal honours:
OBE (Order of the British Empire), 1970.

FWA Footballer of the Year (1972).

Daily Express Sportsman of the Year (1972).

North American Soccer League Most Valued Goalkeeper (1977).

Inaugural Inductee to English Football Hall of Fame (2002).

First 'Sheffield Legend' to be honoured with a Walk of Fame plaque (2006).

A statue erected to him at Stoke City's Britannia ground, unveiled by Pelé and Archbishop Tutu (2008)

Gordon with his 1972 Footballer of the Year award from the Football Writers' Association

BANKS OF ENGLAND

●Alf Ramsey selected Gordon for his first England cap against Scotland on 6 April 1963. Scotland won the match 2-1, with Jim Baxter scoring both Scottish goals – one from the penalty spot.

●Only Banks, Bobby Moore and Bobby Charlton survived from this team to the World Cup final in 1966.

●Played a record 73 times for England between 1963 and 1972 (The previous most-capped England goalkeeper was Ron Springett with 33 caps, with the record now held by Peter Shilton at 125 caps. Ray Clemence was capped 61 times).

●Played 31 times for England at Wembley and was a winner in 21 matches. His full Wembley international record was:

P31 W21 D7 L3

In these Wembley matches he conceded 27 goals while England scored 71. He kept a clean sheet in 14 of the matches.

BANKS OF ENGLAND

●Played 28 matches for England overseas, of which 19 were won. His full overseas international record:

P28 W19 D4 L5

In these games he conceded 19 goals, while England scored 53. He kept a clean sheet in 14 of the matches.

●Played 13 Home Championship matches away from Wembley, of which nine were won. His 13-match record:

P13 W9 D3 L1

In these games he conceded 10 goals, while England scored 27. He kept a clean sheet in 7 of the matches.

●Played 10 Home Championship matches at Wembley, of which seven were won. His 10-match record:

P10 W7 D1 L2

In these games he conceded 15 goals, while England scored 31.

Not quite consenting adults, but Gordon and Nobby Stiles are pleased with each other after England's 2-1 victory over Portugal in the 1966 World Cup semi-final at Wembley.

BANKS OF ENGLAND

● England's full record when Gordon was in goal:

P73 W49 D15 L9 Goals for 152 Against 57

● Banks of England conceded an average 0.78 goals per match.

● The opposition failed to put the ball past him in 35 matches.

● Played in an international match at Goodison Park in January 1966 – a 1-1 draw with Poland.

● Conceded one goal in two England Under-23 matches.

● Gordon's final appearance for England was against Scotland at Hampden Park on 27 May 1972. Alan Ball scored the only goal of the match.

● Only Bobby Moore and Ball remained along with Gordon of the team that won the World Cup at Wembley on 30 July 1966.

More memories from the Banks 1970s scrapbook. It's happy family time above as Gordon and Ursula face the camera with daughters Julia and Wendy and son Robert. And here is Gordon (left) proudly posing outside the beautiful Banks home at Ashley Heath, Market Drayton.

BANKS OF ENGLAND

●During his England career, Gordon had 28 players sharing defensive duties with him. They were, in order of total appearances:

Bobby Moore (68)	Jimmy Armfield (9)
Ray Wilson (39)	Tommy Wright (9)
Jack Charlton (30)	Paul Madeley (7)
George Cohen (28)	Peter Storey (6)
Alan Mullery (24)	Bobby Thomson (5)
Nobby Stiles (24)	Ron Flowers (4)
Keith Newton (19)	Cyril Knowles (4)
Brian Labone (16)	Chris Lawler (4)
Norman Hunter (14)	David Sadler (3)
Maurice Norman (14)	Bob McNab (2)
Terry Cooper (13)	Mike Bailey (1)
Emlyn Hughes (12)	Gerry Byrne (1)
Gordon Milne (11)	Paul Reaney (1)
Roy McFarland (10)	Ken Shellito (1)

THE EARLY YEARS

●Pelé was the first of three children born in near poverty to Joao Ramos do Nascimento and his wife, Dona Celeste in Tres Coracoes (Three Hearts), Brazil, on 23 October 1940.

●On his birth certificate, Pelé is registered as Edison Arantes do Nascimento. He was named after the American inventor Thomas Edison, but has always preferred to call himself Edson.

●He was nicknamed Pelé from his schooldays, and it was a name that he hated. He was happier with his family nickname of Dico, and believes he was called Pelé because he could not properly pronounce the name of a local goalkeeper hero called Bilé, who played for Vasco da Gama. When he said it the name sounded like Pelé, and his schoolmates started calling him that in a mickey-taking fashion.

●He once got suspended from school for a day for punching a classmate for calling him Pelé. It was to become one of the most famous names in the world of sport.

THE EARLY YEARS

●Pele's Fluminense father, known as Dondinho, was a semi-professional centre-forward whose career was cut short by a knee injury. He once scored five goals in a match, all headers.

●Like most in their neighbourhood, the do Nascimento family lived on the edge of poverty, and Dondinho could not afford football boots or a football for his son, who perfected his control by kicking newspapers wrapped in a sock.

●When he was 11, Pelé came under the influence of former Brazilian World Cup player Waldemar de Brito, who coached him as a member of the junior team attached to the Bauru Athletic Club, where Pelé had shined shoes for pennies.

●De Brito recommended him to one of Brazil's major clubs, Santos. When he joined them at the age of 15, de Brito told the club management: "This boy will develop into the world's greatest footballer."

The Best meets The Best. George Best, playing for Los Angeles Aztecs takes on Pelé during a North American Soccer League match against New York Cosmos in 1976.

THE CLUB CAREER

●Pelé made his first-team debut for Santos on 7 September 1956, and scored one and laid on four more goals in a 7-1 victory over Corinthians. He was 16.

●His goals in club football:

Santos   (1956-74)   605 games 589 goals

New York Cosmos   (1975-77)   107 games   64 goals

●Club honours:

Santos Campeonato Paulista: 1958, 1960, 1961, 1962, 1964, 1965, 1967, 1968, 1969 and 1973. Torneio Rio-São Paulo: 1959, 1963 and 1964

Torneio Roberto Gomes Pedrosa (Taça de Prata): 1968

Taça Brasil: 1961, 1962, 1963, 1964 and 1965

Copa Libertadores: 1962 and 1963

Intercontinental Cup: 1962 and 1963

South-American Recopa: 1968

New York Cosmos   NASL championship 1977

THE CLUB CAREER

●Pelé's final haul in all forms of football, including club friendlies, Army matches during National Service and domestic cup and international matches was an extraordinary

1281 goals in 1363 matches

●There is always controversy as to exactly how many he scored, but it is the 1281 goals that are recognized by world-governing body Fifa as the highest total achieved by a professional footballer. It is possible that Artur Friedenreich scored more goals in pre-war Brazilian football, but there are too many doubts about his statistics for his total to be considered official.

●He scored three or more goals in 129 matches, including 91 times in which he netted three goals, thirty-one games when he went on to four, six five-goal hauls and an astonishing one of eight.

●When Santos thrashed Botafogo 11-0 in a Brazilian league game in 1964, Pelé scored eight of the goals including six in a 13-minute burst.

THE CLUB CAREER

●Pelé's peak year for goals was 1958 when he scored 139 times, including his six goals in the 1958 World Cup finals. He was still only 17.

●In 1962, the Brazilian government declared him a national treasure to stop Santos accepting the flood of offers coming from the major clubs in Spain and Italy (this was long before foreign players were welcomed into the English league).

●He was originally known as the Black Pearl (a nickname shared with Eusebio) until it was widely accepted that he should be called "The King of Football" (*O Rei do Futebol*).

●On November 19 1969, Pelé scored his 1000th goal. This was greeted with celebration parties across Brazil. The goal, labelled locally as *O Milésimo* (The Thousandth), was scored in a match against Vasco da Gama and it came from the penalty spot at Pele's favourite ground, the Maracana in Rio which was built for the 1950 World Cup finals. November 19 became known as Pelé Day in Brazil.

THE CLUB CAREER

●In 1967, the two factions involved in the bloody Nigerian civil war agreed to a 48-hour cease fire so that they could watch Pelé play in a friendly with Santos in Lagos.

●Santos 'retired' their No 10 shirt when Pelé hung up his boots in 1972 at the end of his 17th season with the Brazilian club.

●He was persuaded by New York Cosmos to come out of retirement in 1975, and made his debut against Dallas Tornado on May 15 1975, scoring once in a 2-2 draw.

●In his final season with Cosmos he helped them win the NASL title. His last game was a 70,000 sell-out against his old club Santos at the New York Giants stadium. He played for Cosmos in the first-half, scoring from a free-kick. Pelé took part in a half-time ceremony when his No 10 shirt was 'retired' and he handed it to his father. He played the second half for Santos, and Cosmos won the match 2-1.

The King of football becomes Minister of sport for Brazil.

THE PELÉ HONOURS LIST

●Only player to collect World Cup winners' medals at three separate tournaments (1958, 1962 – when he missed the final through injury – and 1970). He was awarded his 1962 medal retrospectively.

●Won a record 32 major team titles with Santos, Brazil and Cosmos.

●Voted Fifa Footballer of the Century, a title shared with Diego Maradona.

●South American Footballer of the Year 1973.

●Awarded an honorary knighthood by the Queen in 1996.

●Voted Athlete of the Century by the International Olympic Committee.

●Recipient of the International Peace Award in 1980.

●Lifetime achievements awards from Laureus (2000) and the BBC (2005)

THE INTERNATIONAL PELÉ

●Pelé made his debut for Brazil at the age of 16 against Argentina in the Roca Cup at the Maracana Stadium in Rio on 7 July 1957. He scored Brazil's goal in a 2-1 defeat.

●He made his first appearance in the World Cup against the USSR in the third match of the 1958 finals. Pelé scored his first World Cup goal in his next game, a quarter-final against Wales, and netted a hat-trick in the semi-final against France.

●Garrincha, the Wing Wizard, made his debut in the same match against the Russians in Gothenburg. Vava scored both goals in a 2-0 victory. Pelé and Garrincha were never on a losing side in 59 international matches together for Brazil.

●Mario Zagola was Pelé's left-wing partner in his World Cup debut. Twelve years later Zagola was manager when Pelé helped Brazil win the Jules Rimet trophy outright in the 1970 final in Mexico with a 4-1 victory over Italy in the Aztec Stadium..

THE INTERNATIONAL PELÉ

●In the 1958 World Cup final Pelé scored twice to help Brazil to a 5-2 victory over host country Sweden. His first goal – catching the ball on his thigh, swivelling around his marker and scoring with a volley – was voted one of the greatest goals in World Cup history.

●At 17, Pelé was the youngest player to collect a World Cup winners' medal. He was also the youngest player to score a World Cup finals hat-trick, and at the time of his debut he was the youngest player to appear in a World Cup finals tournament (a record since taken by Norman Whiteside, who was 17 years 41 days old when he played for Northern Ireland against Yugoslavia in the 1982 finals in Spain).

●In the 1962 World Cup, Pelé pulled a muscle in the second match against Czechoslovakia after scoring in the opening 2-0 victory over Spain. Brazil went on to win the World Cup without Pelé, but he was awarded a medal. Brazil beat Czechoslovakia 3-1 in the final, with Garrincha being voted the player of the tournament.

THE INTERNATIONAL PELÉ

● Pelé considered the 1966 World Cup finals the blackest time of his football career. He was hacked out of the tournament by Portugal after scoring in the first match against Bulgaria. He took such a battering against the Bulgarians that he missed the second match with Hungary, and he limped out of the game against Portugal after a series of scything tackles. Brazil were eliminated without even reaching the quarter-finals, and Pelé vowed he would never again play World Cup football.

● Talked out of World Cup retirement by team manager Joao Saldanha, he scored six goals in Brazil's six qualifying games for the 1970 finals by which time Mario Zagola had replaced Saldanha.

● Brazil's 4-1 victory in their opening match against Czechoslovakia is always remembered for the "nearly" goal. Pelé, on the centre-line, spotted that goalkeeper Viktor was off his line, and he was only inches wide with a sensational lobbed shot that was the talk of the World Cup ... until the Banks save in the next match.

THE INTERNATIONAL PELÉ

●Brazil's 3-1 victory over Uruguay in the semi-finals included yet another magical moment from Pelé. Uruguay goalkeeper Mazurkiewicz raced off his line to try to get to the ball before him. Pelé got there first and, without touching it, produced an outrageous dummy that completely threw the Uruguyan goalie. Mazurkiewicz went for a ball that was not there while Pelé went around him and shot just wide of the far post. It would have been a goal in a million.

●Pelé helped Brazil win the Jules Rimet trophy outright with a succession of classic performances in the 1970 finals in Mexico. His contribution included a superbly headed goal in the final against Italy.

●He scored 12 goals in his four World Cup final tournaments, 14 matches in all. Pelé played his final game for Brazil against Yugoslavia on 18 July 1971, a 2-2 draw. His record in official international matches was:

92 games, **67** wins, **14** draws, **11** defeats, **77** goals

EXTRA-TIME, Second-Half

Iwanted to make this book a real collector's item for all those fans of Pelé and Gordon Banks. Wondering about how to give it a special finish, I said to my co-author Norman Giller: "Wouldn't it be great if we could list every single goal that Pelé scored."

Unflappable Norm said: "No problem, I've got them all on file. Back in the 1960s I worked on the *Daily Express* with Clive Toye, and I succeeded him as chief football reporter when he moved to the United States to join Phil Woosnam in getting the North American Soccer League off the launching pad. Clive and I formed a sportswriting agency called Amsud Features, aimed at the international market. We had just got it established when Clive told me he was having to give up his involvement because he had been appointed General Manager (and later, President) of New York Cosmos. He asked me to put together a compilation of all Pelé's goals. 'What's it for?' I asked. 'Oh,' he said, matter of fact. 'I am about to sign him. I'm off to see Pelé with Henry Kissinger.'

"How about that, Pelé and Henry Kissinger in the same breath! Clive is another great advertisement for the West Country, Terry. You've performed wonders from your base in Dorset. Clive is an Exeter boy who started his sports writing career in Devon. What an adventure he's had!"

So that's the fascinating background to how we are now able to present to you *THE PELÉ GOALS, every one of them ...*

1. THE PELÉ GOALS, Every one of them!

Date	Match result	Pelé	Date	Match result	Pelé
	1956		18-8	Santos F.C. 5-Portuguesa 2	0
7-9	Santos F.C. 7-Corinthians 1	1	20-8	Santos F.C. 2-Combined Bhaiano 2	0
15-11	Santos F.C. 4-Jabaquara 2	1	8-9	Santos F.C. 1-Palmeiras 2	1
	1957		11-9	Santos F.C. 7-Nacional 1	4
12-1	Santos F.C. 1 –AIK(Sweden) 0	0	15-9	Santos F.C. 2-San Pablo 3	1
9-2	Santos F.C. 2-Portuguesa 4	0	22-9	Santos F.C. 1-Portuguesa Santista 1	1
17-2	Santos F.C. 5- America Joinville	0	25-9	Santos F.C. 9-Ipiringa 1	3
1-2	Santos F.C. 3- America Joinville 1	0	29-9	Santos F.C. 6- Juventus-SP 1	1
12-3	Santos F.C. 2-Gremio 3	0	2-10	Santos F.C. 1-Sport 1	0
14-3	Santos F.C. 5-Gremio 0	0	4-10	Santos F.C. 0-Nautico 0	0
17-3	Santos F.C. 5-Riograndense 3	0	6-10	Santos F.C. 2-San Paio Correa 1	2
19-3	Santos F.C. 3-Pelotas 2	0	8-10	Santos F.C. 2-Sport 1	1
22-3	Santos F.C. 2-CRB 2	0	10-10	Santos F.C. 1- Canto do Rio 0	0
24-3	Santos F.C. 1-Guarani 1	1	20-10	Santos F.C. 2-Botafogo 4	0
27-3	Santos F.C. 3-Renner 5	0	23-10	Santos F.C. 2-Portuguesa 2	0
31-3	Santos F.C. 4-Juventude 1	1	26-10	Santos F.C. 4-Palmeiras 3	1
7-4	Santos F.C. 4- Vasco-RJ	0	3-11	Santos F.C. 3-Corinthians 3	3
11-4	Santos F.C. 5-Corinthians 3	1	4-11	Santos F.C. 0-Bandeirantes 3	0
14-4	Santos F.C. 6-Guarani 1	2	6-11	Santos F.C. 3-Portuguesa 1	0
26-4	Santos F.C. 3-San Pablo 1	1	10-11	Santos F.C. 3- XV de Piracicaba 0	1
1-5	Santos F.C. 1-Corinthians 1	0	17-11	Santos F.C. 2-San Pablo 6	0
5-5	Santos F.C. 0-Flamengo 4	0	24-11	Santos F.C. 5-Jabaquara 1	3
9-5	Santos F.C. 2-Portuguesa 4	0	27-11	Santos F.C. 6-XV de Piracicaba 2	2
11-5	Santos F.C. 5-Botafogo1 Rj	0	1-12	Santos F.C. 6-Portuguesa Santista 2	4
13-5	Santos F.C. 1-Botafogo 3 Sp	0	3-12	Santos F.C. 2- San Pablo 2	0
15-5	Santos F.C. 3-Palmeiras 0	2	8-12	Santos F.C. 2-Ponte Preta 1	1
19-5	Santos F.C. 7-Londrina 1	2	15-12	Santos F.C. 6- Portuguesa 0	2
26-5	Santos F.C. 2-Fluminense 2	0	22-12	Santos F.C. 1- Corinthians 0	0
29-5	Santos F.C. 4-America Rj 0	1	28-12	Santos F.C. 4-Palmeiras 1	0
1-6	Santos F.C. 2-Vasco 3	1	29-12	Santos F.C. 10-Nitro Quimica 0	1
9-6	Santos F.C. 7- Lavras 2	4		**1958**	
19-6	Santos F.C./Vasco 6- Belenenses 1	3	19-1	Santos F.C. 4-Bragantino 1	1
20-6	Santos F.C. 3-Rio Branco 2	0	26-1	Santos F.C. 4-Prudentina 0	1
22-6	Santos F.C./Vasco 1 – Dinamo 1	1	30-1	Santos F.C. 2-Atletico MG 5	1
26-6	Santos F.C./Vasco 1-Flamengo 1	1	2-2	Santos F.C. 2-Atletico MG 0	1
29-6	Santos F.C./Vasco 1- San Pablo 1	1	5-2	Santos F.C. 2-Atletico MG 2	0
7-7	BRAZIL 1-Argentina 2	1	7-2	Santos F.C. 4-Botafogo 2	2
10-7	BRAZIL 2-Argentina 0	1	26-2	Santos F.C. 5-America RJ 3	4
14-7	Santos F.C. 5-XV de Piracicaba 3	1	2-3	Santos F.C. 2-Botafogo 2	0
21-7	Santos F.C. 1-Corinthians 2	0	6-3	Santos F.C. 7-Palmeiras 6	1
23-7	Santos F.C. 3-Benfica(Port.) 2	1	9-3	Santos F.C. 2-Flamengo 3	1
25-7	Santos F.C. 7-Ponte Preta 3	3	13-3	Santos F.C. 2-Portuguesa 3	1
28-7	Santos F.C. 3-Arapongas	0	16-3	Santos F.C. 2-San Pablo 4	0
31-7	Santos F.C. 4-Jabaquara 6	0	22-3	Santos F.C. 0- Vasco RJ 1	0
4-8	Santos F.C. 2-Ferroviaria 3	0	23-3	Santos F.C. 2-Noroeste 3	0
11-8	Santos F.C. 4-Botafogo 2	0	27-3	Santos F.C. 1-Corinthians 2	1
15-8	Santos F.C. 8-Guarani 1	4			

2. THE PELÉ GOALS, Every one of them!

Tears of triumph for Pelé as his team-mates celebrate their 1958 World Cup final victory.

Date	Match result	Pelé	Date	Match result	Pelé
4-5	BRAZIL 5-Paraguay 1	1	11-9	Santos F.C. 10- Nacional Sp 0	4
14-5	BRAZIL 4-Bulgaria 0	0	14-9	Santos F.C. 1-Corinthians 0	1
18-5	BRAZIL 3-Bulgaria 1	2	17-9	Santos F.C. 8-Guarani SP 1	1
21-5	BRAZIL 5-Corinthians 0	0	21-9	Santos F.C. 2-Prudentina 2	1
15-6 WC	**BRAZIL 2-USSR 0**	**0**	25-9	Santos F.C. 1-Internacional	0
19-6 WC	**BRAZIL 1-Wales 0**	**1**	28-9	Santos F.C. 0- Gremio 4	0
24-6 WC	**BRAZIL 5-France 2**	**3**	1-10	Santos F.C. 8-Ypiringa 1	5
29-6 WC	**BRAZIL 5-Sweden 2**	**2**	5-10	Santos F.C. 2-Taubete 3	0
16-7	Santos F.C. 7-Jabuaqara 3	2	11-10	Santos F.C. 3- Noroeste 0	0
20-7	Santos F.C. 2- Juventus Sp 0	1	15-10	Santos F.C. 6-Portuguesa 1	3
23-7	Santos F.C. 6-XV de Piracicaba 0	4	19-10	Santos F.C. 5- XV de Piracicaba 0	2
27-7	Santos F.C. 2-Botafogo 2	2	22-10	Santos F.C. 6-Jabuaqara 2	3
31-7	Santos F.C. 1-Comercial 1	1	26-10	Santos F.C. 4-Botafogo 0	3
3-8	Santos F.C. 0-America Sp 0	0	29-10	Santos F.C. 1-Portuguesa 1	0
6-8	Santos F.C. 4-Portuguesa 2	1	1-11	Santos F.C. 0-XV de Jau 0	0
10-8	Santos F.C. 0- Noroeste 1	0	5-11	Santos F.C. 3-America 1	1
13-8	Santos F.C. 4- Ferroviaria 3	1	9-11	Santos F.C. 1-Ferroviaria 2	0
17-8	Santos F.C. 1- San Pablo 0	1	16-11	Santos F.C. 2- Palmeiras 1	1
20-8	Santos F.C. 4- Ponte Preta 0	1	19-11	Santos F.C. 9- Comercial SP 1	4
24-8	Santos F.C. 1-Palmeiras 0	0	23-11	Santos F.C. 2- Ponte Preta 1	0
28-8	Santos F.C. 5- XV de Jau 2	1	27-11	Santos F.C. 4-Portuguesa 3	1
31-8	Santos F.C. 2- Portuguesa 1	0	30-11	Santos F.C. 4-Nacional 3	1
4-9	Santos F.C. 3-Taubale 0	3	7-12	Santos F.C. 6-Corinthians 1	4
7-9	Santos F.C. 4 –Ypiranga 1	0	10-12	Santos F.C. 7-Juventus SP 1	3

Date	Match result	Pelé	Date	Match result	Pelé
14-12	Santos F.C. 7-Guarani SP1	4	7-6	Santos F.C. 3-Nuremberg 3	0
18-12	Santos F.C. 2-San Pablo 2	2	9-6	Santos F.C. 4-Sevette 1	1
21-12	Santos F.C. 1-Coritiba 1	1	11-6	Santos F.C. 6-Hamburgo 0	1
23-12	Santos F.C. 4-Cruzeiro 2	3	13-6	Santos F.C. 7-Sel. Niedersachen 1	3
30-12	Santos F.C. 3-Combinado Paulista	2	15-6	Santos F.C. 5-Sel. Ensechede 0	3
			17-6	Santos F.C. 3-Real Madrid 5	1
	1959		19-6	Santos F.C. 2-Sporting 2	1
4-1-	Santos F.C. 3-Sport Boys 0	2	21-6	Santos F.C. 4-Botafogo 1	1
6-1	Santos F.C. 4-Sporting Cristal 0	2	24-6	Santos F.C. 1-Valencia 4	1
9-1	Santos F.C. 5-Deportivo Mun'al 1	0	26-6	Santos F.C. 7-Internazionale 1	4
11-1	Santos F.C. 3-Emelec 1	2	28-6	Santos F.C. 5-Barcelona 1	2
15-1	Santos F.C. 3-Saprissa 1	2	30-6	Santos F.C. 4-Genoa 0	0
18-1	Santos F.C. 2-Comunicaciones 1	1	2-7	Santos F.C. 0-Viena 3	0
21-1	Santos F.C. 2-Costa Rica 1	0	5-7	Santos F.C. 2-Betis 2	1
29-1	Santos F.C. 4-Guadalajara 2	3	18-7	Santos F.C. 2-Fortaleza 2	2
5-2	Santos F.C. 2-Leon 0	0	19-7	Santos F.C. 0-Sel. Pernambuco 0	0
8-2	Santos F.C. 4-Atlas 1	1	23-7	Santos F.C. 7-Jabaquara 0	1
12-2	Santos F.C. 5-America 0	2	26-7	Santos F.C. 8-XV de Jau 2	3
15-2	Santos F.C. 3- Uka Dukla 4	0	2-8	Santos F.C. 4- Juventus 0	3
17-2	Santos F.C. 3-Sel. Willemstad 2	0	16-8	Santos F.C. 1-Jabale 1	1
19-2	Santos F.C. 4- Spain -Ven- 0	0	19-8	Santos F.C. 0-Ferroviaria 0	0
22-2	Sel. Paulista 1- Sel.Carioca 5	1	21-8	Sel. Guarda Costa 9-G. Docas 0	3
25-2	Sel. Paulista 0-Sel. Carioca 1	0	23-8	Santos F.C. 4-Noroeste 3	3
10-3	BRAZIL 2-Peru 2	1	26-8	Santos F.C. 3-Corinthians 2	1
15-3	BRAZIL 3-Chile 0	2	27-8	Sel. Guarda Costa 7-O.Q.G 0	3
21-3	BRAZIL 4-Bolivia 2	1	30-8	Santos F.C. 3-America SP 2	1
26-3	BRAZIL 3-Uruguay 1	0	5-9	Sel. Guarda Costa 0-Port. Sant 0	0
29-3	BRAZIL 4-Paraguay1	3	7-9	Santos F.C. 5-Portuguesa 0	3
4-4	BRAZIL 1-Argentina 1	1	10-9	Santos F.C. 4-Guarani 1	2
9-4	Santos F.C. 4- Botafogo 2	1	11-9	Sel. Guarda Costa 8-Santos F.C. 4	3
12-4	Santos F.C. 3-Flamengo 2	1	13-9	Santos F.C. 3-Botafogo 1	1
15-4	Santos F.C. 2-Colo-Colo 6	0	17-9	Santos F.C. 7-Chile 0	3
18-4	Santos F.C. 1-Fluminense 1	0	20-9	BRAZIL 1-Chile 0	0
21-4	Santos F.C. 2-Portuguesa 0	0	27-9	Santos F.C. 1-San Pablo 2	0
23-4	Santos F.C. 2-Bahia 1	0	28-9	Guarda Costa 4-FF.AA 2	1
26-4	Santos F.C. 4-San Pablo 3	2	1-10	Santos F.C. 3-Comercial 1	0
30-4	Santos F.C. 3-Corinthians 2	1	3-10	Santos F.C. 7-Palmeiras 3	3
13-5	BRAZIL 2-England 0	0	6-10	Guarda Costa 3-FF.AA 2	1
17-5	Santos F.C. 3-Vasco 0	1	11-10	Santos F.C. 1- Coritiba 0	0
19-5	Santos F.C. 5-Santa Cruz 1	3	12-10	Army A 4-Army B 3	0
23-5	Santos F.C. 3-Bulgaria 3	2	14-10	Santos F.C. 8-America Sp 0	4
24-5	Santos F.C. 2-Bulgaria 0	1	25-10	Santos F.C. 5-XV de Piracicaba 2	2
26-5	Santos F.C. 1-Royal Standard 0	0	27-10	Army 6-Navy 1	1
27-5	Santos F.C. 4-Anderlecht 2	2	29-10	Santos F.C. 6-Noroeste 1	0
30-5	Santos F.C. 1-Gantoise 2	0	1-11	Santos F.C. 6-Comercial 2	1
3-6	Santos F.C. 3-Feyenoord 0	1	4-11	Santos F.C. 4-Comercial Capital 2	1
5-6	Santos F.C. 2-Inter 3	2	8-11	Santos F.C. 0-XV de Jau 1	0
6-6	Santos F.C. 6-Fortuna 4	1	11-11	Santos F.C. 5-Juventus SP 1	2

Date	Match result	Pelé	Date	Match result	Pelé
15-11	Santos F.C. 4-Nacional SP 0	2	27-5	Santos F.C. 9-CSV Alemania 1	3
17-11	Santos F.C. 4-Gemio1	0	28-5	Santos F.C. 6-Anderletch 0	2
18-11	Army 4-Uruguay Army.1	1	31-5	Santos F.C. 10-Royal Haerschoot 1	4
22-11	Santos F.C. 5-Portuguesa1	3	1-6	Santos F.C. 3-Roma 2	1
24-11	Army 2-Argentina Army.1	0	3-6	Santos F.C. 0-Fiorentina 3	0
25-11	Santos F.C. 0-Gremio 0	0	7-6	Santos F.C. 5-States Remis 3	1
29-11	Santos F.C. 1-Palmeiras 5	1	9-6	Santos F.C. 4-Racing de Paris 1	1
6-12	Santos F.C. 5-Ferroviaria 2	2	11-6	Santos F.C. 5-Gaintose 2	2
10-12	Santos F.C. 2-Bahia 2	1	12-6	Santos F.C. 3-Aunterpia 1	0
13-12	Santos F.C. 4-San Pablo 3	2	14-6	Santos F.C. 4-Eintracht 2	2
20-12	Santos F.C. 2-Guarani 3	0	15-6	Santos F.C. 4-Sel.Berlin 2	1
23-12	Santos F.C. 2-Tambate 0	0	17-6	Santos F.C. 3-Stade Remis 1	1
27-12	Santos F.C. 4-Corinthians 1	2	19-6	Santos F.C. 2-Spain 2	0
30-12	Santos F.C. 2-Bahia 0 1	0	23-6	Santos F.C. 3-Toulouse 0	2
			25-6	Santos F.C. 1-Valencia 0	0
	1960		2-7	Santos F.C. 3-Barcelona 4	1
5-1	Santos F.C. 1-Palmeiras1	1	9-7	BRAZIL 0-Uruguay 0	0
7-1	Santos F.C. 2-Palmerias 2	0	12-7	BRAZIL 5-Argentina 1	1
10-1	Santos F.C. 1-Palmeiras 2	1	17-7	Santos F.C. 6-Ponte Preta 3	1
19-1	Sel.Paulista 2-Sel.Bahiana 0	0	21-7	Santos F.C. 1-Portuguesa 1	0
24-1	Sel.Paulista 7-Sel.Bahiana 1	3	24-7	Santos F.C. 2-Guarani 2	0
27-1	Sel.Paulista 4-Sel.Minera 3	1	27-7	Santos F.C. 8-Jabacuama 3	3
31-1	Sel.Paulista 2-Sel.Pernambuco 4	0	31-7	Santos F.C. 1-Corinthians 1	1
3-2	Sel.Paulista 4-Sel.Carioca 1	0	3-8	Santos F.C. 5-Botafogo 1	1
10-2	Sel.Paulista 3-Sel.Pernambuco 1	2	7-8	Santos F.C. 0-Comercial SP 2	0
14-2	Sel.Paulista 2-Sel.Carioca 1	0	10-8	Santos F.C. 4-Noroeste 1	3
16-2	Santos F.C. 2-Universitario 2	0	14-8	Santos F.C. 1-Corinthians 0	1
18-2	Santos F.C. 3-Sporting Cristal 3	0	15-8	Santos F.C. 3-Itau Sport 2	1
24-2	Santos F.C. 2-Alianza 1	0	21-8	Santos F.C. 3-Palmeiras 1	1
26-2	Santos F.C. 2-Universitario 3	0	31-8	Santos F.C. 1-San Pablo 1	0
6-3	Santos F.C. 2-Medellin 1	1	5-9	Santos F.C. 0-Ferroviaria 4	0
9-3	Santos F.C. 1-America COL 0	0	8-9	Santos F.C. 0-Portuguesa 0	0
12-3	Santos F.C. 1-Millonarios 2	0	11-9	Santos F.C. 0-XV de Piracicaba 0	0
13-3	Santos F.C. 4-Dep.Cali 0	1	15-9	Santos F.C. 5-Juventus 2	3
16-3	Santos F.C.1-America COL 0	0	17-9	Santos F.C.0-America SP 1	0
20-3	Santos F.C. 6-LDU Quito 2	0	21-9	Santos F.C. 3-Jabaquara 2	0
19-4	Santos F.C. 2-Portuguesa 2	0	24-9	Santos F.C. 3-Juventus 1	2
21-4	Santos F.C. 1-San Pablo1	0	28-9	Santos F.C. 3-Portuguesa 4	1
24-4	Santos F.C. 0-Vasco 0	0	23-10	Santos F.C. 4-Ponte Preta 1	1
29-4	BRAZIL 5-United Arab Republic 0	0	6-11	Santos F.C. 2-XV de Piracicaba 0	2
1-5	BRAZIL 3-United Arab Republic 1	1	9-11	Santos F.C. 0-Portuguesa 0	1
6-5	BRAZIL 3-United Arab Republic 0	9	13-11	Santos F.C. 3-Noroeste 1	2
8-5	BRAZIL 7-Malmo 0	2	15-11	Santos F.C. 6-Goiana 1	0
10-5	BRAZIL 4-Dinamarca	2	20-11	Santos F.C. 4-Botafogo 2	1
12-5	BRAZIL 2-Inter 2	2	23-11	Santos F.C. 5-Corinthians 0	1
16-5	BRAZIL 5-Sporting PER 0	0	30-11	Santos F.C. 6-Corinthians 1	1
19-5	Santos F.C. 4-Standard Liege 3	1	4-12	Santos F.C. 6-Taubete 1	2
25-5	Santos F.C. 5-Poland 2	1	7-12	Santos F.C. 5-Ferroviaria 0	3

Date	Match result	Pelé	Date	Match result	Pelé
11-12	Santos F.C. 1-San Pablo 2	0	6-9	Santos F.C. 10-Juventus 1	5
16-12	Santos F.C. 2-Palmeiras 1	1	10-9	Santos F.C. 3-Botafogo 0	1
			13-9	Santos F.C. 5-Guaratingueta 1	4
	1961		17-9	Santos F.C. 6-Portuguesa 1	4
8-1-1961	Santos F.C. 6-Uberlandia 1	1	20-9	Santos F.C. 2-Londrina 1	0
10-1	Santos F.C. 10-Guarani 2	2	28-9	Santos F.C. 4-Racing ARG 2	2
14-1	Santos F.C. 3-Colo-Colo 1	2	1-10	Santos F.C. 1-Newell's 1	1
18-1	Santos F.C. 2-Colombia 1	2	4-10	Santos F.C. 3-Colo-Colo 2	1
22-1	Santos F.C. 7-Saprissa 3	1	8-10	Santos F.C. 3-Colo-Colo 1	1
25-1	Santos F.C. 3-Herediano 0	1	15-10	Santos F.C. 4-Botafogo 1	1
29-1	Santos F.C. 4-Guatemala 1	2	18-10	Santos F.C. 5-Portuguesa Santista 2	2
2-2	Santos F.C. 3-Necaxa 4	0	22-10	Santos F.C. 2-Guarani 1	2
19-2	Santos F.C. 6-Guadalajara 2	0	8-10	Santos F.C. 3-Portuguesa 1	2
22-2	Santos F.C. 6-America MEX 2	2	1-11	Santos F.C. 3-Juventus 1	1
24-2	Santos F.C. 2-Atlas 0	0	4-11	Santos F.C. 4-Taubate 2	1
26-2	Santos F.C. 3-America 3	0	8-11	Santos F.C. 4- Guaratingueta 0	3
2-3	Santos F.C. 5-Vasco 1	0	11-11	Santos F.C. 6-America RJ 2	2
5-3	Santos F.C. 3-Fluminense 1	2	15-11	Santos F.C. 1-Flamengo 1	1
11-3	Santos F.C. 7-Flamengo 1	3	19-11	Santos F.C. 6-America RJ 2	2
15-3	Santos F.C. 1-San Pablo	0	21-11	Santos F.C. 4-Comercial 1	1
1-4	Santos F.C. 4-Botafogo 2	2	26-11	Santos F.C. 2-Palmeiras 3	1
5-4	Santos F.C. 3-Atletico 1	2	29-11	Santos F.C. 1-Corinthians 1	0
10-4	Santos F.C. 6-America 1	1	3-12	Santos F.C. 4-Noroeste 2	2
13-4	Santos F.C. 1- Vasco 2	0	6-12	Santos F.C. 7-XV de Piracicaba 2	3
1-6	Santos F.C. 8-Basel 2	3	10-12	Santos F.C. 6-Ferroviaria 2	2
3-6	Santos F.C. 6-Wolfsburg 3	2	13-12	Santos F.C. 4-San Pablo 1	1
4-6	Santos F.C. 4-Aunterpia 4	0	16-12	Sind. Atletas SP 4-Sindic. Atl RJ 1	1
7-6	Santos F.C. 6-Racing FRA 1	1	19-12	Santos F.C. 1-Bahia 1	0
9-6	Santos F.C. 6-Olimpique 2	2	20-12	Santos F.C. 5-Bahia 1	0
11-6	Santos F.C. 3-Israel 1	1			
13-6	Santos F.C. 5-Racing FRA 4	1		**1962**	
15-6	Santos F.C. 6-Benfica 3	2	3-1	Santos F.C. 0-Botafogo 3	0
18-6	Santos F.C. 2-Juventus 0	1	7-1	Santos F.C. 6-Barcelona ECU 2	2
21-6	Santos F.C. 5-Roma 0	2	14-1	Santos F.C. 6-LDU 3	3
24-6	Santos F.C. 4-Inter 1	1	17-1	Santos F.C. 5-Alianza 1	0
26-6	Santos F.C. 8-Karksrhurer 6	3	20-1	Santos F.C. 5-Universitario 2	1
28-6	Santos F.C. 3-AEK 0 1	0	24-1	Santos F.C. 5-Sp.Cristal 1	1
30-6	Santos F.C. 3-Panathinaikos 2	2	27-1	Santos F.C. 3-Municipal 2	1
4-7	Santos F.C. 1-Olimpiakos 2	0	31-1	Santos F.C. 3-Nacional 2	1
23-7	Santos F.C. 0-Taubate 0	0	3-2	Santos F.C. 8-Racing ARG 3	1
30-7	Santos F.C. 2-Palmeiras 1	0	6-2	Santos F.C. 1-River Plate 2	0
6-8	Santos F.C. 4-Jabaquara 0	1	9-2	Santos F.C. 2-Gimnasia Esgrima 2	0
9-8	Santos F.C. 3-Guarani 1	1	14-2	Santos F.C. 3-BRAZIL X1 1	1
13-8	Santos F.C. 7-Noroeste 1	0	18-2	Santos F.C. 4-Municipal BOL 3	0
16-8	Santos F.C. 5-Corinthians 1	1	21-2	Santos F.C. 6-Municipal BOL 1	0
19-8	Santos F.C. 6-XV de Piracicaba 1	3	28-2	Santos F.C. 9-Cerro Porteño 1	2
25-8	Santos F.C. 0-Nacional 1	0	18-3	Santos F.C. 5-Palmeiras 3	2
30-8	Santos F.C. 8-Olimpico 0	5	21-4	BRAZIL 6-Paraguay 0	1
3-9	Santos F.C. 6-San Pablo 3	4	24-4	BRAZIL 4-Paraguay 0	0

Date	Match result	Pelé	Date	Match result	Pelé
6-5	BRAZIL 2-Portugal 1	0	2-2	Santos F.C. 2-Alianza 1	1
9-5	BRAZIL 1-Portugal 0	1	6-2	Santos F.C. 3-Universidad 4	2
12-5	BRAZIL 3-Wales 1	1	10-2	Santos F.C. 5-Talcahuano 0	2
16-5	BRAZIL 3-Wales 1	2	16-2	Santos F.C. 2-Vasco-RJ 2	2
30-5 WC	**BRAZIL 2-Mexico 0**	**1**	20-2	Santos F.C. 6-Portuguesa 3	2
2-6 WC	**BRAZIL 0-Czechoslovakia 0**	**0**	3-3	Santos F.C. 2-Corinthians 0	2
25-7	Santos F.C. 2-Wolsvagen 0	0	7-3	Santos F.C. 6-San Pablo 2	3
5-8	Santos F.C. 2-Prudentina 0	1	16-3	Santos F.C. 5-Olaria 1	0
8-8	Santos F.C. 2-Juventus 0	0	19-3	Santos F.C. 4-Botafogo 3	1
12-8	Santos F.C. 4-Palmeiras 2	1	23-3	Santos F.C. 2-Fluminense 4	1
19-8	Santos F.C. 5-Jabaquara 1	3	31-3	Santos F.C. 1-Botafogo 3	0
26-8	Santos F.C. 1-Guarani 1	1	2-4	Santos F.C. 5-Botafogo 0	2
30-8	Santos F.C. 3-Peñarol 0	2	13-4	BRAZIL 2-Argentina 3	0
2-9	Santos F.C. 3-San Pablo 3	3	16-4	BRAZIL 4-Argentina 1	3
5-9	Santos F.C. 5-Botafogo 2	2	21-4	BRAZIL 0-Portugal 1	0
15-9	Santos F.C. 7-Ferroviaria 2	4	28-4	BRAZIL 3-France 2	3
19-9	Santos F.C. 3-Benfica 2	2	2-5	BRAZIL 0-Holland 1	0
23-9	Santos F.C. 5-Corinthians 2	1	5-5	BRAZIL 2-West Germany 1	1
26-9	Santos F.C. 4-Noroeste 0	2	12-5	BRAZIL 0-Italy 3	0
30-9	Santos F.C. 3-Comercial 1	1	29-5	Santos F.C. 3-Nierdesanschen 2	1
6-10	Santos F.C. 2-Portuguesa 3	1	2-6	Santos F.C. 2-Schalke-04 1	1
11-10	Santos F.C. 5-Benfica 2	3	5-6	Santos F.C. 5-Eintracht 2	4
17-10	Santos F.C. 5-Racing FRA 2	2	8-6	Santos F.C. 3-Stuttgart 1	1
20-10	Santos F.C. 3-Hamburgo 3	2	12-6	Santos F.C. 0-Barcelona ESP 2	0
22-10	Santos F.C. 4-Sheffield Wednesday 2	1	15-6	Santos F.C. 4-Roma 3	2
27-10	Santos F.C. 3-Taubate 0	1	19-6	Santos F.C. 0-Inter 2	0
31-10	Santos F.C. 5-Guarani 0	3	22-6	Santos F.C. 0-Milan 4	0
4-11	Santos F.C. 2-Corinthians 1	1	26-6	Santos F.C. 3-Juventus 5	1
7-11	Santos F.C. 3-Juventus 0	1	21-7	Santos F.C. 4-Noroeste 3	4
11-11	Santos F.C. 1-Noroeste 1	0	24-7	Santos F.C. 1-Portuguesa 1	0
14-11	Santos F.C. 3-Palmeiras 0	1	28-7	Santos F.C. 5-Jabaquara 2	1
18-11	Santos F.C. 1-XV de Piricacaba	0	31-7	Santos F.C. 2- Guaratingueta 2	1
21-11	Santos F.C. 4-Portuguesa 1	2	4-8	Santos F.C. 2-Guarani 1	1
25-11	Santos F.C. 1-Ferroviaria 1	0	7-8	Santos F.C. 1-Palmeiras 1	0
28-11	Santos F.C. 6-Comercial 2	2	15-8	Santos F.C. 1-San Pablo 4	1
2-12	Santos F.C. 8-Jabuaquara 2	4	18-8	Santos F.C. 0-XV de Piracicaba 0	0
5-12	Santos F.C. 5-San Pablo 2	1	22-8	Santos F.C. 1-Botafogo 1	1
10-12	Santos F.C. 2- USSR1	1	1-9	Santos F.C. 4-Botafogo 0	3
12-12	Santos F.C. 1-Botafogo 0	0	4-9	Santos F.C. 1-Ferroviaria 4	1
15-12	Santos F.C. 4-Prudetina 0	2	11-9	Santos F.C. 3-Boca Jrs 2	0
19-12	Sao Paulo X1 4- Rio X1 6	2	18-9	Santos F.C. 2-Boca Jrs 1	1
			22-9	Santos F.C. 2-Prudentina 2	1
	1963		25-9	Santos F.C. 3-Corinthians 1	3
9-1	Santos F.C. 3-Sel.Sergipana 2	2	29-9	Santos F.C. 2-Juventus 1	0
12-1	Santos F.C. 1-Sport 1	0	2-10	Santos F.C. 3-Botafogo1	1
16-1	Santos F.C. 4-Sport 0	0	5-10	Santos F.C. 4-Noroeste 2	1
23-1	Santos F.C. 2-Colo-Colo 1	2	16-10	Santos F.C. 4-Prudentina 0	3
30-1	Santos F.C. 8-Municipal 3	3	24-10	Santos F.C. 2-Milan 4	2

Date	Match result	Pelé	Date	Match result	Pelé
27-10	Santos F.C. 2-Portuguesa 3	1	6-12	Santos F.C. 7-Corinthians 4	4
30-10	Santos F.C. 3-Commercial 0	2	9-12	Santos F.C. 6-San Benito 0	3
2-11	Santos F.C. 2-San Benito 3	1	13-12	Santos F.C. 3-Portuguesa 2	0
7-11	Santos F.C. 0-Juventus 0	0	16-12	Santos F.C. 4-Flamengo 1	3
			19-12	Santos F.C. 0-Flamengo 0	0

1964

1965

Date	Match result	Pelé	Date	Match result	Pelé
16-1	Santos F.C. 3-Gremio 1	1			
19-1	Santos F.C. 4-Gremio 3	3	10-1	Santos F.C. 2-Botafogo 3	0
25-1	Santos F.C. 6-Bahia 0	2	13-1	Santos F.C. 2-Universidad 1	1
28-1	Santos F.C. 2-Bahia 0	2	16-1	Santos F.C. 6-Czechoslovakia 4	3
1-2	Santos F.C. 1-Independiente 5	0	22-1	Santos F.C. 2-River 3	1
6-2	Santos F.C. 0-Peñarol 5	0	29-1	Santos F.C. 3-Colo-Colo 2	0
22-2	Santos F.C. 3-Sport Boys 2	2	2-2	Santos F.C. 3-Universidad CHI 0	0
25-2	Santos F.C. 3-Alianza 2	0	4-2	Santos F.C. 1-River 0	0
28-2	Santos F.C. 2-Colo-Colo 3	0	9-2	Santos F.C. 4-River 3	2
1-3	Santos F.C. 3-Godoy Cruz ARG 2	0	13-2	Santos F.C. 5-Universidad 1	3
8-3	Santos F.C. 2-Talleres -Cba- 1	0	19-2	Santos F.C. 2-Universitario PER 1	0
18-3	Santos F.C. 3-Corinthians 0	1	21-2	Santos F.C. 3-Caracas 1	3
22-3	Santos F.C. 1-Fluminense 0	0	23-2	Santos F.C. 4-Independiente 0	2
25-4	Santos F.C. 3-Botafogo 1	1	26-2	Santos F.C. 1-Universidad 0	1
1-5	Santos F.C. 2-Flamengo 3	1	6-3	Santos F.C. 2-Universitario 1	1
5-5	Santos F.C. 4-Boca Juniors 3	1	10-3	Santos F.C. 4-Portuguesa 1	0
7-5	Santos F.C. 2-Racing 1	1	25-3	Santos F.C. 5-Peñarol 4	1
10-5	Santos F.C. 1-Colon 2	1	28-3	Santos F.C. 2-Peñarol 3	0
30-5	BRAZIL 5-England 1	1	31-3	Santos F.C. 1-Peñarol 2	1
3-7	BRAZIL 0-Argentina 3	0	4-4	Santos F.C. 0-Vasco 3	0
5-7	Santos F.C. 1-America SP 2	1	11-4	Santos F.C. 2-Botafogo 3	0
7-7	BRAZIL 4-Portugal 1	1	15-4	Santos F.C. 4-Corinthians 4	4
19-8	Santos F.C. 6-Guarani 1	1	18-4	Santos F.C. 5-Fluminense 2	1
23-8	Santos F.C. 2-Palmeiras 1	1	21-4	Santos F.C. 2-America 0	0
23-9	Santos F.C. 1-San Benito 1	1	29-4	Santos F.C. 9-Remo 4	5
27-9	Santos F.C. 3-Portuguesa 4	2	2-5	Santos F.C. 6-Bahia 1	1
30-9	Santos F.C. 1-Corinthians 1	1	5-5	Santos F.C. 3-Bahia 1	0
4-10	Santos F.C. 3-America 1	1	8-5	Santos F.C. 6-Don Bosco 2	3
7-10	Santos F.C. 1-Colo-Colo 3	1	11-5	Santos F.C. 4-Comercial 1	3
11-10	Santos F.C. 3-San Pablo 2	1	14-5	Santos F.C. 2-Olimpia 2	1
14-10	Santos F.C. 3-Comercial 2	1	16-5	Santos F.C. 11-Maringa 1	2
18-10	Santos F.C. 4-Atletico MG 1	2	2-6	BRAZIL 5-Belgium 0	3
28-10	Santos F.C. 8-Prudentina 1	4	6-6	BRAZIL 0-Argentina 0	0
1-11	Santos F.C. 6-XV de Piracicaba 3	3	9-6	BRAZIL 3-Algeria 0	1
4-11	Santos F.C. 3-Palmeiras 2	1	17-6	BRAZIL 0-Portugal 0	0
7-11	Santos F.C. 2-Palmeiras 3	0	24-6	BRAZIL 2-Sweden 1	1
10-11	Santos F.C. 4-Palmeiras 0	0	30-6	BRAZIL 3-USSR 0	2
15-11	Santos F.C. 0-Ferroviaria 0	0	4-7	Santos F.C. 6-Noroeste 2	5
18-11	Santos F.C. 1-Guarani 5	0	14-7	Santos F.C. 3-Ferroviaria 1	2
21-11	Santos F.C. 11-Botafogo 0	8	18-7	Santos F.C. 5-Comercial 3	3
29-11	Santos F.C. 3-Noroeste 0	1	21-7	Santos F.C. 6-CRB 0	2
2-12	Santos F.C. 5-Juventus 2	2	25-7	Santos F.C. 3-San Antonio 1	1

Pelé is beseiged by autograph hunters on his arrival in England for the 1966 World Cup.

Date	Match result	Pelé	Date	Match result	Pelé
29-7	Santos F.C. 1-San Pablo 1	0	7-11	Santos F.C. 2-XV de Piracicaba 0	0
1-8	Santos F.C. 2-Portuguesa 0	1	10-11	Santos F.C. 1-Palmeiras 1	1
4-8	Santos F.C. 4-Boca 1	2	14-11	Santos F.C. 4-Corinthians 2	1
8-8	Santos F.C. 2-River 1	0	21-11	BRAZIL 2-USSR2	1
12-8	Santos F.C. 3-Prudentina 1	3	25-11	Santos F.C. 5-Botafogo 0	4
15-8	Santos F.C. 4-Portuguesa 0	3	27-11	Santos F.C. 1-Juventus 0	3
22-8	Santos F.C. 4-Corinthians 3	2	4-12	Santos F.C. 2-Guarani 0	1
23-8	Santos F.C. 7-Botafogo 1	3	8-12	Santos F.C. 1-Vasco 0	1
4-9	Santos F.C. 3-Juventus 1	2	12-12	Santos F.C. 0-Palmeiras 5	0
8-9	Santos F.C. 7-Guarani 0	4			
11-9	Santos F.C. 1-Selección Minera 2	0		**1966**	
15-9	Santos F.C. 0-Palmeiras 1	0	9-1	Santos F.C. 7-SC Abidjan 1	2
19-9	Santos F.C. 4-Ferroviaria 2	0	13-1	Santos F.C. 2- Tucumana X1 0	1
22-9	Santos F.C. 3-Noroeste 0	1	16-1	Santos F.C. 1-Alianza2	1
3-10	Santos F.C. 4-San Benito 2	1	19-1	Santos F.C. 1-Botafogo 2	1
7-10	Santos F.C. 2-Comercial 0	1	22-1	Santos F.C. 0-Botafogo 3	0
10-10	Santos F.C. 3-Portuguesa 0	1	26-1	Santos F.C. 2-Universitario 2	1
13-10	Santos F.C. 0-San Pablo 0	0	28-1	Santos F.C. 4-Alianza 1	1
24-10	Santos F.C. 4-America 0	3	6-2	Santos F.C. 1-Melgar1	0
27-10	Santos F.C. 1-Portuguesa 0	0	9-2	Santos F.C. 6-Universidad CHI 1	3
31-10	Santos F.C. 5-Prudentina 2	5	11-2	Santos F.C. 1-R. Central 0	0
3-11	Santos F.C. 4-Palmeiras2	0	13-2	Santos F.C. 1-Sarmiento 1	0

Date	Match result	Pelé	Date	Match result	Pelé
17-2	Santos F.C. 2-Colo-Colo 2	1	21-2	Santos F.C. 6.U.Catolica 2	4
29-3	Santos F.C. 3-Cruzeiro 4	1	25-2	Santos F.C. 4-Alianza 1	1
31-3	Santos F.C. 1-Atletico 0	1	28-2	Santos F.C. 2-Colo-Colo1	0
19-5	BRAZIL 1-Chile 0	0	8-3	Santos F.C. 1-Atletico MG 0	0
4-6	BRAZIL 4-Peru 0	1	12-3	Santos F.C. 1-Gremio1	1
8-6	BRAZIL 2-Poland 0	0	15-3	Santos F.C. 5-Internacional 1	1
12-6	BRAZIL 2-Czechoslovakia 1	2	19-3	Santos F.C. 1-Flamengo 0	0
15-6	BRAZIL 2-Czechoslovakia 2	1	22-3	Santos F.C. 0-Botafogo 0	0
21-6	BRAZIL 5-Atletico Madrid 3	3	26-3	Santos F.C. 1-Vasco 2	1
25-6	BRAZIL 1-Scotland 0	0	1-4	Santos F.C. 1-San Pablo 1	1
30-6	BRAZIL 3-Sweden 2	0	8-4	Santos F.C. 1-Palmeiras 2	0
4-7	BRAZIL 4-AIK-Sweden 2	2	15-4	Santos F.C. 2-Portugal 2	2
6-7	BRAZIL 3-Malmo 1	2	19-4	Santos F.C. 1-Cruzeiro 3	0
12-7 WC	**BRAZIL 2-Bulgaria 0**	**1**	23-4	Santos F.C. 3-Bangu 0	1
19-7 WC	**BRAZIL 1-Portugal 3**	**0**	30-4	Santos F.C. 0-Fluminense 3	0
17-8	Santos F.C. 1-Juventus 1	0	3-5	Santos F.C. 3-Ferroviario 0	1
21-8	Santos F.C. 4-Benfica 0	1	7-5	Santos F.C. 3-Sel de Ilheus 1	1
24-8	Santos F.C. 1-AEK 0	0	10-5	Santos F.C. 5-Santa Cruz 0	1
28-8	Santos F.C. 1-Toluca 1	0	13-5	Santos F.C. 1-Corinthians 1	1
30-8	Santos F.C. 2-Atlante 2	1	15-5	Santos F.C. 0-Olimpia 0	0
5-9	Santos F.C. 4-Inter 1	1	23-5	Santos F.C. 3-Portugal 2	1
11-9	Santos F.C. 3-Prudentina 1	2	25-5	Santos F.C. 5-Brazil Selection	1
14-9	Santos F.C. 0-Portuguesa 2	0	28-5	Santos F.C. 4-Senegal 1	3
8-10	Santos F.C. 3-Corinthians 0	0	31-5	Santos F.C. 4-Gabao 0	1
13-10	Santos F.C. 7-Comercial 5	0	2-6	Santos F.C. 2-Congo 1	1
16-10	Santos F.C. 2-San Benito 2	1	4-6	Santos F.C. 2-Costa Martin 1	1
23-10	Santos F.C. 3-Portugal 0	1	7-6	Santos F.C. 3-Congo 2	3
26-10	Santos F.C. 4-Noroeste 1	2	13-6	Santos F.C. 5-T.S.V 4	2
30-10	Santos F.C. 1-San Pablo 2	1	17-6	Santos F.C. 2-Mantova 1	1
5-11	Santos F.C. 3-Juventus 0	1	20-6	Santos F.C. 1-Venecia 0	0
9-11	Santos F.C. 2-Nautico 0	1	24-6	Santos F.C. 5-Lecce 1	3
13-11	Santos F.C. 3-Bragantino 2	3	27-6	Santos F.C. 1-Fiorentina 1	0
17-11	Santos F.C. 3-Nautico 5	0	29-6	Santos F.C. 3-Roma 1	1
19-11	Santos F.C. 4-Nautico 1	0	9-7	Santos F.C. 4-San Benito 3	1
23-11	Santos F.C. 2-Palmeiras 0	0	15-7	Santos F.C. 4-Juventus 0	1
26-11	Santos F.C. 2-Guarani 1	0	23-7	Santos F.C. 2-Guarani 1	0
30-11	Santos F.C. 2-Cruzeiro 6	0	6-8	Santos F.C. 1-Palmeiras 1	1
4-12	Santos F.C. 3-Botafogo 1	1	19-8	Santos F.C. 4-Comercial 1	1
7-12	Santos F.C. 2-Cruzeiro 3	1	22-8	Santos F.C. 3-Portugal 1	0
			26-8	Santos F.C. 0-Inter 0	0
	1967		28-8	Santos F.C. 1-Spain 4	0
15-1	Santos F.C. 4-Mar del Plata 1	0	29-8	Santos F.C. 2-Malaga 1	0
19-1	Santos F.C. 4-River 0 1	0	8-10	Santos F.C. 3-America SP 2	1
22-1	Santos F.C. 1-Millonarios 2	0	15-10	Santos F.C. 2-San Pablo 2	1
25-1	Santos F.C. 3-Atletico Jrs 3	0	22-10	Santos F.C. 3-Prudentina 1	2
29-1	Santos F.C. 2-River 4	2	29-10	Santos F.C. 4-Palmeiras 1	1
7-2	Santos F.C. 1-Universidad 1	0	1-11	Santos F.C. 4-Juventus 1	2
10-2	Santos F.C. 2-Vazas 2	1	4-11	Santos F.C. 1- Maranhese 0	0
17-2	Santos F.C. 2-Peñarol 0	0	7-11	Santos F.C. 5-Fortaleza 0	1

Date	Match result	Pelé	Date	Match result	Pelé
11-11	Santos F.C. 1-Comercial 1	1	12-7	Santos F.C. 3-New York 5	0
19-11	Santos F.C. 1-San Benito 1	0	14-7	Santos F.C. 3-Washington 1	0
26-11	Santos F.C. 0-Portuguesa 0	0	17-7	Santos F.C. 4-Sel. Colombia 2	1
3-12	Santos F.C. 1-Guarani1	1	25-7	Santos F.C. 4-Paraguay 0	2
10-12	Santos F.C. 2-Corinthians 1	1	28-7	BRAZIL 0-Paraguay 1	0
17-12	Santos F.C. 3-Portugal 1	1	4-8	Santos F.C. 0-Ferroviaria 0	-
21-12	Santos F.C. 2-San Pablo 1	0	6-8	Santos F.C. 3-Paysandu 1	1
			9-8	Santos F.C. 3-Fast AM 0	1
	1968		11-8	Santos F.C. 2-Nacional 1	1
13-1	Santos F.C. 4-Czech X1 1	0	15-8	Santos F.C. 2-River Plate 1	0
23-1	Santos F.C. 4-Vazas 0	1	18-8	Santos F.C. 4-Benfica 2	0
2-2	Santos F.C. 4-Colo-Colo 1	0	20-8	Santos F.C. 2-Nacional 2	1
3-3	Santos F.C. 4-Ferroviaria 1	2	25-8	Santos F.C. 1-Boca Juniors 1	0
6-3	Santos F.C. 0-Corinthians 2	0	28-8	Santos F.C. 6-Atlanta Chiefs 2	3
9-3	Santos F.C. 5-Botafogo 1	1	30-8	Santos F.C. 3-Oakland 1	2
16-3	Santos F.C. 3-Portugal 0	1	1-9	Santos F.C. 3-Benfica 3	0
19-3	Santos F.C. 3-Goias 3	1	15-9	Santos F.C. 2-Flamengo 0	0
23-3	Santos F.C. 4-Juventus 0	2	18-9	Santos F.C. 0-Palmeiras 0	0
27-3	Santos F.C. 5-San Pablo 2	2	21-9	Santos F.C. 2 –Fluminense 1	1
31-3	Santos F.C. 4-America 3	2	25-9	Santos F.C. 1-Bangu 1	0
7-4	Santos F.C. 8-Comercial 2	2	29-9	Santos F.C. 2-Vasco 3	0
10-4	Santos F.C. 2-Guarani 0	0	6-10	Santos F.C. 2-Corinthians 1	1
13-4	Santos F.C. 1-Palmeiras 0	0	10-10	Santos F.C. 9-Bahia 2	3
18-4	Santos F.C. 1-San Benito 0	0	13-10	Santos F.C. 2-Cruzeiro 0	1
21-4	Santos F.C. 2-Corinthians 0	1	16-10	Santos F.C. 2-Portugal 0	0
24-4	Santos F.C. 3-Juventus 2	2	20-10	Santos F.C. 0-San Pablo 0	0
28-4	Santos F.C. 1- Piracicaba 0	0	23-10	Santos F.C. 3-Internacional 1	1
1-5	Santos F.C. 0-Ferroviaria 0	0	27-10	Santos F.C. 3-Nautico 0	1
4-5	Santos F.C. 1-Portugal 0	0	31-10	BRAZIL 1-Mexico 2	0
8-5	Santos F.C. 0-Flamengo 0	0	3-11	BRAZIL 2-Mexico 1	1
12-5	Santos F.C. 3-Botafogo 1	0	6-11	BRAZIL 2-FIFA X1 1	0
15-5	Santos F.C. 1-Portugal 2	0	10-11	Paulista X1 3-Carioca X1 2	1
19-5	Santos F.C. 3-Palmeiras 1	1	13-11	BRAZIL 2-Curitiba 1	0
23-5	Santos F.C. 0-Boca Juniors 1	0	19-11	Santos F.C. 2-Racing 0	1
29-5	Santos F.C. 5-Comercial 0	1	21-11	Santos F.C. 1-Peñarol 0	0
1-6	Santos F.C. 3-San Pablo 1	0	24-11	Santos F.C. 2-Atletico 2	1
9-6	Santos F.C. 2-Cagliari 1	0	27-11	Santos F.C. 3-Gremio 1	1
12-6	Santos F.C. 2-Alessandria 0	1	1-12	Santos F.C. 2-Botafogo 3	0
15-6	Santos F.C. 4-Zurique 5	1	4-12	Santos F.C. 2-Internacional 1	1
17-6	Santos F.C. 3-Saarbruken 0	1	8-12	Santos F.C. 3-Palemeiras 0	0
21-6	Santos F.C. 4-Napoli 2	1	10-12	Santos F.C. 2-Vasco 1	1
26-6	Santos F.C. 6-Napoli 2	2	14-12	BRAZIL 2-West Germany 2	0
28-6	Santos F.C. 5-Napoli 2	2	17-12	BRAZIL 3-Yugoslavia 3	1
30-6	Santos F.C. 3-St. Louis 2	1			
4-7	Santos F.C. 4-Kansas 1	1		**1969**	
6-7	Santos F.C. 4-Necaxa 3	1	17-1	Santos F.C. 3-Point-Nore 0	1
8-7	Santos F.C. 7-Boston 1	1	19-1	Santos F.C. 3-Congo 2	2
10-7	Santos F.C. 1-Cleveland 2	0	21-1	Santos F.C. 2-Congo 0	0

Date	Match result	Pelé	Date	Match result	Pelé
23-1	Santos F.C. 2-Congo 3	2	15-9	Santos F.C. 4-Radnick 4	1
26-1	Santos F.C. 2-Nigeria 2	2	17-9	Santos F.C. 3-Atl. Madrid 1	0
1-2	Santos F.C. 2-Austria 0	0	19-9	Santos F.C. 1-Zeljesnicar 1	1
4-2	Santos F.C. 2- Medio Orient 1	0	22-9	Santos F.C. 3-Stoke City 2	2
6-2	Santos F.C. 2-Hearts of Oak 0	1	24-9	Santos F.C. 7-Geneva 1	2
9-2	Santos F.C. 1-Algeria 1	0	28-9	Santos F.C. 1-Gremio 2	1
14-2	Santos F.C. 6- Piracicaba 2	2	12-10	Santos F.C. 1-Palmeiras 2	1
22-2	Santos F.C. 4-Portugal 1	1	15-10	Santos F.C. 6-Portugal 2	4
26-2	Santos F.C. 3-Ferroviaria 0	2	22-10	Santos F.C. 3-Curitiba 1	2
2-3	Santos F.C. 2-Paulista 1	0	26-10	Santos F.C. 0-Fluminense 0	0
5-3	Santos F.C. 0-Guarani 1	0	1-11	Santos F.C. 4-Flamengo 1	1
9-3	Santos F.C. 3-San Pablo 0	1	4-11	Santos F.C. 1-Corinthians 4	0
12-3	Santos F.C. 4-San Benito 2	2	9-11	Santos F.C. 1-San Pablo 1	0
15-3	Santos F.C. 2-Juventus 1	1	12-11	Santos F.C. 4-Santa Cruz 0	2
19-3	Santos F.C. 2-America SP 1	0	14-11	Santos F.C. 3-Botafogo 0	1
22-3	Santos F.C. 2-Palmeiras 3	2	16-11	Santos F.C. 1-Bahia 1	0
26-3	Santos F.C. 4-Botafogo 1	1	19-11	Santos F.C. 2-Vasco 1	1
29-3	Santos F.C. 3-Portugal 1	3	23-11	Santos F.C. 0-Atletico Mg 2	0
7-4	BRAZIL 2-Peru 1	0	29-11	Santos F.C. 1-Racing 2	0
9-4	BRAZIL 3-Peru 2	1	2-12	Santos F.C. 1-Peñarol 2	1
13-4	Santos F.C. 0-Corinthians 2	0	4-12	Santos F.C. 1-Estudianets 3	0
23-4	Santos F.C. 3-Portugal 2	0	6-12	Santos F.C. 1-Velez 1	1
27-4	Santos F.C. 1-America Sp 1	1	9-12	Santos F.C. 0-Racing 2	0
30-4	Santos F.C. 1-Portuguesa 2	1	11-12	Santos F.C. 2-Peñarol 0	1
3-5	Santos F.C. 0-Palmeiras 1	0	14-12	Sel. Paulista 2-Sel.Bahiana 1	0
11-5	Santos F.C. 1-Ferroviaria 2	1	17-12	Sel. Paulista 2-Sel.Minera 1	1
21-5	Santos F.C. 1-San Pablo 0	0	21-12	Sel. Paulista 0-Sel.Carioca 0	0
25-5	Santos F.C. 1-Corinthians 1	0			
28-5	Santos F.C. 3-Paulista 2	1		**1970**	
31-5	Santos F.C. 5-Botafogo 1	4	10-1	Santos F.C. 3-Curitiba 1	1
8-6	Santos F.C. 3-Corinthians 1	2	16-1	Santos F.C. 2-Boca Jrs 2	1
12-6	BRAZIL 2 –England 1	0	18-1	Santos F.C. 2-Talleres 0	1
18-6	Santos F.C. 3-Palmeiras 0	1	21-1	Santos F.C. 3-Colo-Colo 4	2
21-6	Santos F.C. 0-San Pablo 0	0	24-1	Santos F.C. 4-Universitario 1	0
24-6	Santos F.C. 1-Inter 0	0	28-1	Santos F.C. 2-Dinamo 2	0
6-7	BRAZIL 4-Bahia 0	1	30-1	Santos F.C. 2-U de Chile 0	2
9-7	Santos F.C. 8-Sergipana 2	0	4-2	Santos F.C. 7-America Mex 0	3
13-7	Santos F.C. 6-Pernambuco 1	1	7-2	Santos F.C. 3-U. De Chile 2	2
1-8	BRAZIL 2-Millonarios 0	0	4-3	BRAZIL 0-Argentina 2	0
6-8	BRAZIL 2-Colombia 0	0	8-3	BRAZIL 2-Argentina 1	1
10-8	BRAZIL 5-Venezuela 0	2	14-3	BRAZIL 1-Bangu 1	0
17-8	BRAZIL 3-Paraguay 0	0	22-3	BRAZIL 5-Chile 0	2
21-8	BRAZIL 6-Colombia 2	1	26-3	BRAZIL 2-Chile 1	0
24-8	BRAZIL 6-Venezuela 0	2	5-4	BRAZIL 4-Sel.Amazonas 1	1
31-8	BRAZIL 1-Paraguay 0	1	12-4	BRAZIL 0-Paraguay 0	0
3-9	BRAZIL 1-Atletico MG 2	1	19-4	BRAZIL 3-Sel.Minera 1	0
10-9	Santos F.C. 3-Estrella 3	1	26-4	BRAZIL 0-Bulgaria 0	0
12-9	Santos F.C. 1-Dinamo 1	0	29-4	BRAZIL 1-Austria 0	0

12. THE PELÉ GOALS, Every one of them!

Date	Match result	Pelé	Date	Match result	Pelé
6-5	BRAZIL 3-Guadalajara 0	1	29-11	Santos F.C. 3-San Pablo 2	1
17-5	BRAZIL 5- Comb de Leon 2	2	2-12	Santos F.C. 5-Bahia 1	1
24-5	BRAZIL 3-Irapuato 0	0	6-12	Santos F.C. 0-Santa Cruz 1	0
3-6 WC	**BRAZIL 4-Czechosl'kia 1**	**1**	10-12	Santos F.C. 4-Hong Kong 0	2
7-6 WC	**BRAZIL 1-England 0**	**0**	11-12	Santos F.C. 4-Hong Kong 0	3
10-6 WC	**BRAZIL 3-Romania 2**	**2**	13-12	Santos F.C. 5-Hong Kong 2	1
14-6 WC	**BRAZIL 4-Peru 2**	**0**	17-12	Santos F.C. 4- Hong Kong 0	2
17-6 WC	**BRAZIL 3-Uruguay 1**	**0**			
21-6 WC	**BRAZIL 4-Italy 1**	**1**		**1971**	
5-7	Santos F.C. 2-Palmeiras 0	0	13-1	Santos F.C. 3-Cochabamba 2	1
8-7	Santos F.C. 0-Ferroviaria 1	0	16-1	Santos F.C. 4-Bolivar 0	2
12-7	Santos F.C. 2-San Pablo 3	0	19-1	Santos F.C. 4-Atl.Marte 1	0
19-7	Santos F.C. 5-Guarani 2	2	23-1	Santos F.C. 4-Martinica 1	1
22-7	Santos F.C. 3-Goias 1	1	26-1	Santos F.C. 2-Guadalupe 1	1
25-7	Santos F.C. 2-Portugal 1	1	28-1	Santos F.C. 4-Transavaal 1	1
29-7	Santos F.C. 9-Sergipe 1	1	31-1	Santos F.C. 1-Jamaica 0	0
2-8	Santos F.C. 2-Corinthians 2	1	2-2	Santos F.C. 1-Chelsea 0	0
5-8	Santos F.C. 5-Guarani 1	1	5-2	Santos F.C. 3-Millonarios 2	2
9-8	Santos F.C. 2-San Pablo 1	0	7-2	Santos F.C. 3-Nacional 1	1
12-8	Santos F.C. 5-Ferroviaria 0	1	10-2	Santos F.C. 1-Dep.Cali 2	1
16-8	Santos F.C. 1-Ponte Preta 0	0	14-2	Santos F.C. 2-Alianza 1	0
19-8	Santos F.C. 0-Botafogo 0	0	17-2	Santos F.C. 2-Haiti 0	0
22-8	Santos F.C. 0-Portugal 1	0	3-3	Santos F.C. 4-Botafogo 0	1
26-8	Santos F.C. 2-San Benito 2	1	7-3	Santos F.C. 1-Ferroviaria 4	1
30-8	Santos F.C. 1-Corinthians 1	0	28-3	Santos F.C. 0-Palmeiras 2	1
2-9	Santos F.C. 2-Gremio 0	1	31-3	Santos F.C. 0 Olympique 0	0
6-9	Santos F.C. 1-Palmeiras 1	0	4-4	Santos F.C. 2-Bahia 3	0
9-9	Santos F.C. 0-Cruzeiro 0	0	7-4	Santos F.C. 2-Galicia 0	1
12-9	Santos F.C. 5-Galicia 1	1	11-4	Santos F.C. 2-Corinthians 4	1
15-9	Santos F.C. 4-All Star 3	0	18-4	Santos F.C. 0-Paulista 0	0
18-9	Santos F.C. 7-Wash. Darts 4	4	21-4	Santos F.C. 1-San Pablo 0	0
20-9	Santos F.C. 2-Guadalajara 1	1	25-4	Santos F.C. 0-Ponte Preta 0	0
22-9	Santos F.C. 2-West Ham 2	2	28-4	Santos F.C. 1-Juventus 1	0
24-9	Santos F.C. 2- Santa Fe 1	0	2-5	Santos F.C. 2-Botafogo 1	1
30-9	BRAZIL 2-Mexico 1	0	9-5	Santos F.C. 1-Paulista 0	0
4-10	BRAZIL 5-Chile 1	1	12-5	Santos F.C. 1-San Benito 0	0
14-10	Santos F.C. 1-Atletico MG 1	1	16-5	Santos F.C. 0-San Pablo 0	0
17-10	Santos F.C. 1-Vasco 5	0	20-5	Santos F.C. 1-Juventus 1	0
22-10	Santos F.C. 1-Ponte Preta 1	1	23-5	Santos F.C. 4-O.Petrolero 3	1
25-10	Santos F.C. 5-Sel. Angona 0	2	26-5	Santos F.C. 2-The Strongest 0	1
28-10	Santos F.C. 0-Atletico PR 1	0	30-5	Santos F.C. 1-Palmeiras 2	0
1-11	Santos F.C. 0-Corinthians 2	0	2-6	Santos F.C. 1-Guarani 0	0
8-11	Santos F.C. 2-Botafogo 2	0	6-6	Santos F.C. 1-Ferroviaria 0	0
11-11	Santos F.C. 1-Palmeiras 1	0	10-6	Santos F.C. 1-Portugal 1	1
14-11	Santos F.C. 0-Flamengo 2	0	13-6	Santos F.C. 2-Ponte Preta 1	1
18-11	Santos F.C. 1-Fluminense 0	0	20-6	Santos F.C. 3-Corinthians 3	1
21-11	Santos F.C. 0-America RJ 0	0	23-6	Santos F.C. 2-Bologna 1	1
25-11	Santos F.C. 2-Universitario 3	0	27-6	Santos F.C. 1-Bologna 1	0
			30-6	Santos F.C. 1-Bologna 0	1

Pelé uses Jairzinho as transport while celebrating his 1970 World Cup final goal.

Date	Match result	Pelé	Date	Match result	Pelé
11-7	BRAZIL 1-Austria 1	1	16-4	Santos F.C. 1-San Pablo 3	0
18-7	BRAZIL 2-Yugoslavia 2	0	23-4	Santos F.C. 0-Guarani 1	0
24-7	Santos F.C. 1-Monterrey 1	0	25-4	Santos F.C. 2-Ferroviaria 0	1
28-7	Santos F.C. 2-Jalisco 1	0	29-4	Santos F.C. 1-Napoli 0	0
30-7	Santos F.C. 3-Hannover 1	0	1-5	Santos F.C. 3-Cagliari 2	2
2-8	Santos F.C. 2-Dep.Cali 2	1	3-5	Santos F.C. 6-Fenerbahce 1	1
4-8	Santos F.C. 5-All Star 1	2	5-5	Santos F.C. 5-Taj.Sports 1	3
8-8	Santos F.C. 0-Bahia 0	0	14-5	Santos F.C. 1-Corinthians 1	0
11-8	Santos F.C. 2-Sport Boys 0	0	17-5	Santos F.C. 1- Piracicaba 0	0
14-8	Santos F.C. 3-San Pablo 1	0	21-5	Santos F.C. 3-Ponte Preta 2	1
18-8	Santos F.C. 0-Botafogo 0	0	26-5	Santos F.C. 3-Japan 0	2
22-8	Santos F.C. 0-America RJ 0	0	28-5	Santos F.C. 4-China 2	0
25-8	Santos F.C. 3-Boca Jrs 0	1	31-5	Santos F.C. 3-Hong Kong 1	1
29-8	Santos F.C. 0-Millonarios 1	0	2-6	Santos F.C. 3-South Korea 2	3
1-9	Santos F.C. 0-Gremio 1	0	4-6	Santos F.C. 4-Newcastle 2	3
5-9	Santos F.C. 1-Atletico MG 2	0	7-6	Santos F.C. 4-Carolina Hill 0	2
18-9	Santos F.C. 0-Portuguesa 0	0	10-6	Santos F.C. 6-Sel. Bangkok 1	1
23-9	Santos F.C. 1-T. Corazones 2	0	13-6	Santos F.C. 2-Coventry 2	0
26-9	Santos F.C. 1-Internacional 1	0	17-6	Santos F.C. 2-Australia 2	1
3-10	Santos F.C. 2-Atletico 1	0	21-6	Santos F.C. 3-Indonesia 2	2
7-10	Santos F.C. 0-Vasco 0	0	25-6	Santos F.C. 7-Catanzaro 1	3
10-10	Santos F.C. 0-Atletico MG 2	0	30-6	Santos F.C. 6-Boston Astros 1	2
16-10	Santos F.C. 0-Internacional 1	0	2-7	Santos F.C. 2-UNAM 0	1
20-11	Santos F.C. 4-Vasco 0	0	5-7	Santos F.C. 4-Toronto 2	0
25-11	Santos F.C. 3-America RN 1	1	7-7	Santos F.C. 5-Vancouver 0	2
4-12	Santos F.C. 2-Botafogo 0	0	9-7	Santos F.C. 5-UNAM 1	2
			11-7	Santos F.C. 4-America -Mex-2	0
	1972		23-7	Santos F.C. 0-San Pablo 2	0
8-1	Santos F.C. 2-America 1	0	30-7	Santos F.C. 1-America SP 0	0
12-1	Santos F.C. 0-Flamengo 1	0	2-8	Santos F.C. 4-Guarani 2	3
15-1	Santos F.C. 0-Palmeiras 4	0	6-8	Santos F.C. 3-Ferroviaria 0	1
30-1	Santos F.C. 3-Dep.Español 1	0	9-8	Santos F.C. 2-Juventus 1	2
2-2	Santos F.C. 1-Saprissa 1	0	13-8	Santos F.C. 0-Palmeiras 1	0
6-2	Santos F.C. 2-Medellin 2	0	15-8	Santos F.C. 2-Avai 1	0
13-2	Santos F.C. 1-Comun'es 1	1	20-8	Santos F.C. 3-Portugal 1	1
15-2	Santos F.C. 0-Olimpia 0	0	27-8	Santos F.C. 0- Piracicaba 1	0
18-2	Santos F.C. 5-Saprissa 3	1	30-8	Santos F.C. 0-Corinthians 1	0
21-2	Santos F.C. 1-Aston Villa 2	0	5-9	Santos F.C. 1-Trini./Tobago 0	1
23-2	Santos F.C. 2-Sheffield Wednesday 0	0	9-9	Santos F.C. 1-Botafogo 1	0
26-2	Santos F.C. 3-Bohemians 2	0	13-9	Santos F.C. 1-Sergipe 1	1
1-3	Santos F.C. 0-Anderlecht 0	0	17-9	Santos F.C. 0-Vitoria 1	0
3-3	Santos F.C. 2-Roma 0	0	24-9	Santos F.C. 1-Fluminense 2	0
5-3	Santos F.C. 3-Napoli 2	2	25-10	Santos F.C. 1-Palmeiras 0	1
8-3	Santos F.C. 1-America 0	0	29-10	Santos F.C. 2-Bahia 0	0
12-3	Santos F.C. 1-Portugal 0	0	12-11	Santos F.C. 0-Portugal 2	0
18-3	Santos F.C. 3-Juventus 2	0	16-11	Santos F.C. 1-Atletico 0	0
26-3	Santos F.C. 1-Palmeiras 2	0	19-11	Santos F.C. 4-Santa Cruz 2	1
30-3	Santos F.C. 2-San Benito 1	0	23-11	Santos F.C. 0-Flamengo 0	0

14. THE PELÉ GOALS, Every one of them!

Date	Match result	Pelé	Date	Match result	Pelé
26-11	Santos F.C. 4-Corinthians 0	0	12-8	Santos F.C. 0-Palmeiras 1	0
29-11	Santos F.C. 2-ABC 0	1	15-8	Santos F.C. 1-Guarani 0	1
3-12	Santos F.C. 1-Ceara 2	1	26-8	Santos F.C. 0-Portugal 0	0
9-12	Santos F.C. 2-Santa Cruz 0	0	29-8	Santos F.C. 0-Vitoria 2	0
14-12	Santos F.C. 0-Gremio 1	0	2-9	Santos F.C. 0-Palmeiras 2	0
17-12	Santos F.C. 1-Botafogo 2	0	9-9	Santos F.C. 1-Flamengo 0	0
			12-9	Santos F.C. 0-Comercial 1	0
	1973		16-9	Santos F.C. 2-Atletico 0	0
2-2	Santos F.C. 2-Vitoria 0	0	19-9	Santos F.C. 0-Atletico 0	0
9-2	Santos F.C. 3-Sel.Ryad 0	2	23-9	Santos F.C. 0-Ceara 2	0
12-2	Santos F.C. 1-Kuwait 1	1	26-9	Santos F.C. 6-America 1	3
14-2	Santos F.C. 3-Nation'l Doha 0	1	30-9	Santos F.C. 3-Nautico 0	0
16-2	Santos F.C. 7-Bahrain 1	2	3-10	Santos F.C. 3-Sergipe 0	1
18-2	Santos F.C. 5-Nation'l Doha 0	2	7-10	Santos F.C. 2-Santa Cruz 3	1
20-2	Santos F.C. 1-Hilal 0	0	14-10	Santos F.C. 1-Vasco 1	0
22-2	Santos F.C. 4-Al Nasser 1	1	17-10	Santos F.C. 0-Goias 0	0
27-2	Santos F.C. 0-Comb Bavaria 3	0	8-11	Santos F.C. 3-Portugal 2	2
4-3	Santos F.C. 2-Bordeaux 2	1	11-11	Santos F.C. 1-Atletico 0	1
6-3	Santos F.C. 1-S. Liege 0	0	14-11	Santos F.C. 1-Guarani 1	1
12-3	Santos F.C. 1-Fulham 2	1	18-11	Santos F.C. 2-Curitiba 1	1
14-3	Santos F.C. 2-Plymouth 3	1	20-11	Santos F.C. 2-Internacional 0	1
25-3	Santos F.C. 2-San Pablo 2	1	5-12	Santos F.C. 4-Huracan 0	1
4-4	Santos F.C. 6-Juventus SP 0	2	9-12	Santos F.C. 1-Palmeiras 1	0
8-4	Santos F.C. 1-Portugal 0	0	12-12	Santos F.C. 4-Gremio 0	2
18-4	Santos F.C. 1-America 0	0	17-12	Santos F.C. 1-San Pablo 0	1
22-4	Santos F.C. 1-Guarani 0	0	19-12	Garrincha X1 2-World X1 1	1
29-4	Santos F.C. 3-Corinthians 0	2			
6-5	Santos F.C. 1-Palmeiras 1	1		**1974**	
13-5	Santos F.C. 2-Botafogo 1	0	9-1	Santos F.C. 4-Palestra 1	1
20-5	Santos F.C. 5-Ponte Preta 1	2	13-1	Santos F.C. 1-Santa Cruz	1
25-5	Santos F.C. 3-Lazio 0	1	20-1	Santos F.C. 3-Botafogo 0	1
28-5	Santos F.C. 4-Lazio 2	2	23-1	Santos F.C. 5-Fortaleza 1	2
30-5	Santos F.C. 6-Baltimore 4	3	27-1	Santos F.C. 0-Gremio 1	0
1-6	Santos F.C. 1-Guadalajara 0	1	29-1	Santos F.C. 1-San Pablo 2	1
3-6	Santos F.C. 2-Guadalajara 1	1	31-1	Santos F.C. 1-Vitoria 0	0
6-6	Santos F.C. 6-Miami Toros 1	1	3-2	Santos F.C. 2-Guarani 0	1
10-6	Santos F.C. 5-Arminia B'fed 0	1	6-2	Santos F.C. 4-Goias 4	0
15-6	Santos F.C. 7-Baltimore 1	1	10-2	Santos F.C. 0-Cruzeiro 0	0
17-6	Santos F.C. 2-Rochester 1	1	22-2	Santos F.C. 2-Vila Nova 1	0
19-6	Santos F.C. 4-Baltimore 0	2	3-3	Santos F.C. 2-Uberaba 0	0
1-7	Santos F.C. 1-Tijucana 0	0	6-3	Santos F.C. 1-Caldense 0	0
4-7	Santos F.C. 1-Goias 2	0	10-3	Santos F.C. 1-Portugal 2	0
8-7	Santos F.C. 2-Botafogo 0	1	17-3	Santos F.C. 2-America 0	0
15-7	Santos F.C. 1-San Benito 0	0	20-3	Santos F.C. 3-Ceub 1	1
22-7	Santos F.C. 1-Corinthians 1	1	24-3	Santos F.C. 2-Guarani 2	2
26-7	Santos F.C. 0-Juventus 0	0	30-3	Santos F.C. 1-Nautico 1	1
29-7	Santos F.C. 0-San Pablo 0	0	3-4	Santos F.C. 2- Guarani 0	0
5-8	Santos F.C. 1-America 0	0	6-4	Santos F.C. 1-Sport 1	1
8-8	Santos F.C. 0-Portugal 1	0	13-4	Santos F.C. 1-Cruzeiro 0	0

The Greatest with The Greatest. Pelé greets Muhammad Ali at his final match for Cosmos on October 1 1977. Pele played one half for Cosmos, and the second half for Santos.

15. THE PELÉ GOALS, Every one of them!

Date	Match result	Pelé	Date	Match result	Pelé
20-4	Santos F.C. 4-Palmeiras 0	1	24-3	NY Cosmos 1-San Diego 1	0
28-4	Santos F.C. 1-Nacional 0	1			
2-5	Santos F.C. 3-Rio Negro 0	1			
19-5	Santos F.C. 1-Corinthians 1	0		**1976**	
2-6	Santos F.C. 1-San Pablo 1	0	28-3	NY Cosmos 1-Dallas T'nado 0	0
9-6	Santos F.C. 1-Atletico MG 2	0	31-3	NY Cosmos 0-San Antonio 1	1
18-7	Santos F.C. 1-Fortaleza 1	0	5-4	NY Cosmos 0-LA Aztecs 0	0
21-7	Santos F.C. 1-Vasco 2	1	8-4	NY Cosmos 5-Honda 0	0
24-7	Santos F.C. 2-Internacional 1	0	10-4	NY Cosmos 3-Seattle S'nd. 1	4
28-7	Santos F.C. 1-Cruzeiro 3	0	11-4	NY Cosmos 1-LA Aztecs 0	2
3-8	Santos F.C. 2-Noroeste 1	0	18-4	NY Cosmos 1-Miami Toros 0	1
11-8	Santos F.C. 0-Portuguesa 1	0	2-5	NY Cosmos 1-Chicago 2	0
14-8	Santos F.C. 2-Botafogo 1	0	5-5	NY Cosmos 3-Hartford Bicn. 1	1
24-8	Santos F.C. 2-Saad 3	0	8-5	NY Cosmos 1-Philadelphia 2	1
31-8	Santos F.C. 0-Spain 2	0	15-5	NY Cosmos 3-Hartford Bicn. 0	1
1-9	Santos F.C. 1-Barcelona 4	1	17-5	NY Cosmos 6-Los Angeles 0	2
3-9	Santos F.C. 3-Zaragoza 2	2	19-5	NY Cosmos 2-Boston 1	0
9-9	Santos F.C. 0-Palmeiras 0	0	23-5	America All Star 0-Italy 4	0
15-9	Santos F.C. 1-San Pablo 1	0	31-5	America All Star 1-England 3	0
18-9	Santos F.C. 1-Comercial 0	0	3-6	NY Cosmos 2-Violette 1	1
22-9	Santos F.C. 2-Guarani 2	1	6-6	NY Cosmos 1-Tampa Bay 5	0
29-9	Santos F.C. 0-Corinthians 1	0	9-6	NY Cosmos 2-Minnesota 1	0
2-10	Santos F.C. 2-Ponte Preta 0	0	12-6	NY Cosmos 3-Portland 0	0
			16-6	NY Cosmos 2-Boston 3	1
	1975		18-6	NY Cosmos 3-Toronto 0	0
15-5	NY Cosmos 2-Dallas Tornado 2	1	23-6	NY Cosmos 1-Chicago 4	0
18-6	NY Cosmos 2-Toronto 0	0	27-6	NY Cosmos 2-Washington 3	1
27-6	NY Cosmos 3-Rochester 0	1	30-6	NY Cosmos 2-Rochester 0	0
29-6	NY Cosmos 9-Washington 2	2	2-7	NY Cosmos 3-St Louis 4	0
3-7	NY Cosmos 1-Los Angeles 5	0	10-7	NY Cosmos 2-Philadelphia 1	1
5-7	NY Cosmos 0-Seattle Sounders2	0	14-7	NY Cosmos 5-Tampa Bay 4	2
7-7	NY Cosmos 2-Vancouver 1	0	18-7	NY Cosmos 5-Washington 0	1
9-7	NY Cosmos 3-Boston 1	0	28-7	NY Cosmos 4-Dallas T'nado 0	0
16-7	NY Cosmos 1-Portland 2	1	7-8	NY Cosmos 1-San Jose 2	0
19-7	NY Cosmos 0-Toronto 3	0	10-8	NY Cosmos 8-Miami Toros 2	2
23-7	NY Cosmos 2-Earthquakes 1	1	17-8	NY Cosmos 2-Washington 0	1
27-7	NY Cosmos 2-Dallas Tornado 3	0	20-8	NY Cosmos 1-Tampa Bay 3	1
10-8	NY Cosmos 1-St. Louis 2	0	1-9	NY Cosmos 2-Dallas Tornado 2	0
27-8	NY Cosmos 2-Earthquakes 3	1	5-9	NY Cosmos 2-Dallas Tornado 1	0
31-8	NY Cosmos 1-Malmo 5	1	6-9	NY Cosmos 3-Dallas Tornado 2	1
2-9	NY Cosmos 3-Alliansen 1	2	8-9	NY Cosmos 1-Canada 1	0
4-9	NY Cosmos 2-Stockholm 3	2	10-9	NY Cosmos 1-Canada 3	0
11-9	NY Cosmos 4-Valaregen	2	14-9	NY Cosmos 1-Paris Germain 3	0
13-9	NY Cosmos 1-Roma 3	0	16-9	NY Cosmos 1-Roy'l Antwerp 3	1
18-9	NY Cosmos 2-Victory 1	0	23-9	NY Cosmos 0-West Japan 0	0
19-9	NY Cosmos 1-Violette 2	0	25-9	NY Cosmos 2-Japan 2	0
21-9	NY Cosmos 0-Santos JAM 1	0	6-10	BRAZIL 0-Flamengo 2	0
26-9	NY Cosmos 12-Puerto Rico 1	1			

Date	Match result	Pelé

1977

Date	Match result	Pelé
2-4	NY Cosmos 9-Victory 0	2
3-4	NY Cosmos 2-Tampa Bay 1	0
9-4	NY Cosmos 0- Quicksilver 1	0
13-4	NY Cosmos 2-Team Hawaii 1	0
17-4	NY Cosmos 2-Rochester 0	1
24-4	NY Cosmos 1-Dallas Tornado 2	0
1-5	NY Cosmos 2-St.Louis 3	0
8-5	NY Cosmos 3-Connecticut 2	0
11-5	NY Cosmos 2-Chicago Sting 1	0
15-5	NY Cosmos 3-Strikers 0	3
22-5	NY Cosmos 1-Chicago Sting 2	0
29-5	NY Cosmos 2-Tampa Bay 4	0
1-6	NY Cosmos 2-Lazio 3	0
5-6	NY Cosmos 6-Toronto 0	0
8-6	NY Cosmos 3-Strikers 0	1
12-6	NY Cosmos 2-Minnesota 1	0
16-6	NY Cosmos 2-Toronto 1	0
19-6	NY Cosmos 3-Tampa Bay 0	3
23-6	NY Cosmos 0-St. Louis 2	0
26-6	NY Cosmos 5-Los Angeles 2	3
10-7	NY Cosmos 0-Seattle S'nd. 2	0
15-7	NY Cosmos 0-Rochester 1	0
17-7	NY Cosmos 2-Portland 0	0
27-7	NY Cosmos 8-Washington 2	0
31-7	NY Cosmos 3-Connect B'cn. 1	0
6-8	NY Cosmos 1-Wash. Dip. 2	0
8-8	NY Cosmos 3-Tampa Bay 0	1
14-8	NY Cosmos 8-Laud Strikers 3	1
17-8	NY Cosmos 3-Laud Strikers 2	2
21-8	NY Cosmos 2-Rochester 1	0
24-8	NY Cosmos 4-Rochester 1	1
28-8	NY Cosmos 2-Seattle S'ders 1	0
1-9	NY Cosmos 5-Caribbean 2	1
4-9	NY Cosmos 1-Portugal 1	0
10-9	NY Cosmos 4-Funkawa 2	1
14-9	NY Cosmos 3-Japan 1	0
17-9	NY Cosmos 1-China 1	1
24-9	NY Cosmos 2-Mohum Bahad 2	0
1-10	NY Cosmos 2-Santos F.C. 1	1

Farewell from The King, the greatest footballer ever to lace up a pair of boots.

A1 SPORTING SPEAKERS

A1 Sporting Speakers is proud to share close relationships with many of the biggest names in sport. With access to hundreds of star turns, we can book you a wide variety of sporting celebrities. Our clients include:

- **JIMMY GREAVES.** Master goal scorer turned master after-dinner speaker.

- **FRANK BRUNO.** The loveable giant is a knockout to meet and greet.

- **SIR GEOFF HURST.** England's World Cup hat-trick hero remains in demand.

- **SIR HENRY COOPER.** The old king of the ring has a fund of great stories.

- **RICKY HATTON.** The Hit Man is always a colossal hit with audiences.

- **GORDON BANKS.** You are in safe hands with this legendary goalkeeper.

- **MARTIN PETERS.** A World Cup final scorer, now scoring on the celebrity circuit.

- **MARTIN CHIVERS.** He played for Saints and Spurs and has lots to tell.

- **PAT JENNINGS.** The first gentleman of football who is always interesting.

- **JACK CHARLTON.** Big Jack (The Giraffe) tells it as it is and is hilarious.

- **RON HARRIS.** Chopper, feared as a footballer, is now very funny as a speaker.

- **RON ATKINSON.** The man with the magnetic personality always draws laughs.

- **STEVE PERRYMAN.** He was the heart of Spurs and is all heart at the mic.

- **MATT LE TISSIER.** His Question and Answer sessions are fascinating.

To book any of these celebrities (and many many more) contact ...

A1 Sporting Speakers
Unit 20, 12 Airfield Road, Christchurch, Dorset. BH23 3TG.
Tel: 01202 475600   Email: terry@a1sportingspeakers.com